J. M. Coetzee's Poetics of the Child

J. M. Coetzee's Poetics of the Child

*Arendt, Agamben, and the
(Ir)responsibilities of Literary Creation*

Charlotta Elmgren

BLOOMSBURY ACADEMIC
LONDON • NEW YORK • OXFORD • NEW DELHI • SYDNEY

BLOOMSBURY ACADEMIC
Bloomsbury Publishing Plc
50 Bedford Square, London, WC1B 3DP, UK
1385 Broadway, New York, NY 10018, USA
29 Earlsfort Terrace, Dublin 2, Ireland

BLOOMSBURY, BLOOMSBURY ACADEMIC and the Diana logo are trademarks of
Bloomsbury Publishing Plc

First published in Great Britain 2021
This paperback edition published 2022

Copyright © Charlotta Elmgren, 2021

Charlotta Elmgren has asserted her right under the Copyright, Designs and Patents Act, 1988, to be identified as Author of this work.

For legal purposes the Acknowledgements on pp. vii–viii constitute an extension of this copyright page.

Cover design: Eleanor Rose
Cover image © Linda Otterstedt

All rights reserved. No part of this publication may be reproduced or transmitted in any form or by any means, electronic or mechanical, including photocopying, recording, or any information storage or retrieval system, without prior permission in writing from the publishers.

Bloomsbury Publishing Plc does not have any control over, or responsibility for, any third-party websites referred to or in this book. All internet addresses given in this book were correct at the time of going to press. The author and publisher regret any inconvenience caused if addresses have changed or sites have ceased to exist, but can accept no responsibility for any such changes.

A catalogue record for this book is available from the British Library.

A catalog record for this book is available from the Library of Congress.

ISBN: HB: 978-1-3501-3842-1
PB: 978-1-3502-4946-2
ePDF: 978-1-3501-3843-8
eBook: 978-1-3501-3844-5

Typeset by Newgen KnowledgeWorks Pvt. Ltd., Chennai, India

To find out more about our authors and books visit www.bloomsbury.com and sign up for our newsletters.

Contents

Acknowledgements	vii
List of Abbreviations	ix

Introduction		1
	The child in Coetzee: A story waiting to be told	1
	Towards a poetics of the child	7
	From Levinas and Derrida to Agamben and Arendt	14
	Writing and the child	19
	The child as the object of writerly desire	21
	The writer as child	25
	Conceptions of the child	29
	'The child' – a fluid concept	30
	The child and the fully human	31
	A figure of openness and possibility	35
	Outline	38
1	The story of the (un)romantic child: Innocence, truth, and first fictions of the self	41
	Fragments of childhoods	44
	(Un)romantic children	46
	Navigating fictions	53
	Moments of openness	60
	Authentic encounters: From self to other	63
2	Ethics of the not-so-other child	65
	The savage-as-child-as-self	71
	Children of iron	81
	Ethics of indeterminacy	92
3	The child between past and future	95
	Natality and the event	101
	Worrying about the child	103

	Getting beyond death	106
	Amor mundi and transmissibility	110
	The interregnum, freedom, and writing	113
	Pedagogy and play	117
	From natality to infancy	122
4	Childish behaviour: The poetics of study	125
	From waiting to 'pressing on'	128
	The incessant shuttling of study	132
	Grasping the potentialities of the present	134
	Impotentiality and the curious state of infancy	136
	Embracing uncertainty	142
	From childish to childlike	145
5	The redemptive nonposition of infancy	149
	The burdensome search for truth	152
	Infancy and language as such	157
	Being like a child: '*The revocation of every vocation*'	159
	Infancy and ethics	162
	Writing and redemption	164

Coda	167
References	171
Index	183

Acknowledgements

This book has emerged under the most favourable conditions imaginable; looking back, I am overwhelmed by how fortunate I am to have benefited from so many invaluable exchanges throughout the journey. I am profoundly grateful to Stefan Helgesson and Pieter Vermeulen, who, with their inspiring scholarly virtuosity, their ever-encouraging enthusiasm for this project, and their valuably different critical perspectives on Coetzee and beyond, have continuously prompted me towards higher levels of precision and clarity in my thinking and writing than I could otherwise have hoped to reach. I wish to express my warmest gratitude to David Attwell, who, as a valued interlocutor for the book in its near-finished incarnation, inspired important final touches; to Carrol Clarkson, without whose vital and insightful recommendations this study would have remained in a much lesser earlier shape; to Jakob Lothe, whose careful and generous reading helped me sharpen my focus; and also to Hermann Wittenberg for valuable comments on an early draft. I am very grateful for the thoughtful and productive comments provided by the anonymous readers of the book proposal; and I wish to extend my special thanks also to the attentive anonymous reviewer for *ARIEL*, whose constructive suggestions were important to developing my thinking on what was later to become Chapter 4.

Over the years during which this book was conceived and developed, the English Department at Stockholm University has provided the most supportive and friendly working environment one could ever wish for. Special thanks are due to Irina Rasmussen for her unfailing kindness and much-treasured mentorship; to Gül Bilge Han whose generous sharing of her experience I continue to appreciate; to Claudia Egerer for her early and sustained encouragement; and to Bo G. Ekelund and Paul Schreiber for, in their different ways, awakening me to what the study of literature can be. I am also thankful for the friendship of Alice Sundman, Maria Zirra, Michaela Vance, Sanja Nivesjö, and Sondos Qutait, who have each helped make of these years such a rich shared journey.

It goes without saying that the writing of this book has affected and depended on family and friends. I want to thank you all for your patience during those long periods of time when everything but this has been put on hold. I wish especially to thank my parents, Lars and Torun Stålberg, for always encouraging and taking an interest in my writing, and for much-appreciated practical support during these years and also all those that came before.

Finally. My family has lived with this book almost as closely as I have myself. Without you three, I could not and would not have accomplished this. I am immeasurably grateful to – and for – my wise and exceptional children: Viktor, for never allowing me to harbour any doubt about my duty to follow this through; and Julia, for your endless patience and for your curiosity about Coetzee and so much else. And, at last, my eternal gratitude to Linus, for knowing me so well, and for assuming the responsibility to enable my – at times quite childish – irresponsibility in pursuing the tos and fros of this study.

Abbreviations

AI	*Age of Iron*
B	*Boyhood: Scenes from Provincial Life*
CJ	*The Childhood of Jesus*
D	*Disgrace*
DBY	*Diary of a Bad Year*
DL	*Dusklands*
DP	*Doubling the Point*
EC	*Elizabeth Costello*
F	*Foe*
GO	*Giving Offense*
GS	*The Good Story: Exchanges on Truth, Fiction and Psychotherapy*
HC	*In the Heart of the Country*
HN	*Here and Now*
IW	*Inner Workings*
LA	*The Lives of Animals*
LE	*Late Essays*
MK	*Life & Times of Michael K*
MP	*The Master of Petersburg*
S	*Summertime*
SM	*Slow Man*
SJ	*The Schooldays of Jesus*
SS	*Stranger Shores*
WB	*Waiting for the Barbarians*
WW	*White Writing*
Y	*Youth*

Introduction

The child in Coetzee: A story waiting to be told

There is a moment in the 'At the Gate' episode of *Elizabeth Costello* (2004) when the aged writer is making her case before the judges guarding the entry to the afterlife. Having been requested to state the precise nature of her beliefs, Elizabeth Costello is doing her best trying to justify her lack of any particular belief, arguing that her ethical responsibility as a writer must be to what she calls her secretarial 'calling' alone (199). Suddenly, one of the judges asks her, seemingly out of the blue: 'What about children?' Slightly taken aback, Elizabeth Costello responds: 'Children? I don't understand.' A short while later, having thought the matter through, she answers: 'I have yet to be summoned by a child, but … I am ready' (202, 204).

If Elizabeth Costello – intellectually preoccupied as she is with questions ranging from animal rights to the realist novel, the state of the humanities, literary censorship, the problem of evil, and so on – does not immediately respond to the idea of the child as the subject of an ethical appeal, she might be forgiven. In fact, Costello's forgetting the child reflects the fact that the child in Coetzee's work – 'the child' here signifying both 'real' child characters and their more abstract counterpart, 'the idea of the child' – has passed strangely below the radar of the otherwise remarkably wide-ranging and profound scholarly engagement with Coetzee's oeuvre over the past three decades. And yet, as this book will argue, the child is a pathway to so many of the concerns that trouble Elizabeth Costello (and, indeed, Coetzee's scholarly devotees) that it seems almost strange for her (and us!) not to have taken it into due consideration.

However, if the child rarely surfaces in the mind of Elizabeth Costello, it certainly does so in the writing of J. M. Coetzee. To begin with, consider the following array of child characters, all of whom, despite sometimes figuring only at the margins of the plot, are important to the dynamics of the novels in which they appear: Martin, Eugene Dawn's small son in *Dusklands* (1974); the nameless children – indeed, the barbarian girl herself is little more than a child – in *Waiting for the Barbarians* (1980); John, Bheki, Hope, and Beauty in *Age of Iron* (1990); Matryona in *The Master of Petersburg* (1994); John, Coetzee's fictional childhood self in *Boyhood* (1997); Pollux, the young rapist in *Disgrace* (1999); Ljuba and Dragos in *Slow Man* (2005); and, last but not least, David/Davíd in the *Jesus* novels (2013, 2016, 2019). Yet the child is visible not only in the form of child characters, but also in the ways that childhood memories and dissonances figure significantly in many of the novels – recall, for example, Magda wondering about her childhood self: 'How can I believe this creature was ever a child, how can I believe she was born of humankind?' (*HC* 41). At other times, it appears in surprising imagery, for example, when a rock as 'big as a child's head' is thrown through Mrs Curren's windscreen during a particularly infernal episode of township violence (*AI* 104).

The child is present also in figures of speech, remarkably often in platitudes where it is unclear if the sentiment expressed is genuine or ironic. Consider, for instance, the ageing narrator J. C.'s reflection in *Diary of a Bad Year* (2007): 'I approve of children, in the abstract. Children are our future. It is good for old people to be around children, it lifts our spirits. And so forth' (*DBY* 213). On the one hand, J. C. approves of children 'in the abstract', attributing to the child a seemingly endless array of clichéd virtues that might be imagined within the appendage 'and so forth'; his tongue-in-cheek tone accentuating the constructedness of such preconceptions. On the other hand, he then reminds himself of the rowdiness of children; his experience of 'real' children cancelling out their ideal counterparts: 'What I forget about children is the unending racket they make. Baldly put, they shout' (213). This same pattern, in which the various abstract conceptions of the child on which Coetzee's narrative figures rely are subverted – either by 'real' children or by alternative constructions – recurs time and time again in Coetzee's fiction.

More often than not, Coetzee's tactic of distancing himself from certain stereotypical figures of the child – such as the above 'children are our future' – is countered by a seemingly serious appeal to the very same ideas. Consider, for example, this tribute a few pages earlier in *Diary of a Bad Year* to the South African poet Antjie Krog:

> Utter *sincerity* backed with an acute, feminine intelligence, and a body of heart-rending experience to draw upon. Her answer to the terrible cruelties she has witnessed, to the anguish and despair they evoke: *turn to the children, to the human future, to ever-self-renewing life.* (199; emphasis added)

Clearly, whereas at first glance the earlier quote might be read simply as making fun of conventional ways of thinking about the child, it becomes less easy to dismiss when juxtaposed to the urgent tone in the above passage on Antjie Krog (although the latter, too, is of course embedded metafictionally in the narrative).

As this book will show, such figurations of the child both participate in and challenge customary ways of presenting the child in literature. However, what is interesting about these various fictional incarnations and invocations of the child is not primarily how they are represented. In fact, with *Boyhood's* John and the *Jesus* novels' David/Davíd as notable exceptions, the child characters themselves are generally opaque and sketchily drawn. Rather, what is significant is the ways in which the presence of children alerts us to how ideas that have come to be associated with the child in the Western imagination open up new perspectives in Coetzee's writing. I will argue that paying attention to the figure of the child enables a reconsideration of core issues in Coetzee's oeuvre: questions related to the self, truth, and writing; the ethical relationship to the other; education and responsibilities towards the past and the future; language and its (im)possibilities; and redemption. By evoking different ideas associated with the child – not least the tensions resulting from the juxtaposition of such ideas – the figure of the child in Coetzee's fiction engenders new ways of seeing and understanding how sometimes seemingly irreconcilable notions feature dialectically in his work. The child highlights the figuring of irresponsibility alongside responsibility, freedom alongside entrapment, responsibility for the old alongside openness to the new, and a desire for transcendence alongside careful attention to the realities of the visible world. Reading Coetzee's work through the figure of the child, then, makes visible the complementarity of seemingly mutually exclusive notions.

Importantly, if the child keeps resurfacing in the novels, it does so elsewhere in Coetzee's writing and thinking as well. In critical essays, notes, interviews, and speeches through the years, Coetzee consistently returns to questions opened up by the figure of the child in ways that demonstrate its potency as a point of entry to the oeuvre. Not only that, the figure of the child is also a striking presence in the work of writers that are often cited as Coetzee's key literary influences, such as Dostoevsky, Beckett, and Kafka.[1] Indeed, the wealth of intertexts raised through the child in Coetzee reminds us of the exceptionally wide-ranging reach of Coetzee's influences and references (basically, the entire canon of Western literature and history of ideas, along with openings to non-Western elements as well). The child in Coetzee points us towards Plato and towards the Bible; it recalls the intensity of experience in Wordsworth's 'spots of time' and reminds us of Blake's intermingling of innocence and experience; it echoes Romantic notions of art's possibility to extend childhood awareness into adulthood and invites us to think about the belief in the child in Goethe; it appears in intricate subversions of colonial discourse; it provokes us to revisit the corruption of innocence in Dostoevsky and Nabokov, and, not least, it returns us to Freud's questions about the very notion of childhood innocence.

The centrality of the child to Coetzee was brought out by Coetzee's Honorary Doctorate acceptance speech at the University of Witwatersrand graduation ceremony in December 2012. Addressing an audience of humanities graduates, Coetzee spoke at length about what the adult might learn from the child, stressing that it is 'good for your soul' to be with children and that children are 'never anything but their full human selves' (Graduation ceremony). Of course, any doubts about the centrality of the child to Coetzee's work were dispelled with the publication in early 2013 of *The Childhood of Jesus* and, in 2016 and 2019, respectively, its sequels *The Schooldays of Jesus* and *The Death of Jesus*, which along with *Boyhood* and *Age of Iron* are the novels to date that bring the figure of the child to the fore most explicitly. Furthermore, David Attwell's book *J.M. Coetzee and the Life of Writing: Face to Face with Time* (2015), the product of Attwell's time spent at the Coetzee

---

1 See, for example, Babuk (2015) on the child in Dostoevsky, Caselli (2005) on the child in Beckett, and Laszlo (2018) on the child in Kafka. See also Georges Bataille's chapter on the 'childish attitude' of Kafka in *Literature and Evil* (2012, 129–45).

archive at the Harry Ransom Center in Austin, Texas (which was opened for research in 2013), shows how the genesis of many of the earlier novels involved Coetzee's thinking and reading about the child. Equally, important passages in Coetzee's dialogue with Arabella Kurtz in *The Good Story: Exchanges on Truth, Fiction and Psychotherapy* (2015) serve to further highlight Coetzee's ongoing concern with ideas related to the child.

However, if the child's presence in Coetzee's work is striking, its relative absence in the accompanying critical conversation is equally conspicuous. It is clearly the case that while the child is not entirely unnoticed in Coetzee scholarship, the ideas mobilized by the child have not been brought together to establish it as the nexus in Coetzee's poetics that it might fruitfully be understood as. A case in point is the edited volume *J.M. Coetzee's The Childhood of Jesus: The Ethics of Ideas and Things* published in 2017, in which not one of the (excellent) essays engages in a sustained manner with the figure of the child as such, despite the child's pivotal role in the novel.[2]

To date, the one sustained engagement with the child – or, more specifically, the *lost* child – in Coetzee is Mike Marais's *Secretary of the Invisible: The Idea of Hospitality in the Fiction of J.M. Coetzee* (2009). Drawing on Maurice Blanchot and Emmanuel Levinas, Marais sets out to show how Coetzee's fiction 'dwells obsessively on an alterity that is figured as being absolute in its irreducibility'; this invisible otherness is contrasted to the visible and 'phenomenal world of history' (xiii). Marais argues that, in Coetzee, the origin of writing lies in the irreducible other that 'can never be accommodated or known', and he posits the quest for the lost child as the key metaphor for the search for this ultimately ungraspable alterity (xii).

In its attention to hospitality in Coetzee, Marais's argument approaches Derek Attridge's influential ethics of reading, the latter laid out in the

---

2 Sue Kossew's essay 'J.M. Coetzee and the Parental Punctum' comes closest, with its reflections on parenthood. There are other instances of research that specifically pay attention to the parent/child relationship in Coetzee. Gillian Dooley devotes the chapter 'Parents and Children' in her book *Coetzee and the Power of Narrative* (2010) to the bond between parents and children, reflecting on motifs of lost children, childlessness, and the absence of happy childhood memories. Equally, in a 2003 essay, Paola Splendore explores filial relations in Coetzee's work, finding in the many examples of failed parental love a figure for the failure of the colonial system; suggesting also that Coetzee's focus on parenthood serves to remind us of our responsibility towards the other. Interestingly, many moments in David Attwell's *J.M. Coetzee and the Life of Writing* link Coetzee's creative processes to his own familial relationships.

companion works *The Singularity of Literature* and *J.M. Coetzee and the Ethics of Reading* (both published in 2004); Attridge's thinking also forms an important point of departure for my own work.[3] In these seminal contributions to literary criticism in general, and to Coetzee scholarship in particular, Attridge compellingly shows how Coetzee's novels call for a particular ethical response.[4] He observes that 'Coetzee's works both stage, and are, irruptions of otherness into our familiar worlds', and that they ask – of their characters and of their readers – 'what is our responsibility toward the other?' (2004a, xii). The 'other', to Attridge, is a relation between the self and 'that which, in its uniqueness, is heterogeneous to me and interrupts my sameness'; in other words, the 'other' could equally be, for example, an encountered person, a future event, or a literary work (2004b, 33). Noting how Coetzee's novels resonate with Jacques Derrida's writing on hospitality (in its turn inspired by the work of Emmanuel Levinas), Attridge develops an ethics of reading throughout the two volumes, emphasizing the reader's responsibility to be responsive to her experience of reading a literary work, in order for that work's singularity and otherness to be acknowledged. For Attridge, unlike for Marais, 'the other' is not an absolute or transcendent alterity; although it 'cannot be apprehended by the old modes of understanding', it has the potential to be at least partially grasped by the responsive subject, whose world is slightly remade in the process (2004b, 29). Like Attridge, I see the dramatization of a felt responsibility towards the other (along with the possibilities and impossibilities experienced in trying to assume this responsibility) as a prominent feature of Coetzee's work, accounting for much of the striking ethical potency of his oeuvre. Moreover, and like Marais, I believe that Coetzee's writing simultaneously often strives towards something 'beyond' that cannot be grasped, and that this movement is staged partly through figurations of the child. However, while I find Marais's and Attridge's respective accounts compelling in many places, I also find them insufficient. This brings me to my central claim; *alongside*

---

[3] Attridge continues to develop his ethics of reading in *The Work of Literature* (Oxford University Press, 2017).
[4] Another noteworthy intervention in the context of Coetzee and ethics is Stefan Helgesson's *Writing in Crisis: Ethics and History in Gordimer, Ndebele and Coetzee* (2004), which offers a Levinasian reading of Coetzee.

the persistent tendency to follow or feel responsible for the other (whether or not that other is understood to be transcendent), *Coetzee's writing manifests an equally persistent element of freedom, irresponsibility and play.* It is the dialectic between these seemingly contradictory forces – and how this interplay evokes notions of imagination, innocence, irony, natality, and impotentiality – that constitutes the core of what I call 'Coetzee's poetics of the child'.

Towards a poetics of the child

The episode that opens this book, in which Elizabeth Costello finds herself at the gate to the afterlife, is also the scene that inspires the title and opening of Marais's book. Unwilling to sign up for any specific cause, Costello calls herself 'secretary of the invisible'; in Marais's reading she is alluding to the ethical responsibility implied in her position of writing from *within* history about the 'invisible' other *beyond* history that cannot be grasped (*EC* 199). As Marais points out, this writerly predicament seems analogous to what Coetzee himself has described as the writer's 'responsibility toward something that has not yet emerged' (*DP* 246). In a series of close readings (from *Dusklands* to *Slow Man*), Marais traces an ethics of writing through metaphors in Coetzee's work, the most important of which, he argues, is the figure of the lost child. Marais states as part of his purpose to

> relate the recurrent quest for the lost child to the metaphor of following the invisible: the child is a deeply self-reflexive metaphor for the invisible. … The writer writes in order to render visible what is invisible … s/he bears a parental responsibility for the child. S/he has no option but to try to find the child. The writer must write. Nevertheless … to render visible the invisible is to destroy the invisible. Hence the salience of the figure of the damaged child and the theme of betrayal in Coetzee's writing. (2009, xiv)

I agree with Marais that the figure of the child is tightly linked to the ethics of Coetzee's writing. This important common denominator aside, my reading of the child in Coetzee is very different from Marais's; it is the persistent *presence* of the child that is striking, not primarily its absence or its figuration as 'lost, abandoned, deformed, dead or unborn' (xiv). By articulating the implications of this divergence at some length here, I will start to establish what I mean by Coetzee's poetics of the child.

A good place to begin this discussion is the aforementioned quote from the interview in *Doubling the Point* (1992), in which Coetzee speaks to David Attwell about the differences between writing fiction and literary criticism. The full quote reads as follows: 'The *feel* of writing fiction is one of freedom, of irresponsibility, or better, of responsibility toward something that has not yet emerged, that lies somewhere at the end of the road' (*DP* 246; emphasis in original). For Marais, it is the *second* half of what Coetzee is saying here – the idea of writing as 'responsibility toward something that has not yet emerged' – that is of interest and that forms the basis for the ethics he finds in Coetzee's novels (2009, xiii). Attridge, too, focuses exclusively on the second part of the quote, when he establishes the link between responsibility and artistic creation in Coetzee (2004b, 124; 160 n1). However, picking up on responsibility alone does not reflect the full significance of what Coetzee is saying here. Notice how Coetzee uses the word 'responsibility' in the above quote as a *better way of expressing* 'freedom' and 'irresponsibility'; in other words, to Coetzee 'responsibility' and 'irresponsibility' are two sides of the same coin; two different ways of understanding the '*feel*' of writing fiction. The importance of the aspect of 'freedom' is underlined elsewhere in the same passage of the interview, when Coetzee says that 'stories are defined by their irresponsibility', and that writing fiction, for him, involves 'liberating' and 'playing with possibilities' (*DP* 246). Also, in a different interview, this time revolving around the idea of community, Coetzee talks about freedom in terms of the 'unimaginable':

> I am someone who has intimations of freedom (as every chained prisoner has) and constructs representations – which are shadows themselves – of people slipping their chains and turning their faces to the light. I do not imagine freedom, freedom *an sich*; I do not represent it. Freedom is another name for the unimaginable, says Kant, and he is right. (*DP* 341; emphasis in original)

Here, 'freedom'/'the unimaginable' verges on the meaning of the earlier 'something that has not yet emerged'; *ergo*, Coetzee as a writer claims to be driven by a sense of responsibility towards a sense of freedom. The relation, then, between these notions of 'responsibility' and 'freedom', both obviously fundamental to writerly inspiration in Coetzee, is important; it reflects the interplay between what I see as the two crucial dimensions of Coetzee's writing: an attitude marked, at times, by entrapment in language (or 'history') and failure to grasp the 'other', on the one hand, and the image of 'slipping … chains', a more affirmative approach to writing and being in the world, on the other.

My reason for dwelling so extensively on this point is that the figure of the child brings to light how Coetzee's writing is driven *both* by responsibility towards the 'other' *and* by an unyielding sense of freedom and irresponsibility. However, to my mind, the influential strand of Coetzee criticism that we might loosely classify as Derridean/Levinasian readings (encompassing between themselves, of course, a range of quite diverse interventions), with its focus on hospitality towards the other, has come to eclipse the equally important element of irresponsibility and play.[5] The need to address this imbalance becomes especially pronounced in the light of Coetzee's latest work, the *Jesus* novels (2013, 2016, 2019), in which an ethics of hospitality is addressed in a sometimes near-comical way, while what we might call 'childish' attributes of openness and irresponsibility are treated more seriously. (Importantly, Marais's and Attridge's books predate the publication of these novels.) I believe that both sides of the dialectic that is so clearly at play in Coetzee deserve to be articulated, and the key rationale behind this book is that the figure of the child provides a privileged vantage point from which to do so.

Let me highlight, here, two noteworthy critical interventions that offer valuable perspectives on those dynamics in Coetzee's work that converge in what I call the 'irresponsibility' aspect of Coetzee's poetics of the child. In *J.M. Coetzee and the Novel: Writing and Politics after Beckett* (2010), Patrick Hayes illuminates 'the highly wrought tension' in Coetzee's writing 'between the serious and the comic', claiming that Coetzee's '"jocoserious" play with the rules and boundaries that govern political discourse' constitutes an attempt to articulate a serious position for literature in relation to politics (2010, 2; 4).[6]

---

[5] I refer elsewhere, too, to 'Derridean/Levinasian readings', grouping them together for the sake of simplicity, to intend readings of Coetzee that focus on an ethics of alterity.
[6] Hayes points out that Coetzee borrows the term 'jocoserious' from James Joyce's *Ulysses* (1922).

My focus here is not primarily the relation between literature and politics, yet the 'nonposition' that Hayes locates throughout Coetzee's works – and that Coetzee also addresses himself in his essay 'Erasmus: Madness and Rivalry' in *Giving Offense* (1996) – approximates the stance of responsible irresponsibility that is evinced through the child especially in Coetzee's later works and that I will discuss in Chapter 5 (Hayes 2010, 133). Equally, Jan Wilm's *The Slow Philosophy of J.M. Coetzee* (2016) explores a mode of approaching Coetzee's work, which, while it involves 'naïve questioning', 'does not ask what a text means ... it does not primarily wish to get reading over with, but it wants to remain in reading' (2016, 80; 45). There are important affinities between such 'slow reading' and the mode of openness and experimentation that I find in Coetzee's childish poetics of 'study', which is the subject of Chapter 4.

Locating the child at the centre of Coetzee's poetics, then, highlights the tensions in Coetzee that I have started to sketch above. The child calls to mind *both* the otherness towards which the writer or subject strives (whether due to 'parental' responsibility or desire) *and* the liberation from any such compulsions. Bringing this dialectic into view has implications for our reading of Coetzee, especially with reference to the subject's relation to language, the ethics of the other, and the ethics of reading.[7] Clearly, reading the quest for the lost child as a metaphor for following the invisible (as Marais does) does not even begin to (nor, of course, does it aim to) address all the complexities that the child in Coetzee brings to light.

Let me illustrate how the figure of the child in Coetzee can simultaneously evoke the failure to grasp the other – with an ensuing sense of ethical responsibility for that other – on the one hand, and an affirmative ethic of freedom and irresponsibility, on the other. Consider the second section of *Life & Times of Michael K* in which the medical officer and the camp commander unsuccessfully try to understand who Michael K is, and to grasp the reason for his presence on the farm where he has been apprehended. Seeking alternately to interpret and construct K's story, the frustrated medical officer refers to K as an 'unborn creature' (*MK* 135). Marais reads Coetzee's 'use of the child-image' here in terms of a '*failure* ... to "give birth" to K, to invest his alterity

---

7 I use the term 'dialectic' interchangeably with 'dynamic' or 'interplay' to signify the to-and-fro movement between positions in Coetzee.

with form and substance in language' (2009, 49; emphasis in original). In Marais's reading, the medical officer, Coetzee and the reader alike – indeed, even K himself – are trapped within the confines of language when confronted with the enigmatic character: 'Words', writes Marais, 'fail to present K; they fail to do what they are supposed to do' (54). He argues that the inability to make sense of K induces a sense of responsibility for the former in the medical officer (and the reader), along with a sense of loss and grief 'without term' for the child that is never born (57). The child, then, is beyond the reach of language and, in its ungraspability, becomes the object of the writer's, and the reader's, responsibility and unfulfillable desire. I find this reading compelling. However, I propose that the episode should also be read in reverse; the medical officer's failure to accommodate Michael K *at the same time* constitutes the triumph of the latter's condition of freedom from being contained in language. Equally, if the unfathomable K prompts an *impossible desire to grasp*; he *at the same time* provokes the reader's endless *curiosity, experimentation and openness to different possibilities of thought*. The same inversion figures in many of Coetzee's novels, perhaps most vividly in *The Childhood of Jesus*. Simón and the Novillian educational authorities fail to understand the child David within their conventional frames of reference, but their failure is at the same time the radical openness inherent in the Bartleby-like child's state of not yielding to any particular explanation. (For the sake of the analogy, it is worth pointing out that Michael K, too, was imagined as a child by Coetzee at various points of the drafts (Attwell 2015, 137–9).) So while writerly – and readerly – inspiration is driven by the unfulfillable desire to accommodate the other, it also involves the abandonment of that desire; in more affirmative terms, writing and reading ultimately necessitate the irresponsible embracing of uncertainty, curiosity and experimentation. Metaphorically speaking, such irresponsibility is *childish* behaviour; indeed, as I will argue, Coetzee's poetics partly implies the figurative mobilization of a lingering *childlike* state of openness.

Let me comment briefly on my use of the terms 'childish' and 'childlike'. The Oxford English Dictionary tells us that the former can be understood either as 'of, like, or appropriate to a child or to childhood; childlike', or 'with reference to a person who is no longer a child: not befitting maturity; puerile, foolish, silly'; while the latter appears 'frequently with reference to the innocence, charm, etc, of children', in 'contrast to the depreciative use of childish'. In other words, 'childish' tends to be understood as disparaging, while 'childlike' suggests adult approval. While I do use the terms distinctively – employing 'childlike' to retain the associations with innocence (and, sometimes, redemption), and 'childish' to connote playfulness and irresponsibility – neither is favoured over the other or treated pejoratively in my discussion, or, I venture, in Coetzee's poetics. (If anything, Coetzee questions the very notion of innocence; this is discussed in Chapter 1.) Ultimately, these distinctions serve to remind us of the multifarious ideas associated with both the child and adult responses to the child.

Another example, now, of how the figure of the child draws out apparently conflicting aspects of Coetzee's writing: While Michael K – let us stay with him as an illustrative figure of the child[8] – can indeed be read as an 'unborn' story or something 'other' beyond what can be described, we must not forget that he is also very much 'within' history. He has a mother; he experiences racial injustice and political violence; he is hungry and plants pumpkin seeds from which to live. The child in Coetzee is both within and beyond history (history, here, to be understood loosely as the visible world as circumscribed by language). And while the quest for the lost child works well as a metaphor for 'following the invisible' in the case of, say, Susan Barton's search for her lost daughter in *Foe* (1986), and Dostoevsky's longing for the deceased Pavel in *The Master of Petersburg*; it does not suffice to account for the many worldly children present in Coetzee's fiction. Consider, as another example, *Age of Iron*. In Marais's reading, the lost child is a figure for Mrs Curren's original self, lost in her construction of an identity that is inevitably tainted by the apartheid state. When Mrs Curren tries to render the enigmatic vagrant Verceuil understandable in her own terms by naming him and bringing him into her world, she implicates herself in the 'discourses of history' and 'deforms the child', that is, herself (Marais 2009, 100). Again, I find myself agreeing with Marais's reading; undoubtedly, the difficulties in relating responsibly to the other is a – if not *the* – central theme in the novel, and Mrs Curren's longing

---

8 Of course, Michael K is not literally a child (although, as I remarked above, early drafts show that he was originally conceived of as such). However, when approaching Coetzee's poetics of the child, I am curious not only about the staging of child characters (understood here as characters of ages ranging from infancy to early adolescence), but also about the many figurative evocations of the child. The medical officer's thinking about Michael K as an 'unborn child' is an example of the latter.

for the innocent child reflects her desire for a state of being that is unspoiled by violent history. But still, what about the *actual* children in the fictional world of the novel – John and Bheki, Hope and Beauty? What about Mrs Curren's failure to grasp the experience of these 'other' children *within* history? They are not metaphors for something lost; they are very much *there* (on the ontological level of the story world). Also, what about how the presence of child figures destabilizes (post)colonial self-other boundaries, as in the encounter between Jacobus Coetzee and the Khoi children in *Dusklands*, or between David Lurie and the child-rapist Pollux in *Disgrace*? Certainly, the 'other' child in Coetzee – the (post)colonial child that is present, not absent, lost, or 'beyond', and that disrupts the understanding of the self – is a story waiting to be told.

The child figure in Coetzee surfaces also in the negotiation of past, present, and future. Coetzee's protagonists frequently find themselves in the fraught position of feeling answerable both to the past and the future; wanting at once to safeguard the old and to welcome that which exceeds the current imagination. The character Elizabeth Costello's observation that the past is 'a shared story' while the future is 'a structure of hopes and expectations', might serve to illustrate the incommensurability between the two, and the child emerges as a significant force in this intersection (*EC* 38). While it is true that the unknowability of the future – epitomized by the child and the new that it might bring – is a source of frustration, even anxiety, in many of Coetzee's novels, it is also the case that the birth of the new is welcomed in gestures of responsibility towards a common human world. Indeed, in yet another incarnation of the interplay sketched out earlier between responsibility and irresponsibility, impossibility and possibility, Coetzee's characters tend to shuttle between the desire to ensure cultural transmission between the past and the future and its apparent opposite, the embracing of uncertainty. The tension between continuity and discontinuity – and especially how it is made visible in episodes dealing with education and pedagogy – has not yet been fully critically articulated, somewhat surprisingly considering the attention that Coetzee affords issues related to teaching and learning.[9] This too, is a story

---

9 Pedagogy and education are not entirely unexplored themes in Coetzee criticism. Barnard (2014) provides a useful overview of educational scenes in Coetzee; Michael Bell has a chapter 'The Lecturer, the Novelist, and the Limits of Persuasion: Elizabeth Costello and J. M. Coetzee on The Lives of Animals and Men' in his *Open Secrets: Literature, Education and Authority from J.J. Rousseau to*

waiting to be told, and for this reason, scenes of pedagogy will be crucial in my discussions.

From Levinas and Derrida to Agamben and Arendt

I have started to sketch out above how the child in Coetzee is, on the one hand, a figure of ungraspability and impossibility and, on the other hand, a figure of openness, experimentation and possibility, and how the figure of the child can thus illuminate the interplay between these different forces in Coetzee's poetics. While this book acknowledges both sides, so to speak, it places particular focus on an 'affirmative' reading where the child in Coetzee signifies freedom, irresponsibility and possibility (recalling Coetzee's words about writing fiction as 'playing with possibilities' (*DP* 246)). There are two reasons for this: First, it seems to me that Derridean/Levinasian readings of Coetzee have already been well (and repeatedly) articulated. Second, I firmly believe that the figure of the child in Coetzee's late work – I am thinking especially of the *Jesus* novels – privileges more 'joyful' readings, inviting us to reconsider also his earlier fiction from such perspectives.

In the light of this more affirmative slant to my reading of Coetzee, it makes sense to enlist the aid not of discourses of alterity (and, by extension, of 'impossibility'), but rather of those who set up the child as a figure of irresponsibility and possibility. The figure of the child is central to many philosophers, but I have found Giorgio Agamben and Hannah Arendt to be the thinkers whose respective work most helpfully elucidates the patterns in Coetzee's poetics opened up by the child.

Let us consider Agamben first: his idea of infancy – a notion at the core of his thinking about language, potentiality, and the messianic since the volume *Infancy and History: The Destruction of Experience* was first published in 1978 – offers a range of fruitful intersections with ideas generated by the figure

---

J.M. Coetzee (2007) that offers useful perspectives on Coetzee's work in terms of the limits of the teachable and the erosion of the authority of Bildung in contemporary culture. Also, Zimbler (2014) reflects on postcolonial pedagogy alongside *Disgrace*, considering the ethical challenges in teaching the other. Aparna Mishra Tarc's *Pedagogy in the Novels of J.M. Coetzee* (Routledge Research in Education, 2020) also offers fresh perspectives on this topic.

of the child in Coetzee. In Agamben's thought, infancy refers to a condition of openness to that which has not yet been written, the state of having the capacity to speak but not yet having spoken (infancy derives from *infantia* signifying the inability to speak).[10] As Arthur Willemse puts it, 'Agamben's philosophy of infancy exposes our existence within language, and thus repeats the infant experience of discovering a world that is yet to be named, foregrounding the being of language' (2018, 13). In his discourse on infancy (which I will draw on extensively in Chapters 4 and 5), Agamben evokes the child as a figure of openness:

> His voice still free from any genetic prescription, and having absolutely nothing to say or express, sole animal of his kind, he could, like Adam, name things in his language. In naming, man is tied to infancy, he is for ever linked to an openness that transcends every specific destiny and every genetic calling. (1995, 96–7; emphasis in original)

Infancy, in other words, signifies freedom from determination, from 'every specific destiny'. Agamben also refers to this condition as *impotentiality*, to designate the circumstance of having a certain potentiality that is not yet – and that may never be – realized. In Agamben's understanding, infancy does not refer to being *beyond* or *prior to* or *eluding* language, but rather of being in a state of freedom *in* language before anything has been determined – of experiencing language *as such*. Put differently, to Agamben, being in a relationship to language in infancy is not a state of entrapment, but an opening to multiple possibilities. This idea of infancy resonates well with my reading of the child in Coetzee.

I invoke Agamben, then, to help me convey the aspect of irresponsibility and openness in Coetzee's poetics of the child, with the intention of complementing existing Derridean/Levinasian readings. A helpful way to think about the relation between Derrida and Agamben here – and about the dialectic that this book wishes to highlight – is in terms of 'a confrontation between … difference

---

10 Agamben's notion of infancy originated as 'a way to expand on Benveniste's distinction between semiotic and semantic', locating infancy in the space in between the two (Bertolini 2011, 105). In *Countervoices* (2013), Carrol Clarkson traces how the linguistic and formal nuances in Coetzee's writing translate into an ethics of address; a point of departure for her discussion is Coetzee's bringing together of Émile Benveniste (linguistics) and Martin Buber (ethics) in his 1977 essay 'Achterberg's "Ballade van de gasfitter": The Mystery of I and You' (*DP* 69–90).

and impossibility and … indifference and possibility – between the *trace* as the miracle of interpretation and the *remnant* as the paradigmatic opportunity for thought' (Willemse 2018, xiii; emphasis in original). I find this quote (and, indeed, much of Willemse's book *The Motif of the Messianic: Law, Life, and Writing in Agamben's Reading of Derrida* (2018)) very helpful in pinpointing the central tension I find in Coetzee's poetics of the child.[11] Without delving too deeply into the intricacies of 'traces' and 'remnants', the difference between the two condenses into the issue of whether language implies the responsibility to something presupposed, or rather a freedom from presupposition.[12] From one perspective, the child is an unattainable object of desire, and, while a source of inspiration, can at best partially be grasped through interpretation; from the other perspective, the child points rather towards the remnant of a state of openness before the divisions of metaphysical thought have been imposed, leaving open the potential for all directions of thinking. It should be noted that the relationship between Derrida's responsibility and Agamben's irresponsibility is not one of direct opposition, but rather one of *complication*; this is also how I view this dynamic in Coetzee's poetics. The crucial distinction is this: while Derridean/Levinasian responsibility by definition *necessitates* irresponsibility – in order to welcome the other, I must be unconditionally hospitable, thus unconditionally open – this discourse on hospitality does not share the affirmative and emancipatory nuance that I find in Agamben's notions of infancy and impotentiality.

To date, while Coetzee has been extensively and productively read in dialogue with Agamben, the scholarly work bringing the two together has focused mainly on how the latter's biopolitical framework, with his concepts of *homo sacer*, 'bare life' and 'state of exception', opens up ethicopolitical interrogations in novels such as *Life and Times of Michael K* and *Waiting for the Barbarians*, as well as on the resonances between Coetzee's and Agamben's thinking on the relation between human and non-human animals.[13] However,

---

11 For another useful study of the dialogue between Agamben and Derrida, see Attell's *Giorgio Agamben: Beyond the Threshold of Deconstruction* (2015). See also Watkin's chapter 'Derrida and Agamben: *Différance* Makes Indifference Communicable', in *Agamben and Indifference* (2014).
12 Agamben writes: 'Language is what must necessarily presuppose itself' (1999b, 41; emphasis in original).
13 For perspectives on how Agamben's biopolitical framework informs readings of Coetzee, see, for example, Caton (2006), Bartnik (2014), and Barney (2016); for perspectives on the intersection between salvation and non-human animals in Coetzee and Agamben, see Restuccia (2017).

there are compelling reasons to read Coetzee alongside Agamben in broader contexts than has so far been the case. Although Coetzee and Agamben, to my knowledge, do not refer to each other anywhere, the correspondence between Coetzee's poetics of the child and Agamben's work on infancy, language, and potentiality brings to light the common dimension of freedom, hope, and possibility in their respective work, in a way not unlike that explored by Anke Snoek in her book *Agamben's Joyful Kafka: Finding Freedom Beyond Subordination* (2012). Against the generally more pessimistic understanding of Franz Kafka's influence on Agamben, Snoek argues that 'Agamben uses Kafka not so much to support his dark political theories as to show a way out', in that they both point towards 'a possibility or potential that lies enclosed within the current situation' (2012, 2). Similarly, I find that the child in Coetzee, like infancy in Agamben, suggests a way out *within* the confines of language, thus challenging the sometimes bleaker readings of both.

Although they are not explicitly concerned with infancy, there are instances of 'emancipatory' readings of Coetzee in dialogue with Agamben that gesture in similar directions. Let me mention some examples: Daniele Monticelli (2016) sets out to explore how in *Life and Times of Michael K* 'the traditional idea of a foundational telos as the essence of human political existence is … replaced by the idea of a void to be shown and inhabited' (619, 624). Drawing on Agamben's terminology, Monticelli understands K's existence in terms of a '"central emptiness" which must be shown as the place where all separations and articulations are called into question', arguing that 'for both Agamben and Michael K/Coetzee, the possibility of a different form of life (and politics) for human beings is essentially related to the opening and maintenance of this kind of place' (625–6). While Monticelli's interest lies in the 'political potentiality of Coetzee's novel', the patterns that emerge out of his reading of the 'inoperativity' at work in *Michael K* form a compelling analogy to how I see infancy evinced in Coetzee's work (Monticelli 2016, 619). Similarly, when Catherine Mills (2006), also drawing on Agamben, finds in K 'a modest figure of hope – as a man who persists in relation to [the law]', this too is an analogy to the being *in a relation to language as such* that is the hallmark of Agamben's infancy (189). Another example is Chris Danta, who invokes Agamben to highlight the presence in Coetzee's writing of a 'potentiality to create that remains pending' (2013, xix).

Agamben's sustained engagement with the child through infancy and related concepts such as (im)potentiality has only recently come to be explored as such. Among the most significant contributions to date on Agamben and the child are Tyson Lewis's *On Study: Giorgio Agamben and Educational Potentiality* (2013) and Joanne Faulkner's *Young and Free. [Post]colonial Ontologies of Childhood, Memory and History in Australia* (2016); both these works have proved important in opening up my readings of the child in Coetzee's fiction, as has Katrien Vloeberghs's helpful contextualization of Agamben's concept of infancy (2004). Additionally, several valuable interventions in Agamben scholarship place infancy (and its analogical concepts in Agamben's thought) at the centre of their argument, although infancy is not explicitly foregrounded as the object of study. Among these, two works that I have found especially productive are the already mentioned Arthur Willemse's *The Motif of the Messianic: Law, Life, and Writing in Agamben's Reading of Derrida* (2018), and Colby Dickinson's *Agamben and Theology* (2011); another example is William Watkin's *The Literary Agamben: Adventures in Logopoeisis* (2010).

In addition to Agamben, the thinker who has proven particularly elucidating in my readings of the child in Coetzee is Hannah Arendt. Her role in my account, presented in Chapter 3, might be articulated in terms of a *hinge* between discourses of responsibility and irresponsibility – a hinge that is premised on the care for a shared human world. In other words, if Derrida/Levinas are figuratively understood in terms of responsibility *towards* the child, and Agamben in terms of the irresponsibility *of* the child; Arendt's thought forms a compelling way of articulating the necessary complementarity of the two.

Arendt's thinking on *natality* (her term for man's unique capacity for new beginnings) and *amor mundi* (love of the world, a concept Arendt finds in Augustine) captures an affirmative nuance in Coetzee's approach to both the new and the world that I find missing in existing critical readings. Arendt's natality shares its emphasis on welcoming the new with Derrida's Levinasian notion of hospitality and, hence, Attridge's discourse on the event, but with *amor mundi* Arendt makes explicit the inextricable link between the birth of the new and the safeguarding of the common human world. My readings show how encounters with the child in Coetzee's fiction, not least in educational episodes, have in common such a care for the world. The adult character feels responsible both for protecting the world and for the possibility of its being changed; this tension – constantly reminding us that Coetzee is himself a teacher – is wonderfully elucidated by Arendt's writing on education, which, to my knowledge, has not yet been activated in Coetzee scholarship.[14] Equally, Arendt's natality offers a counterweight to *mortality*, and thus a way to help articulate how the anticipation of death in Coetzee's novels is interrupted by the child and the possibility of the new.

Writing and the child

This book is born out of the conviction that the idea of the child constitutes a particularly productive, yet surprisingly unexplored, site for engaging with Coetzee's oeuvre. As the study has developed, it has come to focus specifically on how the child might help our thinking about the poetics of Coetzee's oeuvre, both in terms of the genesis of the writing and in terms of the particular modes of reading that the writing invites.

My interest in the writing as such means setting aside a range of other possible approaches to the child in Coetzee's work, most notably, perhaps, political mobilizations of the child. Over the past few decades, postcolonial, feminist, and queer theorists have continued to explore the boundaries imposed on and challenged by the idea of the child and approach its constructedness – 'colonization', even – from the point of view of different emancipatory ideological agendas.[15] Jo-Ann Wallace, for example, argues that the child figure, while enabling imperialist discourse (I will return to the (post)colonial child in Chapter 2), also functions as an image of possible future empowerment, thus offering 'both an explanatory *and* an emancipatory potential' (1994, 176, 183). This is exactly the sort of doubleness that is at work

---

14 Beyond natality, there are some references to Arendt in Coetzee criticism. For example, Niemi (2017) reads *Waiting for the Barbarians* and observes points of convergence between Arendt and Coetzee with regard to individual responsibility and radical thinking; and Ryan (2005) finds Arendtian intertexts specifically concerned with issues of banality, evil, and thinking in *Elizabeth Costello*.
15 Jo-Ann Wallace's 'De-scribing the Water-Babies: "The Child" in Post-Colonial Theory' (1994), Lee Edelman's *No Future: Queer Theory and the Death Drive* (2004) and Kathryn Stockton's *The Queer Child, or Growing Sideways in the Twentieth Century* (2009) are some examples.

in Coetzee's fiction. Equally, the once self-evident association between the child and the promise of the future is sometimes called into question; Aṣhis Nandy claims that 'childhood has become a major dystopia for the modern world', the fear of regression to childhood a constant in a society geared towards 'perfect adulthood' and 'ultra-normality' (1987, 56, 65). This political condition seems to be what Coetzee is responding to, in part, although he himself is clearly also part of the 'adulthood' that he resists.[16] Other voices observe that in late-modern society, the child is associated with a longing for the social bonds and solidity of times past – the result of a disenchantment with the current condition and a lack of sense of purpose. Sociologist Chris Jenks suggests that the child symbolically represents the uncertain identity that follows from a postmodern lack of authority: 'Children have become … the way in which we explore missing, unexpressed and disempowered aspects of ourselves' (Jenks 2005, 150). A question that remains unanswered in this book is whether the affirmative inclination I locate in Coetzee's poetics might also be translated into an analogous political attitude more broadly speaking.

What I explore here, then, is the generative capacity of the child figure for Coetzee's poetics. I use the term 'poetics' to signify abstract configurations of dynamics that appear in Coetzee's writing across his different works. Indeed, there is a sense in which this book itself is part of the process of reading and writing – of childlike openness and childish experimentation – that the poetics of the child in Coetzee sets in motion. Reading *like* a child, I wonder about patterns and tensions in the texts, carefully analysing the ways in which the child (child figures or the 'idea' of the child) surfaces in the texts, and asking questions rather than seeking to explain. This mode of curious reading requires paying particular attention to what I see as striking tensions, paradoxes, and ambiguities in the writing.

What is it, then, that makes the child such a compelling figure to think alongside in relation to the dynamics of literary representation? Essentially, the child's special potency in this regard has to do with how, as Roni Natov writes in her introduction to *The Poetics of Childhood*, 'the poetics of childhood

---

16 See, for example, Coetzee's apprehension about the increasing instrumentality of higher education in his foreword to John Higgins's book *Academic Freedom in a Democratic South Africa: Essays and Interviews on Higher Education and the Humanities* (2014).

draws attention to the ways in which we might see the flux of our imaginations more clearly' (2003, 5–6). Indeed, thanks to the close relationship between writerly creation and the idea of the child, the child makes visible the dynamics of the writing itself; when different qualities associated with the child are set in conflict with each other in the novels, the tensions that emerge help us visualize the forces of literary creation. In other words, by virtue of its various connotations – of otherness, inaccessibility, and unrepresentability, on the one hand, and of openness and indeterminacy, on the other – the child figure helps us see the interplay between responsibility and irresponsibility that, I argue, is a (if not the) central dynamic in Coetzee's poetics.

The child as the object of writerly desire

Literary critics often return to the notion of the child as a figure for that which is somehow out of reach – the child as an object of writerly *desire* (or, analogously, responsibility). An early intervention exploring this idea, often referred to as a milestone in the field of literary childhood studies, is Jacqueline Rose's *The Case of Peter Pan or the Impossibility of Children in Children's Fiction* (1993).[17] Rose makes the case that the representation of children in children's fiction is driven by the adult desire to master the child, a desire in its turn driven by the hope that the adult might thus be granted the child's 'special access' to a 'primitive or lost state' (Rose 1993, 9). 'It is', she writes, 'as if the child serves to sanction that concept of a pure origin because the child is seen as just such an origin in itself. The child is there, and the original meaning is there – they *reinforce* each other' (19; emphasis in original). In other words, if the writer can grasp the innocent child, she can at the same time grasp an unmediated access to meaning.[18] Pertinently, Rose observes that the idea of 'a true and primary meaning' is also 'the ultimate fantasy of much literary criticism' – hence, perhaps then, the critical desire to grasp the child (19).

---

17 Although Rose's argument focuses on children's literature, she continues to be widely cited also by literary critics dealing with child figures in fiction in a broader sense.
18 For discussions on childhood innocence in literature, see Ellen Pifer's *Demon or Doll: Images of the Child in Contemporary Writing and Culture* (2000), James R. Kincaid's *Erotic Innocence: The Culture of Child Molesting* (1998), and Karin Lesnik-Oberstein's *Children's Literature: Criticism and the Fictional Child* (1994).

Rose traces the beginnings of the critical connection between the child and original meaning to the writings of Sigmund Freud. Crucially, however, she suggests that Freud himself gradually abandoned the idea of childhood as something distinct that can be located and interpreted. Instead, she argues that the main insight to be taken from Freud is that 'childhood … persists as something which we endlessly rework in our attempt to build an image of our own history' (12). Central to Rose's account is that, for Freud, 'neither childhood nor meaning can be pinned down – they shift, and our identity with them' (16–17). Rose critiques the notion of interpretation that 'presupposes a form of original innocence of meaning which the act of criticism can retrieve – the very notion of how meaning (and childhood) operate which Freud himself had had to discard' (Rose 1993, 19).[19]

Considering that (mis)readings of Freud are central to critical approaches to the child in literature, it seems relevant to consider how Freud's thought might be seen to inform Coetzee's poetics. Although overt references to Freud's *Interpretation of Dreams* surface in relation to the child especially in the early fiction – the Magistrate thinking, 'Somewhere, always, a child is being beaten' (*WB* 88), and Mrs Curren imagining the dream scene in which the child appears by his sleeping father's bedside saying, to no avail, 'Father, can't you see I'm burning' (*AI* 110) – such moments are not presented as central to the writing as such.[20] In a conversation with David Attwell, Coetzee expresses his reservations about the ethical potential of Freudian psychoanalysis and confirms his 'lack of interest in the psychological as a field for fiction to exercise itself in' (*DP* 249). Although Coetzee also clarifies that he is not anti-Freudian – 'Far from it – the traces of my dealings with Freud lie all over my writings' – it would seem from his 'Confession' essay and other comments that he embraces neither the pessimistic 'endlessness' of Freudian psychoanalysis nor the more

---

19 Rose suggests that Freud's psychoanalytic writings can be read as a challenge to the idea 'that psychic life is continuous, that language can give us mastery, or that past and future can be cohered into a straightforward sequence and controlled'. She writes: 'Above all, it throws into question the idea that the child can be placed at the beginnings of this process (origins of culture, before sexuality and the word), or, indeed, at the end (the guarantee for continuity for ourselves and our culture over time)' (Rose 1993, 134).
20 For valuable readings of these Freudian intertexts, see, for example, Attwell (2019) on wish-fulfilment in *Waiting for the Barbarians*; Kaplan (2011) on failures of witnessing in *Age of Iron* and *Disgrace*; and Durrant (2006) on Freud, Lacan, and the limits of the sympathetic imagination in *Waiting for the Barbarians* and *Age of Iron*.

optimistic notion that the child as origin might be reached (*DP* 244–5). More recently, in *The Good Story* (2015), Coetzee refers to his doubts raised when reading 'Freud in his less pessimistic moments', – presumably the early Freud who still believed that there was such a thing as childhood that might be accessed – and reacting against the 'rather unquestioning way' in which Freud prescribes 'You shall know the truth, and the truth shall set you free' (*GS* 7). In the book's ensuing dialogue with Arabella Kurtz on the impossible negotiation between accessing *the* truth of self and the poetic freedom to narrate *a* truth of self, Coetzee seems to settle for *authenticity* as an alternative yardstick: 'The question is not whether somewhere there is a child who is crying; the question is whether the memory of the crying child is true and truly felt' (27). In the discussion of *Boyhood* in Chapter 1, I reflect on how the notion of authenticity seems to function as the pivot between the writer's desire for truth, on the one hand, and the writer's fictions of the self, on the other.

Closely related to the child figure's unreachability, is its function as a challenge to the practice of representation. Expanding on Rose's discussion of the unknowable child, Susan Honeyman argues in *Elusive Childhood: Impossible Representations in Modern Fiction* (2005), that, paradoxically, in novelistic representations of the child, it is its very unrepresentability that attracts writers to the child figure. Honeyman suggests that childhood offers a space for the writer's desire to 'escape dependence on linear thought and language', reflecting 'a desire for something antithetical to [the writer's] own art' (2005, 17, 27). In other words, the child figure holds an appeal as an antidote to entrapment in language, discourse and linearity, aesthetically gesturing towards the availability also to the adult of a condition outside rationality and instrumentality.[21]

Its perceived inaccessibility is undoubtedly why the child in literature is frequently rendered as a figure of otherness. Often, it is the foregrounding of the child's constructedness that emphasizes this otherness. After all, if the child is not innocent (as the Romantic story goes), what is it then?[22] Coetzee

---

21 This idea of continuity between childhood and adulthood is expressed by Gaston Bachelard when he writes that 'childhood lasts all through life', and that poetry can 'help us find this living childhood within us' (1992, 20).
22 In Anglophone literature, Henry James was an early pioneer in the exploration of the idea of the child as a figure of otherness. By drawing attention to the constructedness of the Romantic idea of childhood innocence, James's writing inspires ambiguous responses from the reader, who is destabilized and unsure what to believe. James, writes Honeyman, was so 'transparently troubled

never attempts to represent the child's perspective (other than at a distance through an adult narrating voice in the fictional autobiography *Boyhood*), yet the ambiguous ways in which child characters figure in his writing often prompt reflection on the constructedness of both self and other. Indeed, – and this is a simple but integral aspect of Coetzee's poetics of the child – the figure of the child alerts us to how encounters with the other are always also encounters with the self. In Chapter 2, I discuss this idea at length in relation to (post)colonial child encounters in *Dusklands*, *Disgrace* and *Age of Iron*.

A pivotal link between the child and literary representation, then, is to be found in the child as the object of the writer's unfulfillable longing for an ultimately unrepresentable essence. It is apparent how this writerly desire for the child can be understood as analogous to the Derridean/Levinasian desire to accommodate alterity in an ethics of hospitality; indeed, this is exactly the point Mike Marais makes about the 'lost child' in Coetzee, although he does not articulate this in terms of the qualities associated with the literary child figure as such. Equally, as I have also suggested, if the child as the object of writerly responsibility is a compelling figure for the desire to accommodate the other, it is also helpful to our understanding of the longing for an out-of-reach truth of *self* that constitutes such a central aspect of Coetzee's poetics. (Chapter 1 discusses how the child makes visible the impossible quest to attain a truth of self in Coetzee's '*autre*biographical' writing.)

The connection between the child and the self was cemented in the nineteenth century, when the figure of the child became a way of structuring new abstract ideas about interiority and selfhood. In *Strange Dislocations: Childhood and the Idea of Human Interiority* (1995), Carolyn Steedman shows how the child figure provided the means 'for thinking about and creating a self: something grasped and understood: a shape, moving in the body … something *inside*: an interiority' (1995, 20; emphasis in original). Steedman proposes that it was the incompleteness of the child figure – its own lack of a story – that prompted

by the challenge children present to realist representation' that he foregrounded his method of external focalization to expose and confront this challenge (22). In *What Maisie Knew*, James offers the limited perspective of the innocent (and partly ignorant) child, producing the double effect of exposing the inconsistencies and hypocrisy of adult discourse while leaving the reader 'aware of the impossibility of knowing what Maisie knows' (Honeyman 2005, 22). In his representations of the child, James draws attention to the limits of figural narration and to the 'one-sided and unchecked power of adult discourse when constructing children' (30).

adults to invest it with a narrative of what was lost in the self: 'the child *was* the story waiting to be told', both recalling and expressing the individual past of the adult (11; emphasis in original). The child was taken to personify a certain meaning, bestowed on the child figure by the adult imagination. Joanne Faulkner observes that it was in this interiorized self-as-child that 'a *spiritual* dimension of subjectivity, otherwise denied by empiricism, could be preserved' (Faulkner 2016, 13; emphasis added).

The child as a figure for the self can also be considered in light of the proximity between confession and the child figure in literary history. In *The Child Figure in English Literature* (2008), Robert Pattison observes the simultaneous appearance of autobiographical narrative and the child as the object of theological dispute, first in Augustine's *Confessions* and later in Wordsworth's *Prelude* and Rousseau's *Confessions*. Pattison traces the emergence of 'an introspective and confessional attitude which finds an outlet in autobiography and first-person narratives in general' to early Church debates about the child and original sin, arguing that Augustine's doctrine (connecting childhood with sin and free will) 'laid the foundation for the child as a literary image' (2008, 108–9; 19). He suggests that the child's potency as a figure lies in the fact that it is connected to both the essence and expiation of original sin, in both senses 'nearer the unsullied truth than the adult' (119). Clearly, the child is conceived time and again in literature – including, occasionally, in Coetzee – as a redemptive figure serving as a guide towards a state of grace or its secular equivalent. While it is compelling to consider the urge of writing one's way towards the child – or the truth – in terms of redemption, I suggest in Chapter 5 that it is in the childish poetics of irresponsibility – manifested especially in the later novels – that the most conspicuous redemptive gestures in Coetzee's writing may be found.

The writer as child

If the child as the object of writerly desire constitutes one side of the poetics I wish to illuminate with this book, the other side, of course, is imagining the child as the *subject* of writerly creation; in other words, imagining the *writer as a child* approaching the uncertainties of the world and the self. Susan Honeyman makes the valuable point that the child figure inspires the writer's creativity precisely in how it prompts the exploration of 'the process of acquiring language and crossing boundaries of cultural knowledge'. She writes:

> The artist attempts to channel despair into creation and turns to the child … as a source of inspiration. The creativity of the child consists in the fact that he passes from a state of complete ignorance at birth to a state of knowledge. It is the actual moment of transition from ignorance to knowledge which bears witness to creativity; knowledge once obtained becomes automatic and loses its value. (Fiona Björling quoted in Honeyman 2005, 44)

Boyhood's child character John is a compelling figure for such a 'transition from ignorance to knowledge'. The child figure helps us see clearly how epistemological uncertainty, the navigation between the fictions constituting the world and the self, fuels also the adult writer's inventiveness.

More than anything, perhaps, the idea of the writer as 'child' is linked to the association between the child and the notion of 'play', which has frequently been evoked in literary and philosophical discourses to describe a dynamic and holistic way of being in the world. The German Romantic poet and philosopher Friedrich Schiller says: 'Man plays only when he is in the full sense of the word a man, and *he is only wholly Man when he is playing*' (1984, 80; emphasis in original). To Schiller, it is through play that we manage our simultaneous immersion in and distance from the world; the way in which passion and reason, the true and the good are balanced against each other, leading to the creative expansion of meaning. Infant psychoanalyst D. W. Winnicott similarly points to the concept of play as a reconstructive force, taking place in a 'transitional space' both inside and outside the world; play the experience of continuously shifting the boundaries between the self and the world through at once active form-giving and passive perception.[23] In Chapter 3, I look at Coetzee's many references to play, considering them particularly

---

23 Along the same lines, John Wall defines play as the 'passive-active tension with the world that makes it possible to create meaning at all' (2010, 49). Drawing on Richard Kearney, Wall proposes the notion of 'play as creativity', which he distinguishes both from Hans Gadamer's 'tragic' notion of play, whereby history unfolds itself within each individual consciousness; and from Jacques Derrida's 'comic' view of human being as 'the play of traces' in the endless deferral of meaning. Wall describes this 'creative' phenomenology of play as 'tragicomic', 'neither already structured into meaning nor something whose meaning is forever escaping, but rather an endless process of becoming' (Wall 2010, 51).

in relation to Arendt's notion of natality and to the uncertain interregnum between past and future where writing takes place.

I mention Schiller as a theorist of play, but of course, there are countless references to Romantic work in Coetzee's writing.[24] It seems important to ask, then, how Romantic approaches to the child and writing might be seen to inform the interplay between responsibility and irresponsibility that I find in Coetzee's poetics?

Importantly, although it is possible to speak in general terms about the 'Romantic child', often used interchangeably with the 'modern idea of the child', as a figure of natural sensibility, innocence, and truth – 'gesturing ahead', as Ann Rowland writes, to 'the ideas of childhood that will dominate Western culture well into the twentieth century' – different Romantic thinkers emphasize different aspects of the child and its relation to writing (2012, 9). It is fair to say, though, that the child's redemptive potential is at the very centre of the Romantic elevation of the child. Peter Coveney describes how the Romantic poets in response to 'a world given increasingly to utilitarian values and the Machine' found in the child 'the symbol of Imagination and Sensibility, a symbol of Nature … Through the child the artist could express his awareness of the conflict between human Innocence and the cumulative pressures of social Experience' (Coveney 1967, 31). Certainly, Coetzee's skepticism at aspects of modern society, such as 'binary thinking' and instrumentalism in higher education, resonates with Romantic evocations of the child figure that foreground feeling and the imagination against the Enlightenment's privileging of the empirical and rational thought.[25]

Coetzee's work exhibits traces of especially William Blake's spiritual longing and William Wordsworth's desire for unity with nature, both sharing the idea of art's capacity to extend the redemptive potential associated with childhood into adulthood. In Blake's view, the child figure symbolized the disharmony he felt with the times, but also offered the possibility of renewed harmony

---

24 For scholarship on Romantic resonances in Coetzee's writing, see, for example, Smuts (2014), Beard (2007), and Vermeulen (2007).
25 See, for example, Coetzee's piece 'On Literary Thinking' (2016) in which he expresses concern about the digital age's 'binary thinking', and the corresponding spread of a form of mental constraint that conceives of itself quite innocently as freedom'; and Coetzee's apprehension about the increasing instrumentality of higher education in his foreword to John Higgins's book *Academic Freedom in a Democratic South Africa: Essays and Interviews on Higher Education and the Humanities* (2014).

and salvation; by resisting or unlearning the corruptive influences of nature and experience, the adult might develop a higher innocence. An important parallel to Coetzee is how, in Blake's best-known work *Songs of Innocence and Experience* the states of innocence and experience coexist and interrupt each other; Roni Natov writes of the 'permeable boundaries' between the two states, and of how Blake's two poems, when read alongside each other, 'suggest not synthesis or reconciliation but a [sustained] tension' (2003, 13). This tension is a central dynamic also in Coetzee's poetics, made visible through the never-quite-innocent and never-quite-knowing child.

Wordsworth found the child figure's redemptive potential instead in its unity with nature. In his understanding, the child's natural state of innocence affords it an immediacy of experience and totality of vision (the 'eye among the blind') that is lost to most adults but can be maintained by the poet through his imaginative capabilities.[26] Wordsworth highlighted the potential inherent in the adult's *remembrance* of childhood, in how it could evoke a longing 'for the immediate transcendence and joy available to … adults through the vision of childhood' (Pattison 2008, 62). Wordsworth's famous 'spots of time', flashes of childhood memories, evoked in *The Prelude* are manifestations of such adult access to the truth of feeling in connection to nature that Wordsworth attributes to childhood. In *Boyhood* and elsewhere, Coetzee explores this Romantic idea of the child's fullness of experience in privileged moments.[27] Of course, the idea of childhood evoking adult longing speaks directly to the sense of writerly responsibility towards the child described earlier.

It is equally clear how the Romantic idea of the child informs the tension I outline between Derrida and Agamben in Coetzee's writing, in how it figures literary language as at once entrapment and emancipation. Ann Rowland describes how the Romantic period engendered a discursive shift, the 'infantilization of literary culture', a key aspect of which was the attempt

---

26 Considering the interest that Coetzee affords to ageing, it is worth noting the affinities between childhood and senescence in this regard. Judith Plotz points out that Romantics such as Charles Lamb separated both the very young and the very old, with their shared values and characteristics, from the world of normal adulthood, that 'darkness of sense and materiality' (2001, 115–16). Similarly, Jane Missner Barstow notes recurring 'womb/tomb' images of harmony in both Charles Dickens, Marcel Proust, and Günter Grass (1978, 153).
27 Coetzee has remarked on the centrality of Wordsworth's thought to his writing: 'Wordsworth is a constant presence when I write about human beings and their relations to the natural world' (*Dagens Nyheter* 2003).

'to bring the unvoiced, gestural and non-semantic elements of language' into literature (2012, 5). In Romantic times, the 'prattle' or meaningless chatter of children served as an image of 'poetic inspiration and linguistic innocence', reflecting eighteenth-century debates on the origins of language (Rowland 2012, 17). Such prattle was also an image for the ability of children to 'turn significant language back into insignificant noise', and Rowland observes how, through the child figure, *'Romantic writers confront the shaping influence language and history have on the individual at the same time as they imagine a way to slip free of their determinative force'* (21; emphasis added). The child thus conjures up both the entrapment in language, and a state outside such entrapment. The reader will recognize how this doubleness is at play in Coetzee; certainly, one noticeable feature of the child in Coetzee is how it interrupts linear and teleological ways of thinking, privileging instead uncertainty and openness. Importantly, in the interplay between responsibility and irresponsibility outlined earlier, it seems to be sometimes in the desire for the unrepresentable and unknowable, and sometimes in the *abandonment* of that desire, that the writing takes place.

Conceptions of the child

Central to my argument is the point that Agamben's notion of infancy is distinct from the Romantic ideal of an originary innocence: Where the latter suggests that the child provides a certain direction towards which the writer might strive in a quest for redemption, aesthetic fulfilment or self-actualization; the former is about being in thought – and writing – with an openness to infinite possible directions. In order to understand this distinction, it is helpful to think about different ways in which the child has been imagined in Western intellectual history.[28] I turn first to enduring theological and philosophical conceptions

---

28 Although my chapters discuss certain openings to non-Western understandings of the child in Coetzee's writing, the present section deals mainly with conceptions of the child in Western/European intellectual history, as this is the cultural lineage to which Coetzee counts himself and where he finds his central influences. It should be noted, though, that as María J. López and Kai Wiegandt point out (2016), Coetzee emphasizes 'his own "colonial" and "provincial" condition', and occupies a 'complex and uncertain position ... in relation to different Western literary traditions and intellectual affiliations' (114). For a discussion on the strong South African resonances especially in Coetzee's earlier works, see Jarad Zimbler, who argues that 'if Coetzee's *material* necessarily

of the child in relation to different ideals of the 'fully' human, and then to notions in contemporary philosophy of the child as a site of openness and possibility. First, though, I make some brief remarks on the constructedness of the concept of 'the child'.

'The child' – a fluid concept

There is broad agreement today that 'the child' should not be understood as a biological entity with a fixed set of qualities but as a dynamic sociocultural construct; French historian Philippe Ariès's *Centuries of Childhood* (1960, in French) has been pivotal in shaping our understanding of the concept of childhood as a construct shifting in meaning across time and place. (Although my focus here is the idea of the child rather than the idea of childhood as a period in the individual's life, the concepts are closely related and, of course, share their constructedness.) Ariès famously argues that the Western idea of childhood can be traced to early-modern times, when new attitudes to children coincided with an increased focus on the nuclear family and the removal of the child from the public sphere.[29] In a mainly French setting, Ariès traces society's attitude towards childhood from early modernity onwards, using examples from art, language, history of games, and schooling to show an increasing separation between the worlds of childhood and adulthood. Although Ariès has since been criticized both for his method and his claims, there is broad agreement today on his main contribution: the insight that our conception of childhood is an evolving sociocultural construct.[30]

---

incorporates the products of centuries of literary labour in several European languages, his *field* is South African' (2014, 14; emphasis in original). Also, Coetzee's critical enterprise demonstrates his ongoing engagement with the work of non-European writers; see, for example, his anthology of South African writing *A Land Apart* (1986), coedited with André Brink, and his essays collected in *Stranger Shores* (2002) on writers such as Caryl Phillips, Naguib Mahfouz, and Ali Mazrui.

29 The idea that childhood was 'invented' in early modern times is by no means uncontroversial. Partly due to misinterpretation (the French original wording 'sentiment de l'enfance' implies both idea of and feelings/attitude towards childhood), historians have attributed to Ariès the claim that pre-modern society did not have an idea of childhood as a separate life stage, reminding us of distinctions made between adult and child in both ancient and medieval times (Hanawalt 2003, 24; Cunningham 2005, 27). Another common criticism is that what Ariès takes to be changing attitudes to childhood are in fact changes in art practices.

30 The constructedness of childhood means that its very existence is sometimes challenged. In *The Disappearance of Childhood* (1982), Neil Postman connects the emergence of childhood as a category to the birth of the printing press in the mid-fifteenth century, which created unprecedented boundaries between children and adults. With literacy, a new symbolic world emerged, from which children were excluded, relegated to a separate realm of 'childhood' until 'adulthood' was

Their constructedness notwithstanding, the divisions made between the categories of adult and child invariably display certain persistent traits. In a very basic sense, the child is understood as that which the adult is not, in a privative or a positive sense. The distinction has often been built on deficiencies in the child: the one who is not yet mature enough to be counted as a full-fledged human being or citizen; not yet physically developed and not yet in possession of reason; thus vulnerable, dependent, and lacking the capabilities required for full moral and civic responsibility. However, the child has also often been accorded a special nature, with certain prized qualities distinguishing it from the adult.

The child and the fully human

Philosophers, theologians, and educational thinkers since Plato have, more or less explicitly, approached the idea of the child as sometimes embodying and sometimes failing to embody an ideal view of humanity. Conflicting conceptions of the child often coexist within the doctrine of individual thinkers, making it difficult to discern a chronological path of evolving views of the child. Instead, it is helpful to heuristically distinguish between three basic ontological and teleological models into which philosophical and theological conceptions of the child and the desired trajectory towards adulthood are often organized, both within and outside of the Christian traditions. In each case, the conception of the child implies a corresponding view of education: the unruly child needs to receive discipline, or grace, to develop in a desired direction; the pure child may or may not preserve its innocence into adulthood – indeed, it might serve as a model for the adult to aspire towards; and the child as undeveloped potentiality might progressively acquire the faith or rationality needed to actualize its potential into adulthood. While we may recognize here the debate on original sin that has marked

---

reached. From his late-twentieth-century vantage point, Postman predicts the disappearance of the categories of childhood and adulthood as a consequence of the rise of new communication channels, rendering 'information uncontrollable' and erasing the boundaries that previously limited children's access to the adult world (71). Similarly, Jean Baudrillard argues in 2002 that 'the child is no longer a child', attributing the disappearance of childhood to factors such as artificial reproductive technologies and the accelerated tempo of life, disrupting the genetic and symbolic order (103).

Christianity since at least Augustine, these alternate views of the child go back to ancient Greece, giving us an idea of their resilience as cultural conceptions.[31]

First, consider the notion of the child as unruly or sinful. This idea dates back to Plato, to whom the child is brutish and irrational; the *Laws* and the *Republic* detail civilizing and moral training required for the child in order to maintain a rational and just society.[32] The idea of the child in need of discipline is also a recurrent theme in the Bible: in Adam and Eve's weakness when confronted with the serpent's corruption; in the Old Testament's fifth commandment to 'honour thy father and thy mother'; and in Paul's call in the Corinthians for the adult to 'put away childish ways' (Cor. 13.11). Also in this tradition, of course, is Augustine's famous assertion in his *Confessions* that even day-old infants show sinful tendencies inherited since Adam's original transgression, establishing what was to become the idea of original sin to be rectified only with divine grace.[33] Later, Martin Luther and Jean Calvin each theorized original sin, although Calvin also believed that adults should strive to emulate the lack of malice in the child.

Second, the view of the child as inherently innocent and pure is reflected in many places in the Bible; in the Old Testament's examples of children prophesying or modelling faith, and especially in the New Testament, where both Jesus and children in general are associated with wisdom and divinity. The value of a childlike nature is highlighted in the Gospels, when Jesus says to his disciples: 'Except ye be converted, and become as little children, ye shall not enter into the kingdom of heaven' (Mt. 18.3). Different strands of Christian theology have in common their elevation of the child as a model for the adult, in opposition to the Augustinian doctrine of original sin; both the Protestant theologian Friedrich Schleiermacher (1768–1834) and the Roman Catholic theologian Karl Rahner (1904–1984) professed childlike qualities of presence and openness as desirable elements of adulthood.

---

31 This framework is developed by John Wall in his *Ethics in Light of Childhood* (2010), as a way of viewing ethical thinking from a child-centred perspective. Wall labels the historical categories 'top-down', 'developmental', and 'bottom-up', and points out that each of these tendencies remains influential today (30–1).
32 Relatedly, we might remember Plato's – or at least Socrates's – aversion to 'that *childish* passion for poetry' (1997, 1212; emphasis added).
33 Augustine's conversion to Christianity took place following the voice of an unseen child prompting him to 'pick up and read' the Bible, the child thus at once a bearer of original sin and a spiritual guide (2008, 152).

In post-Enlightenment times, the child was established as also a secular figure of natural virtue. Jean Jacques Rousseau's *Émile* (1762, in French) served as the key source of inspiration for the modern idea of the child that we have come to associate with the Romantic Movement and its reaction against the period's rationalism and materialism. In *Émile*, Rousseau emphasizes the child's association with an originary state of nature, arguing that the child should be brought up in nature, learning about the world through experience and the senses rather than from books and instruction.[34] To Rousseau, the child is important in itself, not just as an adult-in-the-making; and he argues that the child's education should build on its special nature. Importantly, however, just as Rousseau does not 'seek the man in the child', it is made clear in *Émile* that he also does not look for the child in the man: 'We must consider the man in the man, and the child in the child' (46).[35]

Finally, the third enduring conception is that of the child as neither good nor bad, but rather incomplete, an undeveloped potentiality from which rational humanity can unfold gradually over time. This view was first articulated by Aristotle, to whom human nature is *pre*-rational, with the possibility of actualizing its not-yet-fulfilled potential with the development of reason. In the thirteenth century, the philosopher and theologian Thomas Aquinas synthesized the Aristotelian view with Christianity, outlining 4 seven-year phases of ethical evolution by way of which reason can gradually evolve. Like Aristotle, Thomas sees the adult as the actualization of the 'potential adult' in the child. Later, the sixteenth-century Catholic humanist Erasmus discussed childhood in terms of rational and moral potential, which may be actualized with a good education but also risks being corrupted over time by ignorance and neglect. In the eighteenth century, the Protestant thinker Johann Gottfried von Herder conceived of childhood as the beginning of the human road towards full-fledged humanity, proclaiming that 'we *are* not yet human beings, but are daily *becoming* so' (quoted in Wall 2010, 28; emphasis in original). The Aristotelian open-ended view of the child as an unformed person with

---

34 In *Émile*, Rousseau, expresses his disdain for 'words, words, nothing but words' and argues that *Robinson Crusoe* is the only book necessary in the education of a child (73, 163).
35 However, Rousseau does envisage the possibility of a new form of innocence in adulthood, when in his *Confessions* he sets himself the task to achieve, in Coetzee's words, 'total self-revelation' (*DP* 264).

an inherent rational potential was resurrected by John Locke, against the then predominant Reformation view of children as essentially unruly. In *Some Thoughts Concerning Education* (1693), Locke highlights the child's naturally endowed potential to acquire moral reason, which can be fulfilled through gradually increasing individual liberty.[36] Only with the actualization of this potential can full-fledged citizenship be acquired – but, for Locke, in a liberal society rather than in the 'kingdom of God' envisaged by Erasmus.

Coetzee's work is imbued with references to these fundamental notions of unruliness, innocence, and potentiality, which are often evoked in his work with a mix of seriousness and playfulness. Coetzee is quite explicit in his aversion to the disciplining of the 'unruly' child in the authoritarian Calvinist schooling he was subjected to himself, but there is a measure of ambiguity in his approach to both innocence and potentiality. Think of how, in *The Childhood of Jesus*, Simón tends to reason about education in terms of the child fulfilling its potential, while at the same time the novel appears to endorse the human possibility of *withholding* potential (what Agamben calls *impotentiality*), an option that the Aristotelian tradition makes possible but does not pursue; this forms a central part of the discussion in Chapter 4. Or think of Mrs Curren's lamenting of departed childhood innocence in *Age of Iron*; such fictional moments certainly do not present unequivocal positions on the idea of the child and its relation to adulthood. The chapters in this book reflect on different instances in which competing ideas of the child are picked up and discarded in Coetzee's fiction, and on their effects in terms of the subject's relation to the self, the other and the world. Indeed, these conflicting – yet in Coetzee's writing often coexisting – conceptions of the child bring us to a pivotal question: What does Coetzee *mean* when he says at Wits that 'children are never anything but their full human selves?'[37] Equally, how are we to understand the character

---

36 Although Rousseau is conventionally associated with the innocent child at one with nature, and Locke with the child as a *tabula rasa* to be inscribed with experience, they both share an optimistic view of the potential for the child to develop into an ideal citizen under appropriately regulated circumstances; this shows that the distinction between innocence and potentiality as different ways of viewing the child and its relation to adulthood is not entirely clear-cut.
37 Jean-François Lyotard asks a similar question in *The Inhuman: Reflections on Time* (1991): 'What shall we call the human in humans, the initial misery of their childhood, or their capacity to acquire a "second" nature which, thanks to language, makes them fit to share in communal life, adult consciousness and reason?' (3)

Eugene Dawn in *Dusklands* when he says 'I speak in troubled times and tell you how to be as children again', or the character Elena in *The Childhood of Jesus* when she, from a different vantage point, urges Simón to 'try to be like a child again' (*DL* 29, *CJ* 143)? These questions are central since they bring us to core moments in Coetzee's fiction in which literature, philosophy and – sometimes – theology intersect – moments in which the child prompts us to think about language, truth, and redemption.

Notice how the three narratives above – the unruly child, the good child, and the child as potentiality – all invest the child with certain meaning that reinforces the discourse in which the child appears. Also, each of these approaches to the child follows a teleological pattern. With an impetus to strive towards a certain end, whether it is the replication of order, the retaining/regaining of childhood purity or the actualization of human potential, each conception prompts a movement towards the future, or, sometimes, a nostalgic desire for the past.[38] As I will show, neither of these 'foundational fictions' – to borrow Coetzee's phrase from his reflection on innocence in *Giving Offense* (1996) – fully captures the figuration of the child in Coetzee (14). The child in Coetzee is never merely innocent, bad or a figure of potentiality; equally, it resists deterministic narratives and predictable outcomes.

A figure of openness and possibility

In contrast to the above understandings of the child in its relationship to a human ideal, a range of voices in contemporary philosophy advance the child instead as a site of radical openness and possibility. I have already put forward Giorgio Agamben's thinking on infancy as 'an openness that transcends every specific destiny and every genetic calling' (1995, 97). Katrin Vloeberghs observes that Agamben's infancy 'echoes ... but subverts' Modernity's central constructions of childhood; both 'the Enlightenment idea of progressive continuity and linear development ... and ... the Romantic, to some extent deterministic conception of harmonious deployment', both of which support the idea of 'development as a potential to be actualized' (Vloeberghs 2004,

---

38 As Susan Honeyman writes, 'the romantic view simply inverts the temporal pattern of development, reversing the direction of a supposedly fixed and still lineated process' (2005, 26).

73). In opposition to these traditional conceptualizations, Agamben's idea of infancy presents 'an alternative understanding of potentiality and ... a particular transformation of the habitual understanding of temporality' (73).[39] Vloeberghs notes that Agamben's idea of infancy is situated within the tradition of twentieth-century literature and theory that 'although highly critical of totalitarian visions of a utopian future as well as of a homogenous historical narrative ... continue to activate [the] association between the figure of the child and the potential of redemption' (76):

> In a tradition grounded in Nietzsche, the condition of *infantia* stands for an ideal and utopian final destination of human kind which can only be reached precisely when the concept of progressive development is given up ... [Agamben] envisages an alternative utopian idea [in contrast to the utopian Enlightenment and Romantic narratives of childhood and growing up] which no longer stands for some final resting point that is to be reached and upon which all movement will stand still, but rather as the eventual actualisation of a potentially permanent renewal. (Vloeberghs 2004, 76)

Other noteworthy philosophers elevating the child as a liminal figure of openness and possibility, and similarly positing the child as an interruption to linear development, include Jean-François Lyotard, to whom the child is that which 'in the midst of man, throws him off course ... the possibility or risk of being adrift'; Gilles Deleuze and Félix Guattari, to whom the child is 'the becoming-young of every age', a condition of possibility that the adult can inhabit; and Michel Foucault, to whom the child, as Claudia Castañeda puts it, is 'the embodiment of experience free of any historical or social anchoring', the child's time-space 'the experience of possibility itself' (Deleuze and Guattari 1987, 277; Lyotard 1992, 101; Castañeda 2002, 146).[40]

---

39 Agamben's idea of messianic time is captured in his principle of *kairology*, which, 'based on the rhetorical concept, *kairos*, roughly meaning "the opportune moment for intervention", ... aims to transform every moment in history into an opportune moment' (Maxwell 2011, 64). Agamben's kairology is a continuation of Walter Benjamin's conception of '*Jetztzeit* [now-time]', as 'the relationship of *instant* to *continuum*'; as Leland de la Durantaye puts it, Agamben's temporal model is one of 'a moment of truth: a moment of decisive intervention that interrupts a continuum and changes the course of history' (2009, 115–16). I will return to Benjamin's and Agamben's ideas of messianic time in Chapter 4.

40 For a discussion of the respective child figurations of these particular thinkers, see Castañeda (2002, 144–6). For an overview of how the child is figured as a site of possibility in postmodern thought, see McGavran (1999).

David Kennedy – who has written extensively on subjectivity and the philosophy of childhood – describes how the child has come to represent 'no longer an *incomplete* but an *alternative* epistemology' (2002, 157; emphasis in original). This alternative epistemology, Kennedy suggests, echoes Julia Kristeva's notion of the 'subject-in-process', the postmodern self under perpetual reconstruction – the adult, like the child, an unfinished and 'experimental being' in which the elements of self are in constant dialogue with each other and the external world (158). As I have begun to argue in the earlier section of this Introduction, the figure of the child in Coetzee points towards both an ungraspable alterity *beyond* language and an emancipatory state *in* language; the condition of 'experimental being' outlined here approximates such an emancipatory state.[41]

If the child in such philosophical discourses gives us a figure of human life as always in the process of becoming, of disruption and resistance, it also underlies the notion of *learning from the child* that is very much in focus in the fields of educational philosophy and philosophy of childhood. As childhood philosopher Walter Omar Kohan puts it, children, 'because of their briefer exposure to oppressive institutions ... are closer to that state in which they can really think for themselves' (Kohan 2011, 349). From this perspective, education is as much about educating the child in the adult as about educating the actual child in the world, a dynamic that is staged in the *Jesus* novels.

With the above synthesis of historical and contemporary perspectives on the child and the literary child figure, I have tried to account for the optic through which I approach the child in Coetzee's work. The idea of the child draws attention to concerns related to the nature of humanity, language, truth, and ethical responsibility, and, equally, the ways in which literature engages with these questions. Readers of Coetzee will know that such reflections bring us to the very core of his oeuvre. For while, in Coetzee, questions prompted

---

41 Relatedly, different conceptions of childhood are linked to different conceptions of time. Walter Omar Kohan suggests that the view of childhood as a stage of life coincides with a chronological conception of time (*chronós*); while the idea of childhood as an intense form of being throughout life presupposes a non-chronological *aionic* conception of time introduced by Heraclitus: 'Time [*aión*] (is) a child childing (playing); its realm is one of a child' (Heraclitus quoted in Kohan 2011, 341). Kohan glosses for us that Heraclitus's point is that childhood and this particularly intense experience of time emerge *together* as non-chronological; in other words, childhood is understood as not only a period of life but 'a specific strength, force or intensity that inhabits a qualitative life at any given chronologic time' (342).

by the idea of the child are not always about the child itself, they invariably prompt us to think about what it is to be human in the world.

Outline

This book is thematically divided into five chapters, each of which discusses a specific aspect of Coetzee's poetics of the child. The first three chapters discuss tensions elucidated by the child that resurface across several works, while the last two chapters read mainly the first two *Jesus* novels in dialogue with Agamben, reflecting my intuition that the latter's thought is a particularly relevant point of entry to ideas that are becoming increasingly pronounced in Coetzee's work. The chapters in this book suggest a certain shift in Coetzee's poetics, where, figuratively speaking, the idea of the writer as adult (with the ungraspable child as the object of responsibility) gradually – but never completely – gives way to the idea of the writer as irresponsible child.

Chapter 1 explores how Coetzee evokes the figure of the child to problematize the link between the self, truth, and fiction. It does so by engaging with the idea of the innocent child in Coetzee's critical writing, and by observing how, in *Boyhood*, the not-quite-innocent yet never-fully-knowing child in his desire to be true – or 'responsible' – towards his self and the world, navigates – one might say childishly, or playfully, or 'irresponsibly' – between fictions of the self and of the world, offering thus a compelling figure for Coetzee's writing of fiction in the search for a never available truth of self.

Chapter 2 moves from child-as-self to child-as-other and notes how Coetzee's stagings of (post)colonial self-other encounters figure both accommodating and othering impulses made visible through the child. The chapter argues that fictional encounters with 'other' child figures within history are ethical in their destabilization of boundaries between self and other and in their foregrounding of ironic remainders highlighted through different constructions of the child.

Chapter 3 explores how the possibility of the new is intimated in Coetzee's fiction through the figure of the child, enlisting Hannah Arendt's thinking on natality, *amor mundi* and education to reflect on how Coetzee's characters move in the difficult gap between past and future in the South African interregnum and beyond. The chapter argues that the child calls attention to how Coetzee's working through of the uncertainties of new beginnings is closely linked to a care for the world. The inclusion of Arendt as the central theoretical touchstone in this chapter has a particular rationale; her thinking makes visible the hinge not only between the past and the future, and between the child and the world, but, significantly, between responsibility and irresponsibility; the ideas outlined in this chapter, then, constitute also the hinge of this book and of Coetzee's poetics of the child.

Chapter 4 finds a childish poetics of perpetual study and experimentation in Coetzee's late work. The chapter places *The Childhood of Jesus* in dialogue with Agamben's reflection on study, bringing together the latter's foundational thinking on infancy, (im)potentiality, and the messianic. It shows how *The Childhood of Jesus* prompts its readers towards the pursuit of infinite openings to thought in the present moment, inviting a different mode of reading than the future-directed Derridean/Levinasian ethics of hospitality through which Coetzee's work has often been read.

Chapter 5 argues that *The Schooldays of Jesus* proposes the childlike as a redemptive state, a 'nonposition' beyond the taxonomies of Western metaphysics. Observing how the novel gestures towards infancy through the making visible of the experience of language as such, the chapter sees a movement from responsibility to irresponsibility in Simón's trajectory from trying to explain himself truthfully to abandoning that quest and becoming like a child.

The coda reiterates and synthesizes the interrelatedness of the main ideas discussed in the chapters: innocence, irony, natality, infancy, and redemption. I reflect here on how Coetzee's imaginings of the not-quite-innocent child evoke the epistemological mode of uncertainty that prompts the creation of new stories of selves and of the world. This dynamic site of not-quite-knowing is where the ethical force of irony is at play; where the interregnum between the old and the new gives intimations of freedom; where impotentiality – the capacity not to commit – is not dismissed but embraced; and where, possibly, something approaching grace might appear. I conclude by emphasizing again the significance of childish openness and childlike experimentation in approaching the generative (ir)responsibilities of Coetzee's poetics.

1

The story of the (un)romantic child: Innocence, truth, and first fictions of the self

In a dialogue with psychoanalyst Arabella Kurtz published in 2015, Coetzee remarks on his own 'dogged concentration … on the ethical dimensions of truth versus fiction' (77). 'Dogged' indeed, as Coetzee's preoccupation with the boundaries between truth and fiction is fundamental not only to *The Good Story* (aptly subtitled *Exchanges on Truth, Fiction and Psychotherapy*) in which the quote appears, but also to the ethics and poetics of his entire oeuvre, ever since *Dusklands* was published in 1974. In fact, *Dusklands* is a case in point; its embryo was a project titled 'Lies' (Attwell 2015, 50). In his non-fiction as in his fiction, Coetzee returns insistently to the epistemological quandary of the impossibility of truth in narratives of the self; a dilemma well captured in his by-now axiomatic remark that 'all autobiography is storytelling, all writing is autobiography' (*DP* 391). This remark is a comment on the essay 'Confession and Double Thoughts' (1985), in which Coetzee, reading Tolstoy, Rousseau, and Dostoevsky, discusses the idea of confession as an infinite regression of 'self-serving fiction[s]', the idea being that there is always an underlying motive for presenting a certain narrative of the self, and that any truth that might emerge can only be provisional and 'tainted with doubt' (*DP* 280, 293). In Coetzee's writing, the telling of a story, regardless of genre, can never be done with complete authority as the truth of the self – the narrator's and the writer's – is always in question. This means, as Coetzee tells David Attwell, that 'all autobiography is *autre*-biography' (Attwell and Coetzee 2006, 216).

Yet, alongside this sense of a truth of self perpetually out of reach, Coetzee's writing simultaneously manifests a persistent self-professed 'longing or nostalgia for the one and only truth' (*GS* 68). It is this paradox that brings about what Coetzee refers to as the 'tragic double awareness' that arises in writing when 'one *believes sincerely in the truth of what one is writing* at the same time that *one knows it is not the truth*' (*GS* 76; emphasis added). Often pronounced in relation to ethical responsibility – notably the fraught position of the gendered white South African subject – the nostalgia for an absolute truth can perhaps best be understood as the desire for *authenticity* – trying to be true to one's self – rather than a transcendent longing. To David Attwell, sensitively bringing together Coetzee's life and work in his study of Coetzee's manuscripts and notebooks in *J.M. Coetzee and the Life of Writing* (2015), Coetzee's writing – Attwell includes both the novels and the autobiographies here – is 'a huge existential enterprise', and he points precisely to Coetzee's 'fear of living inauthentically' as a driving force (2015, 26–7). Indeed, when Coetzee reflects on the question of whether 'among the fictions of the self' yielded by a life of writing there are 'any that are truer than others', he is interested not primarily in 'truth to fact', but in 'something beyond that', which we might understand, perhaps, as the notion of authenticity (*DP* 17). However, Coetzee's work also displays momentary impulses towards transcendence, reminding us of the aforementioned 'Confession' essay, according to which the possibility of undoing of the infinite regress of self-serving fictions must rely, finally, on grace or its secular equivalent.

It is this central point of departure for Coetzee's poetics – that writing originates in a desire to reach *the* truth of self, while such a truth is never fully available; and that the acknowledgement of this impossibility is itself the mark of authenticity – that I approach in this chapter through the idea of the child. The obvious starting point for this discussion is Coetzee's fictionalized autobiographies. In a conversation with Joanna Scott, Coetzee speaks of his memories of childhood as 'the childhood I have constructed for myself in retrospect', which implies that when he approaches his childhood in *Boyhood* (and, equally, his young adult life in *Youth*), the premise is that the true account of the boy John's experience is not available to Coetzee the writer (Coetzee and Scott 1997, 83). Critics have shown how the distance between the adult writer and the young focalizer is highlighted in both works through free indirect discourse, and particularly through the unconventional combination of third-person narration in the present tense.[1] Coetzee himself has pointed out how '[rewriting] *Boyhood* and *Youth* with *I* substituted for *he* throughout would leave you with two books only remotely related to their originals' (Attwell and Coetzee 2006, 216). Taking her lead from this remark, Carrol Clarkson experiments with replacing the third person with the first person in a passage from *Boyhood*. She shows how substituting 'I' for 'he' creates the implausible impression that the child is revealing his secret thoughts at the time of narration. In Clarkson's words, '[situating] both narrating and narrated consciousness in the present of the utterance' produces an effect of 'phoniness' (2013, 26). She shows how this problem is circumvented in the third-person narrative of *Boyhood*, in which the depiction of the child as a distant 'he' creates, instead, a feeling of authenticity.

It is, indeed, striking how in *Boyhood* (as in *Youth*), Coetzee establishes an acute sense of truthfulness in his rendering of a narrative that he at the same time is careful to frame as, ultimately, not quite true. In this chapter I would like to complement existing discussions of the narrative techniques by means of which this sense of authenticity is achieved, by exploring the thematic staging in *Boyhood* of the child's quest towards authenticity. I will argue that the child's approach both to the self and the world – with the fictions encountered, dismantled, and created in this process – offers a compelling figure for Coetzee's poetics; the playful irresponsibilities inevitably entangled with the sense of responsibility inherent in the writerly endeavour to grasp the unreachable.

My claim, then, is that the figure of the child – specifically the child-figure John in *Boyhood* – provides an invaluable optic for approaching Coetzee the writer's never-quite-successful effort to reach a definitive truth of self. There are several reasons for this: First, I am assuming that the literary child figure is a singularly productive 'means for thinking about and creating a self', in Coetzee just as in the nineteenth-century imagination as per Steedman's account discussed in the introduction (Steedman 1995, 20). Also, the strong connection between the child and the aesthetic imagination established in Romantic thought highlights the pertinence of linking the child to the

---

[1] For key references on the choices of narrative techniques in *Boyhood* and *Youth*, see Clarkson (2009) and Lenta (2003).

conundrum of the boundaries between truth and fiction. However, the most compelling reason to look closely at *Boyhood*'s John in a discussion of truth and fiction in Coetzee is found in the following passage:

> He knows he is a liar, knows he is bad, but he does not change. He does not change because he does not want to change. His difference from other boys may be bound up with his mother and his unnatural family, but is bound up with his lying too. *If he stopped lying* he would have to polish his shoes and talk politely and do everything that normal boys do. In that case *he would no longer be himself.* If he were no longer himself, what point would there be in living? (*B* 34–5; emphasis added)

What we learn from this passage is that the child John tells lies – and 'lies', of course, is another way of saying 'fictions' – *as a way of being true to himself*. In fact, this is very close to what Coetzee says about authenticity here: 'Being authentic includes being able to lie and steal and cheat *as long as you don't pretend to yourself* that you are not a liar and a thief and a cheat' (*GS* 85; emphasis added). Importantly, *Boyhood* also dramatizes how, for the child, the creation of these first fictions of the self is tightly linked to navigating the fictions presented by the world. Crucially, and as I will show, these encountered fictions are often fictions about childhood itself.

Fragments of childhoods

Let me now follow some traces of Coetzee's engagements with the idea of the child, insofar as they connect to my subsequent discussion on the child, truth, fiction, and the self. Drawing on biographical fragments alongside Coetzee's critical discourse placed in dialogue with illustrative episodes in Coetzee's fiction, I sketch a brief story of Coetzee's 'story of the child'. It should be said that if navigating the field of figurations of childhood is a thorny enterprise in itself – the figure of the child carrying abundant and oft-contradictory meanings, as I have shown in the introduction – this is no less the case when exploring the figure of the child within the realm of Coetzee's oeuvre. As is true for many aspects of Coetzee's exceptionally erudite writing, his evocations of the child draw on a wide range of cultural sources and resist confinement to theoretical silos. A wealth of traces of Socratic, Biblical, Romantic, Freudian, African, and other figures of the child or childhood are at play in the different works, complicating the task of discerning overarching ideas pertaining to the child.

Coetzee's own childhood in the ethnically segregated South Africa of the 1940s and 1950s was shaped by the peculiar circumstance of being born into an English-speaking family with an Afrikaans name and ancestry, neither comfortably fitting in with the Afrikaner sociocultural heritage nor bearing an organic relation to being 'English'; belonging neither here nor there. Coetzee has remarked that 'by the age of twelve' he had 'a well-developed sense of social marginality' (*DP* 393). If – as it seems fair to assume – the fictional autobiographies bear resemblance to Coetzee's own early life, Coetzee experienced the uncomfortable intersection of, if not exactly irreconcilable, then at least highly incongruent, stories of childhood; on the one hand, variations of the Romantic child – cherished Rousseauan episodes of 'roaming the veld as free as wild animals' (*S* 108); exposure at home to British Romantic poetry and a mother inspired by Steiner and Montessori and concerned with fostering his natural talents; on the other hand, authoritarian Neo-Calvinist schooling attempting to form him 'as congregant, as citizen, and as parent to be' (*S* 252); as well as distant encounters with – in the child character John's eyes – enigmatic coloured children who fit into neither of these paradigms of childhood:[2]

> With Coloured people in general, and with the people of the Karoo in particular, he simply does not know when they cease to be children and become men and women. It seems to happen so early and so suddenly: one day they are playing with toys, the next day they are out with the men, working, or in someone's kitchen, washing dishes. (*B* 86)

As this passage shows, South Africa around 1950 imposed very different versions of childhood on different children, adding, as we will see, to the complication of the idea of the child to *Boyhood*'s John. (The juxtaposition

---

2 In the South African context, 'coloured' is a term that has sometimes been understood as pejorative, but generally not, used to designate a racially diverse group including descendants from the Khoi and San tribes and their mixing with Dutch colonists, slaves from West Africa, the Dutch East Indies, and India. In the Population Registration Act of 1950, a coloured person was defined as a person who was not white or black. During apartheid, coloureds had a slightly more favourable position than blacks in the racial hierarchy, but the blurred racial boundaries meant that coloureds were sometimes designated 'white' or 'black', causing confusion and family tragedies.

of childhoods far removed from each other on both sides of 'the great divide', contrasting 'children scorning childhood' against 'children of paradise, blond, innocent', is presented with particular force in *Age of Iron* (7).)

Attwell observes that Coetzee's own childhood was one of social and cultural isolation, illustrating this sentiment with notes from the drafts of *Summertime*:

> He asks his mother (somewhat accusingly) why she impressed it on him that the world was hostile, that his education should be devoted to making a nest for himself where he would be invulnerable. It strikes him that the children's books that had most enthralled him had revolved around stockades and fortresses: *Treasure Island, Robinson Crusoe*. (Attwell 2015, 149)

Readers of *Boyhood* will recognize the young John's building a 'nest' or 'fortress' of invulnerability in response to an uncomprehending and incomprehensible world. If, as the above passage suggests, Coetzee partly questions this Romantic influence on his upbringing – the idea of the insulated child is a highly Romantic notion – it is nevertheless clear from the published version of *Summertime* that he is grateful to his mother for providing him with 'the kernel of his resistance' to being formed 'in some predetermined image' by the Dutch Calvinist schooling that he was subjected to (252–3). Certainly, Coetzee's biographical experience *as* a child of different 'truths' and 'fictions' *of* the child underline the relevance of making visible these matters in Coetzee's poetics by paying attention to the child figure's approach to truth and fiction in *Boyhood*. Before moving to *Boyhood*'s John, however, I take a brief look at stories of the child throughout Coetzee's oeuvre. As this overview will make clear, double-edged approaches to Romantic notions of the child are a recurrent feature of Coetzee's novels from *Dusklands* and onwards.

(Un)romantic children

I discussed in my introduction how in Romanticism the child is associated with an originary state of being with unmediated access to truth and nature. Episodes in many of the novels show Coetzee playing with Romantic notions of innocence and transcendence. Eugene Dawn, the narrator of *Duskland*'s first section 'The Vietnam Project' harbours a Romantic longing for being liberated from rational discourse into 'wordless being, under the influence of birdsong and paternal love and afternoon walks', but at the same time cannot abide his young son's innocent vulnerability: 'Children will not grow up if they are treated like children' (*DL* 35, 38). In *In the Heart of the Country*, Magda's unstable subjectivity is mirrored in different versions of a childhood self: abject images of a 'baby in a black diaper waving [her] rickety little legs, clutching at [her] black knitted bootees, wailing', and 'an infant, a grub, a white shapeless life with no arms, no legs, nothing even to grip the earth with, a sucker a claw'; the image of the child as primitive with 'unthinking animal integrity'; but also, intriguingly, the near-Wordsworthian notion of a child 'transported out of [herself] for an instant and [having] a vision of [herself] as [she] really was' (*HC* 43–4, 55).

Coetzee's sustained interaction with Romantic ideas of the child is confirmed by Attwell's account of the genesis of the different works. For example, in the process of writing *Life and Times of Michael K*, Coetzee makes 'notes about the boy in Chaucer's *The Prioress's Tale*. Wordsworth's 'Immortality Ode' is mentioned and he speculates about Rudolf Steiner's educational doctrine, remembering the songs used by Waldorf school pupils about angelic children' (Attwell 2015, 137). While he is described as 'a baby, asleep all your life', and as 'an unbearing, unborn creature', the character Michael K in the published novel is not a child, although, as mentioned in the introduction, he was *imagined* as a child at various points in the drafts (*MK* 88, 135). Yet K's resistance to violent history and his ungraspability, the latter at once attracting and unnerving the medical officer, are both related to his childlike qualities. Importantly, the medical officer seems to believe that Michael K has access to some form of transcendent truth unavailable to himself: 'people like Michaels are in touch with things you and I don't understand', he tells his colleague Noël (*MK* 155). The complexity of Coetzee's engagement with the Romantic child comes across also in notes from a 1983 draft of *Foe*. In his writing process, Coetzee is in dialogue with the idea of the child at one with language as a figure of inspiration; at one point in his draft notes, Susan Barton 'feels as if [she] were a cherub flying down from high, but full of words already, piping them' (Attwell 2015, 151). (As Attwell points out, the cherub here is derived from the introduction of William Blake's *Songs of Innocence*.) Coetzee tries to find a way into the 'cleanliness and simplicity' of Defoe's language which is 'incapable of knowing itself', and reflects on Defoe as 'a man who lives in his world, in his language *like a fish in water*' (Attwell 2015, 152; emphasis added). To Coetzee, it is the tension between being in 'language like a fish in water' and the desired *departure* from that innocent state that, he hopes, will animate the novel-to-be. Relatedly, and as I will show, the child figure in *Boyhood* makes visible the creative impetus that lies in the navigation between not-knowing and knowing – albeit without these Romantic resonances.

The Romantic ideal of being in language 'like a fish in water' reminds us of the Magistrate's lament for an imagined childhood unity of being in *Waiting for the Barbarians*, in which the child's link to nature is offered as a counterpoint to 'history': 'What has made it impossible for us to live in time like fish in water, like birds in air, *like children*? It is the fault of Empire! Empire has created the time of history' (*WB* 146; emphasis added).[3] The Magistrate's escapist vision of innocence is certainly not endorsed by the novel, but I will return in Chapter 3 to how the child, nevertheless, is figured as a site of resistance to the determining progress of history. The idea of the child's affinity with nature is brought to life also in those moving moments in *Boyhood*, when John reflects on his feeling more at home on the Karoo farm Voëlfontein than anywhere else: 'He wants to be a creature of the desert, this desert, like a lizard' (*B* 83). Although the Wordsworthian communion between child and nature is not often explicitly visible in Coetzee's work – rather, it lingers under the surface – it does appear at times. In *Disgrace*, lines from a passage in Wordsworth's *Prelude*, linking the child's poetic spirit to its relation to the natural world, surface rather incongruously in David Lurie's mind at the point when his disgrace has become public: 'Blest be the infant babe. No outcast he. Blest be the babe' (*D* 46). Also, towards the end of *Disgrace*, Lurie turns in an affirmative move to Victor Hugo, the latter, like Wordsworth, famous for his celebration of the child's relationship to nature. Alluding to Hugo's collection of poems on childhood innocence, *How to Be a Grandfather* (*L'Art d'être Grand-Père*), Lurie thinks: 'He must have a look again at Victor Hugo, poet of grandfatherhood. There may be things to learn' (*D* 218).

---

3 For a discussion on the tension in Coetzee between mediated social reality and the Romantic vision of subject formation guided by nature, see Smuts (2014).

It is in *Age of Iron* that Coetzee most notably troubles conceptions of childhood as a time of innocence. The novel traces how Mrs Curren gradually – but never wholly – relinquishes her idea of childhood innocence as a consequence of her sociopolitical awakening; her overflowing exposition on innocuous white childhoods illustrates how the novel approaches the idea of the innocent child in an at once distanced and immersive manner; ironic yet never *merely* ironic:

> Swimming lessons, riding lessons, ballet lessons; cricket on the lawn; lives passed within walled gardens guarded by bulldogs; children of paradise, blond, innocent, shining with angelic light, soft as *putti*. Their residence the limbo of the unborn, their innocence the innocence of bee grubs, plump and white, drenched in honey, absorbing sweetness through their soft skins. Slumbrous their souls, bliss-filled, abstracted. (*AI* 7, emphasis in original)

As Mrs Curren comes to realize, the 'real' children Bheki and John that figure in the inferno of apartheid-induced township violence rendered in the novel are anything but 'slumbrous', 'bliss-filled' or 'abstracted', and I will return in Chapter 2 to a consideration of how (post)colonial child figures complicate the narrative of the innocent child.[4]

Romantic notions of the child surface ambiguously also in *Slow Man*, in which especially the boy Drago, but also his younger sister Ljuba, on multiple occasions evoke the sense of something 'angelic' and mystical to the central character Paul Rayment (39, 146, 188). This idea is picked up in the novel in Elizabeth Costello's puzzling monologue about the child:

> From the beginning you have glimpsed something *angelic* in Drago, and I am sure you are not wrong. Drago has remained in touch with his *otherworldly origins* longer than most children. Overcome your disappointment, your irritation. Learn from Drago while you can. One of these days the *last wisps of glory that trail behind him* will vanish into the air and he will simply be one of us. (*SM* 182; emphasis added)[5]

---

4 See Dominic Head on competing ideas of childhood in *Age of Iron* (2010, 134–6).
5 The references to the child as otherworldly in *Slow Man* and the *Jesus* novels are clearly intertextually linked to Rudolf Steiner's anthroposophical teachings. It is also interesting to note that Coetzee's son, Nicolas, began his education in a Waldorf school in Cape Town (Attwell 2015, 254 n.22).

It is tempting to read Costello's (and Coetzee's) exposé of the Romantic idea of the 'other-worldly' child trailing 'wisps of glory' as ironical. Certainly, the comical tone is reinforced by Costello's following enumeration of platitudes:

> You think I am crazy, don't you, or deluded? But remember: I have raised two children, real-life, unmystical children; you have raised none. I know what children are for; you are still ignorant. *So pay heed when I speak, even when I speak in figures. We have children in order that we may learn to love and serve. Through our children we become the servants of time.* (SM 182; emphasis added)

Interestingly, Coetzee foregrounds the *effect* of this ironical treatment of the other-worldly child in such a way that it is unclear what response is elicited from the reader. Paul Rayment reflects: 'Speaking in figures. Angels from on high … She believes what she is saying, it would seem' (*SM* 182). No wonder that Paul Rayment – much like Coetzee's reader – 'never knows, with the Costello woman, when he is being treated seriously and when he is being taken for a ride' (230). If the reader draws the same conclusion as Paul Rayment here, namely that Elizabeth Costello *does* believe that children are the key to learning 'to love and serve', to becoming 'the servants of time', the implication might well be that Coetzee, too, is serious. In this way, *Slow Man* leaves the reader with an authentic remainder of the formulaic figure of the 'angelic' child, despite having created ironic distance to this figure throughout the narrative. Indeed, when Elizabeth Costello says to Rayment, 'Nothing that happens in our lives is without a meaning, Paul, as any child can tell you', we might understand her as referring to precisely the authentic remainder that emerges out of the at once ironic and serious treatment of the Romantic idea of the child (96). (I will return in more detail to ironic figurations of the child in Chapter 2.) As mentioned in the introduction, a similar pattern is visible also in *Diary of a Bad Year*, in which the narrator J. C. alternates between platitudes about the child and a seemingly serious appeal to the very same ideas.

Coetzee's late work manifests a sustained interest in the child as a conduit to absolute selfhood. An important instance of this attentiveness to the child is the already mentioned graduation ceremony speech that Coetzee held at the University of the Witwatersrand in December 2012. In his address, Coetzee urged the young male graduates in particular to consider a career in teaching, highlighting the individual reward to be found in the encounter with the child, the 'nakedness to experience' to be found in a classroom of young children:

> It is not hard to make the case that it will be good for you, good for your soul, to be with small children. One of the dreary facts about jobs in what we call the real world – jobs in which you sell things to people, or buy things from people, or stare all day at a computer monitor fiddling with numbers and figures – is that you are haunted by the feeling that what you are doing is not real, that most of the people you deal with in your work are not real human beings but shadowy figures playing roles and wearing masks.
>
> Well, if you work with young children, I promise you will never have that feeling. Children can be exhausting, they can be irritating, but they are never anything but their full human selves. There is a nakedness to experience in the classroom that you will not encounter in the world of adult work. (Coetzee 2012; emphasis added)

Bewildered by the unexpected simplicity of this message (and, of course, ever cautious, mindful of Coetzee's renowned 1997 Tanner lectures delivered in the name of his fictional persona Elizabeth Costello), critics responded to Coetzee's speech with a certain consternation, some naming it 'the worst convocation speech ever', others attempting to uncover some postmodern prank.[6] However, attentive to the fact that Coetzee's pronouncements about children are never not partly serious, the essence of the Wits lecture is anything but trivial. What Coetzee does in this speech, in placing his emphasis on children as 'never anything but their full human selves', contrasted with an adult world of illusions, is to reaffirm the importance of Romantic notions of the child to his thought. (Of course, the Wits speech could also be read as the preservation of an adult fiction about the child's supposed fullness of being; in fact, it is worth noting that Coetzee subsequently talks in *The Good Story* about 'pitting oneself day after day against children' in the classroom as 'soul-destroying' (162).)

The story of the child in Coetzee continues with the publication of *The Childhood of Jesus* and its sequel *The Schooldays of Jesus*. These novels, too, place the story of the child at the centre of attention, and, just as *Boyhood* does, they put forward the world as a place where the child – and also, importantly,

---

6 See, for example, Poplak (2013).

the adult – navigates between fictions, creating their own stories. I will discuss in Chapters 4 and 5 how the desire to arrive at an absolute truth seems to be backgrounded in these later novels, in favour of the 'shuttling' itself, so to speak. Significantly, though, in the *Jesus* novels, Coetzee foregrounds the adult desire for the child's supposed access to truth, rekindling the Romantic idea of the child that is if not rejected then at least revised in *Boyhood*. However, although the child David writes '*Yo soy la verdad*, I am the truth' on the classroom blackboard, the reader is given no particular reason to believe that the novel itself endorses the idea of the child as possessing some originary access to truth (*CJ* 225). As in earlier novels, the tension between different approaches to the child is evident in *The Childhood of Jesus*; the belief in the child – sometimes expressed through explicit Romantic allusions such as the child David singing Goethe's famous 'Erlkönig' poem, which is precisely about believing in the child – is set against the need for the child to conform to the 'real' world mediated through language and education. This idea is continued in *The Schooldays of Jesus*, in which, as I will argue in Chapter 5, the central character Simón is at once drawn to and sceptical of the idea of a childlike state of wholeness and openness.

The above examples serve to illustrate that Romantic ideas of the child as a figure of wholeness of being, innocence, and transcendence are constantly present and problematized throughout Coetzee's oeuvre. Clearly, Coetzee's personal and writerly histories, intertwined as they are, suggest that his ongoing engagement with Romantic ideas of the child is anything but straightforward.[7] Indeed, Coetzee's characters frequently display frustration with childishness rather than desire for the childlike, and tendencies to mourn or place hope in the child are treated with ambivalence – yet always with a measure of seriousness; Elizabeth Costello, for example, seems decidedly ambivalent towards the possibility that she might have retained a 'childish faith' in 'the artist and his truth' (*EC* 207). I move now to the intersection between the child, truth, and the creation of fictions, to explore how *Boyhood's* John might help us think about 'the artist and his truth' in Coetzee's poetics.

---

[7] A tangent: The character John Coetzee in *Summertime* is posthumously described by his former colleague Sophie as the proponent of 'old-fashioned Romantic primitivism' (*S* 231).

Navigating fictions

As I have already suggested, the child character through whom the interplay between fictions is brought to light most vividly in Coetzee's work is John, the ten-year-old protagonist of *Boyhood*. John is, by his own account, 'a liar', prone to deliberately telling untrue stories about himself: 'He is not honest, straight, truthful' (*B* 34, 100). Leaving aside, for the moment, the point that Coetzee the writer, while striving to be authentic, can never be entirely truthful in his account of his childhood – remembering that 'all autobiography is storytelling' – *Boyhood* is very much a story about childhood as a time of lying, pretending, and concealing. Significantly, *Boyhood* firmly links John's compulsion to make up stories to the circumstance that he finds himself surrounded by stories that he either does not understand or does not believe in. First and foremost among these is the story of childhood itself:

> Childhood, says the *Children's Encyclopaedia*, is a time of innocent joy, to be spent in the meadows amid buttercups and bunny-rabbits or at the hearthside absorbed in a storybook. It is a vision of childhood utterly alien to him. Nothing he experiences in Worcester, at home or at school, leads him to think that childhood is anything but a time of gritting the teeth and enduring. (*B* 14)

Notice how the narrated child figure knows that the narrative of childhood is precisely that – 'a vision of childhood'. This narrative of childhood is alien to the ten-year-old John – the idea of childhood as 'a time of innocent joy' so clearly a fiction bearing no resemblance to his own experience – however, he feels no more affinity with the nationalist Afrikaner version of childhood:

> He thinks of the Afrikaans songs they are made to sing at school. He has come to hate them so much that he wants to scream and shout and make farting noises during the singing, particularly during 'Kom ons gaan blomme pluk', with its children gambolling in the fields among chirping birds and jolly insects. (70)

The disjunctions between stories of childhood in these passages and John's own experience enable me to make the important point that Coetzee's story of the child is as much about dismantling fictions as it is about creating them, starting precisely with the 'foundational fiction' itself: the Western construction of the innocent child.

As a part of his argument in the essay 'Taking Offense' (published in 1996, the year before *Boyhood*), in which he considers the ethical dimensions of censorship, Coetzee questions the adult world's true motives in wishing to 'preserve the childhood of children by protecting them' from information and sights that they are not deemed ready for (*GO* 13):

> Children are not, *qua* children, innocent. We have all been children and know – unless we prefer to forget – how little innocent we were, what determined efforts of indoctrination it took to make us into innocents, how often we tried to escape from the staging-camp of childhood and how implacably we were herded back.[8] ...
>
> Innocence is a state in which we try to maintain our children; dignity is a state we claim for ourselves. Affronts to the innocence of our children or to the dignity of our persons are attacks not upon our essential being but upon constructs – constructs by which we live, but constructs nevertheless. This is not to say that affronts to innocence or dignity are not real affronts, or that the outrage with which we respond to them is not real, in the sense of not being sincerely felt. The infringements are real; what is infringed, however, is not our essence, but a *foundational fiction to which we more or less wholeheartedly subscribe*. (*GO* 14; emphasis added)

It is worth dwelling for a moment on the concept of innocence here. Etymologically, the term evokes the idea of the child as 'not guilty' (*in- nocere* from the Latin 'not harmful'), but also (albeit incorrectly) the idea of the child as 'not knowing' (*in- noscere* from the Latin 'to know'); and the myth of the Garden of Eden, of course, suggests innocence as a state prior to both knowledge and sin. Given that the context to Coetzee's point above is an interrogation of censorship – and within that larger argument, a discussion of pornography – it seems fair to assume that innocence here approximates ignorance, intending a lack of knowledge and experience.

---

8   With regard to the being 'herded back' to the 'staging-camp of childhood', it is worth noting that Coetzee uses very similar imagery in *Summertime* to describe 'the Worcester of his schooldays, where once a week all the children, from youngest to oldest, were herded into the school hall to have their brains washed' (252). In that instance of indoctrination, however, it seems to be the neo-Calvinist Afrikaner nationalist rhetoric that is intended, rather than the idea of childhood innocence that is at stake here.

What Coetzee is saying, then, in this essay and in *Boyhood*, is that while the adult world *wishes to believe* the fiction that children are innocent, children already know and desire to know more than the adult world acknowledges and allows.⁹ This point is distinctly un-Romantic, of course, in establishing that, rather than '[beginning] to close/ Upon the growing Boy', as Wordsworth has it, the 'shades of the prison-house' were there all along; in other words, there never was a point at which the child was entirely free from experience of the world (2008, 67–8). Relatedly, Michiel Heyns observes in his piece on confession in white South African writing how *Boyhood*'s John is aware of his complicity in apartheid power-relations as a 'simple fact'; the child 'is from the start outcast from paradise, and thus never innocent' (Heyns 2000, 52).

However, and in a way that is less paradoxical than it may seem at first glance, Coetzee elaborates elsewhere on the ethical implications of the point that children *are* innocent – not culpable and not-yet-knowing. The following passage is from an interview with David Attwell, in which Coetzee reflects on Vladimir Nabokov's (to Coetzee's mind) naïve mourning of his lost Russian childhood:

> I too had a childhood that – in parts – seems ever more entrancing and miraculous as I grow older. Perhaps that is how most of us come to see our childhood selves: with *a gathering sense of wonder* that there could once have been such an innocent world, and *that we ourselves could have been at the heart of that innocence*. It's a good thing that we should grow fond of the selves we once were – I wouldn't want to denounce that for a minute. The child is father to the man: we should not be too strict with our child selves, we should have the grace to forgive them for setting us on the paths that led us to become the people we are. Nevertheless, we can't wallow in comfortable wonderment at our past. *We must see what the child, still befuddled from his travels, still trailing his clouds of glory, could not see.* We – or at least, some of us, enough of us – must look at the past with a cruel enough eye to see what it was that made that joy and innocence possible. Forgivingness but

---

9   Interestingly, then, the *adult* world is *authentically* committed to the 'lie' about the innocent child. Coetzee expounds on authenticity in *The Good Story*: 'I suspect that the word *authentic* came into wider usage precisely to capture what the word *sincere* fails to ... the phenomenon of the person who holds a belief in all sincerity yet is not committed heart and soul to that belief' (*GS* 85; emphasis in original).

also unflinchingness: that is the mixture I have in mind, if it is attainable. First the unflinchingness, then the forgivingness. (*DP* 29; emphasis added)

The 'joy and innocence' that Coetzee speaks of here may seem as alien to readers of *Boyhood* (which was yet to be written, at the time of the interview) as the entry in the *Children's Encyclopaedia* was to young John. Indeed, Coetzee himself is invoking, here, the 'foundational fiction' about the innocent child to which the adult world 'more or less wholeheartedly [subscribes]' to repeat his words from the earlier quoted passage from *Giving Offense*. But although speckled with Wordsworthian references, the above is not a Romantic view of the child either, but an inversion of Wordsworth. In Wordsworth's 'Ode' the child comes 'trailing clouds of glory' from the 'Heaven [that] lies about us in our infancy', possessing, in other words, an immediate but inarticulate connection to the truth, which will decline with the assimilation of language (64, 66). To Coetzee, instead, the child, rather than bearing a clarity of vision that will gradually recede, is 'still befuddled', held back by the 'clouds of glory', not yet able to see clearly or think rationally. If we read this together with the passage from *Giving Offense*, Coetzee is saying that while, on the one hand, children are not innocent as such, for they always already possess some knowledge of the 'real', on the other hand, the knowledge they have of the world is always incomplete.[10]

What the two passages say, in other words, is that children are neither innocent about the world nor 'visionary'. Yet while 'our child selves' should be forgiven for not fully seeing beyond the fictions, our duty remains to try to approach the 'truth'. Coetzee reiterates the same ethical point in a different interview: 'I try not to lose sight of the fact that we are children, unreconstructed … to be treated with the charity that children have due to them (charity that doesn't preclude clear-sightedness)' (*DP* 249). Reminding us of our own not-knowing, the child who is only ever partly knowing – which, as Coetzee suggests here, is also a figure of what it is to be human – emerges as a central figure for the poetics that animates Coetzee's work; the quest – and duty – to navigate between fictions and truth, of the world and of the self, in an incessant endeavour to approach authenticity.

---

10 Susan Honeyman writes that 'the modern romantic figuration of childhood is prelapsarian, but not entirely unknowing – at once celebrated for innocence and curiosity' (2005, 100).

Coetzee thus emphasizes that children are never-fully-innocent and never-fully-knowing, and reminds us to be charitable in view of the child's – and our own – lack of clarity of vision. In *Boyhood*, the young John is clearly not innocent, yet he is a figure of certain 'befuddledness'. In fact, it is in this very circumstance that we find the root of his inner conflict: although he has exposed the illusion of childhood innocence as precisely that, he is nevertheless himself immersed in this 'foundational fiction'. In school, he is 'greedy to see more' of 'the cruelty and pain and hatred raging beneath the everyday surface of things', yet sees himself as 'too young, too babyish and vulnerable, for what he [is] being exposed to' (139). He recognizes his condition as a construction; he is angry with his mother for 'turning him into something *unnatural*, something that needs to be protected', and is frustrated by the Nationalist party's 1948 ban on Captain Marvel and Superman comics, allowing only the import of 'comics intended to keep one a baby' (8, 70; emphasis added). At the same time, John attributes the idea of childhood innocence to children other than himself: 'Afrikaans children are almost like Coloured children he finds, unspoiled and thoughtless, running wild, then suddenly, at a certain age, going bad, their beauty dying within them' (56). Thus he wanders in and out of the story of the innocent 'unspoiled' child, sometimes resisting the story, sometimes endorsing it, knowingly or unwittingly.

Remarkably – and this is one of the key points of this chapter – in *Boyhood*, the collision of divergent fictions of the child, and the feeling of dissonance between these fictions and his own experience, serves as the impetus to John's creation of his own fictions of the self. In this way, *Boyhood* engages thematically with the point that Coetzee later articulates in *The Good Story* that 'our engagements are with a constantly changing interplay between shadows (fictions) and glimpses of the real' (*GS* 142). Indeed, a careful reading of stories 'of' and 'by' the child in *Boyhood* reveals a distinct pattern where the child's telling of stories emerges as a way of dealing with the – often conflicting – narratives by means of which the 'truth' of the 'real' world is presented or withheld; fictions obscuring but not diminishing a dogged desire for authenticity and for a better understanding of the world.

The notion of innocence, centering as it does on shielding the child from certain truths, produces fictions both on the part of the adult trying to hide certain things, and on the part of the child trying to make sense of the world that is being concealed. (An example of the former is how, in *The Schooldays of Jesus*, Simón makes up 'the easiest, most bearable story he can' to answer the child Davíd's questions about the murder that takes place in the novel (226).) The child himself, however, can never know the extent of his innocence (or ignorance), which is shown in *Boyhood* through the stories that John *does* believe:

> He is not ignorant. He knows how babies are born. They come out of the mother's backside, neat and clean and white. So his mother told him years ago, when he was small. He believes her without question: it is a source of pride to him that she told him the truth about babies so early, when other children were still being fobbed off with lies. (*B* 57)

Through passages such as this, Coetzee stages the child's lack of insight at his own ignorance, and, equally, the child's insight that people, including himself, present different versions of the world. The reader is reminded that the child – as a figure for the self – cannot always distinguish between truth and fiction. Importantly, in all its examples of making up stories, *Boyhood* stages how the disjunction between the conventions of what childhood should be, on the one hand, and John's actual experience and desire, on the other, causes him to lie in order to be faithful to his own experience. So adults construct the child, and the child continues in the same way, constructing his own story, paradoxically, to get closer to the truth.

In his own eyes, this sense of disjunction between the ruling story of the child and his own experience sets the young John apart from other children: 'Among all this innocence and normality, he is the only one who desires' (57). He is painfully aware that the self he presents to the world is a fiction. Eager to conform to expectations, he writes a paper in school elaborating how he polishes his shoes in the morning, although the embarrassing reality is that, in contrast to his classmates, he has never brushed his own shoes; his mother does it for him. Another fiction: on the first day of school, he signs up to be Roman Catholic 'on the spur of the moment' when asked what religion he is (18):

> He chose to be a Roman Catholic, that fateful morning, because of Rome, because of Horatius and his two comrades, swords in their hands, crested

helmets on their heads, indomitable courage in their glance, defending the bridge over the Tiber against the Etruscan hordes. Now, step by step, he discovers from the other Catholic boys what a Roman Catholic really is. A Roman Catholic has nothing to do with Rome. Roman Catholics have not even heard of Horatius. (*B* 20)

Poignantly, such stories – lies – are borne out of precisely the childhood innocence that they taint. At the same time, as I have argued, the lying is a pathway to authenticity: out of the choices of religion available, 'Roman Catholic' resounds the most with John's understanding of himself: a boy who is captivated by Horatius. However, out of the childhood predicament of being at once not-innocent and not-yet-knowing, and of lying in order to be true to himself, a 'burden of imposture' is created, causing John to feel 'damaged' and to dream of getting 'beyond childhood, beyond family and school, to a new life where he will not need to pretend anymore' (9, 13–14). For in the present of *Boyhood*, John's lying in order to be true to himself is a significant source of anxiety:

> If the worst were to happen, he thinks now, facing the worst, if the Catholic priest were to visit his mother and ask why he never comes to catechism, or – the other nightmare – if the school principal were to announce that all boys with Afrikaans names were to be transferred to Afrikaans classes – if nightmare were to turn to reality and he were left with no recourse but to retreat into petulant shouting and storming and crying, into the baby behaviour that he knows is still inside him, coiled like a spring – if, after that tempest, he were as a last, desperate step to throw himself upon his mother's protection, refusing to go back to school, pleading with her to save him – if he were in this way to disgrace himself utterly and finally, revealing what only he in his way and his mother in her way and perhaps his father in his own scornful way know, namely that he is still a baby and will never grow up – *if all the stories that have been built up around him, built by himself, built by years of normal behaviour, at least in public, were to collapse, and the ugly, black, crying babyish core of him were to emerge for all to see and laugh at, would there be any way in which he could go on living?* (*B* 111–12; emphasis added)

Notably, the 'ugly, black, crying babyish core' that John imagines at the heart of his being, is linked to being a child, 'still a baby'. Of course, this abject image bears no resemblance to the Romantic idea of the child's wholeness of being as a point of origin. Instead, the possibility of approaching absolute selfhood is linked to *leaving* childhood and growing up, as when John thinks: 'Whoever he truly is, whoever the true "I" is that ought to be rising out of the ashes of his childhood, is not being allowed to be born, is being kept puny and stunted' (140). However, while the child character John imagines that, with adulthood, authenticity will no longer depend on making up stories, Coetzee's comments on truth and writing in *Doubling the Point* and *The Good Story* suggest that the adult writer's predicament is the same as the child's: also for the adult, it is in the creation of fictions that the 'truth' can be approached.

Moments of openness

I outlined earlier in this chapter how Coetzee seems not to direct his characters towards childhood as a space of unmediated truth other than in rare moments; this is certainly the case in *Boyhood*. To invert Wordsworth again, heaven pointedly does *not* lie about the young John in his infancy. Instead, it is the child's approach to the world and varying stories about that world that forms the backdrop to his gradual creation of his own story. Relatedly, when Coetzee reminisces in *The Good Story* about his own storytelling as a child, he understands it as a way of '[handling] the real world':[11]

> I remember at the age of eight or nine becoming aware of myself as a child given inordinately to fantasy ... I compared myself with other children of my age, contrasting the ease with which they handled the real world with my own ineptitude. Nonetheless, I never thought of giving up my fantasy life and attaching myself to the real. Rather, I accepted fantasising as a kind of affliction that had been visited on me at birth, a congenital disease that I was doomed to carry. (*GS* 156)

---

11 For a discussion about the imagination as a way of dealing with the epistemological problem of knowing reality in Coetzee, see Su (2011).

We are reminded of *Boyhood*'s John, busy navigating the 'real world' by creating those stories of the self that appear most truthful to him at each juncture. The 'affliction' of fantasizing is also attributed to the character David in *The Childhood of Jesus*. But, other than their shared propensity to tell stories, John and David are very differently rendered. David displays flashes of 'rapt, distant' transcendence; instants when his guardian Simón looks into his eyes, and, 'for the briefest of moments, sees something there' (151, 186). Similar episodes recur also in *The Schooldays of Jesus*. Interestingly, these scenes bear uncanny resemblance to Coetzee's account in *Inner Workings* (2008) of the childhood recollections of Bruno Schulz. Coetzee recounts with great attentiveness how Bruno Schulz attributes his creative powers to otherworldly images from the inner life of his childhood, moments of 'creative rapture', a 'mythologised childhood "when everything blazed with godly colors"'; and, not least, Schulz's trance-like vision of the Erlkönig story (which Coetzee has David sing out of the blue on a bus ride in *The Childhood of Jesus*) (*IW* 65, 71, 77). However, unlike David, *Boyhood*'s John does not have such trance-like visions of transcendence. Instead, he has moments of '[seeing] the *world* as it really is' (*B* 160; emphasis added):

> Sometimes the gloom lifts. The sky, that usually sits tight and closed over his head, not so near that it can be touched but not much further either, *opens a slit, and for an interval he can see the world as it really is*. He sees himself in his white shirt with rolled-up sleeves and the grey short trousers that he is on the point of outgrowing: not a child, not what a passer-by would call a child, too big for that now, too big to use that excuse, yet still as stupid and self-enclosed as a child: childish; dumb; ignorant; retarded. In a moment like this he can see his father and his mother too, from above, without anger: not as two grey and formless weights seating themselves on his shoulders, plotting his misery day and night, but as a man and a woman living dull and trouble-filled lives of their own. *The sky opens, he sees the world as it is, then the sky closes and he is himself again, living the only story he will admit, the story of himself.* (*B* 160–1; emphasis added)

This striking evocation of a fleeting moment of seeing 'the world as it really is' represents a different mode of seeing – and writing – than the idea of the transcendent clear-sightedness of the child (which is how David appears to the adult Simón in *The Childhood of Jesus*). It is precisely the representation of such 'heightened openness' to the world that Coetzee describes admiringly in his essay on Doris Lessing's autobiographical writing, which, he writes, belongs 'among the great pieces of writing about childhood' (*SS* 295–6).[12] He notes how certain of Lessing's childhood passages 'celebrate special moments, Wordsworthian "spots of time", in which the child is *intensely open to experience and also aware of heightened openness*, aware that the moment is privileged' (*SS* 295–6; emphasis added).[13]

Remarkably, it is the foregrounding of the *gap* between John's 'story of himself' and his experience that can never quite be captured that produces a sense of authenticity. Perhaps we might find here an affinity between Coetzee and the Australian writer Patrick White, whom Coetzee portrays as a 'Great Writer in the Romantic mould', in that he 'had the typically great-writerly sense of being marked out from birth for an uncommon destiny and granted a talent ... which it is death to hide, the talent in his case consisting in a heightened power to *see through appearances to the truth behind them*' (*LE* 218; emphasis added).

I set out in this chapter to propose the child's navigation and creation of fictions in a quest towards authenticity as a compelling figure for Coetzee's poetics. In *Boyhood*, the child's clarity of vision emerges not in a Romantic fullness of experience and the absence of social stories, but in the *friction* between experience and stories of childhood; a *revised* Romanticism, then. This friction, or gap, is where fictionalizing takes place. Indeed, one way to understand the particular interaction between fiction and truth evinced by the child is through Coetzee's retrospective reflection on his childhood photography: 'I believe I was interested in being present at the moment when

---

12 The essay on Lessing appeared originally in the *New York Review of Books* in 1994, at a time when Coetzee had temporarily abandoned his early work on *Boyhood*.
13 Coetzee's early (1993) notes for *Boyhood* suggest the challenges involved in trying to evoke such openness to experience in his own writing of childhood:

> Who is this *he* who will not speak his name? Why will he not bring the story to life? What puritanism keeps him from evoking those wet winter mornings, wind-still, droplets on every leaf, mist over the roads, the glow of headlights and the soft swish of approaching tyres, and the boy on his bicycle breathing, breathing in mist and breathing out mist; the velvety softness of the mist? Why not live with this living boy? (Attwell 2015, 153; emphasis in original)

truth revealed itself, a moment which one *half discovered* but also *half created*' (Coetzee and Wittenberg 2017; emphasis added).

Importantly, the point that the storytelling in *Boyhood* emerges in the friction between experience and stories of childhood is another way of saying that the storytelling emerges in a social realm. I noted earlier in this chapter how, in the notes for *Summertime*, the character John questions the fact that 'his education should be devoted to making a nest for himself', and, equally, how he is struck by the fact that 'the children's books that had most enthralled him had revolved around stockades and fortresses' (Attwell 2015, 149). Yet, as I have shown, the journey towards self-discovery staged in *Boyhood* is not one of Romantic insulation, but one of constant dialogue or play between the self in search of authenticity and the stories of others; as I have argued, it is out of such interactions that fictions of the self keep emerging. In Chapter 3, I will return to how the child in Coetzee gestures towards the importance of the shared human world as a space for dialogue and renewal.

Authentic encounters: From self to other

I have argued in this chapter that the rendering in *Boyhood* of the child's approach to the self and the world shows how the quest for authenticity takes place in the form of a constantly evolving dialogue between stories of the self and other stories of childhood and of the world. Inevitably, in Coetzee's novels, being attuned to the world while trying to be truthful to the self puts particular ethical pressure on the white South African subject. One of the most ethically charged scenes in *Boyhood* may serve to illustrate this point. The episode in question figures John celebrating his birthday, feeling 'princely' and treating his three best friends to ice cream sundaes at a local café, when, suddenly, the magic is broken and the occasion 'spoiled by the ragged Coloured children standing at the window looking in' (*B* 72). The silent encounter reminds John of his own privileged position: 'On the faces of these children he sees none of the hatred which, he is prepared to acknowledge, he and his friends deserve for having so much money while they are penniless' (72). If John were someone else, he thinks, he would ask to have the children chased away. But although he wishes that the onlookers, 'like children at a circus, drinking in the sight', would disappear, he cannot bring himself to say to the café owner, 'they are spoiling my birthday, it is not fair, it hurts my heart to see them' (73). Either way, he reflects, 'whether they are chased away or not, it is too late, his heart is already hurt'. Importantly, although John's initial disappointment is caused by the appearance of the 'other' children, his discomfort – his 'hurt' heart – is produced by his own ethically fraught response to this interruption. Chapter 2 turns from trying to reach a truth of self to relating to the (post)colonial other – and to the ethical implications of the ambivalent responses brought out by the child in such encounters.

2

Ethics of the not-so-other child

Magda, the spinster sheep farmer's daughter of *In the Heart of the Country*, is one of the protagonists in Coetzee for whom the lack of a reciprocal relation to the (post)colonial other is most overtly linked to an unstable sense of self. Trapped in her 'father-tongue', a 'language of hierarchy, distance and perspective', her failure to grasp the self at the core of her being is as pronounced as her failure to know the 'others' living on the farm (*HC* 106). Magda's predicament of knowing neither self nor other is presented partly through conflicting invocations of the child scattered through the narrative, sometimes underlining and sometimes undermining (post)colonial self-other boundaries in the early-twentieth-century time of pre-apartheid master-servant relationships in rural South Africa.[1] Her fragmented tale weaves between visions of sameness and difference, inscribed in alternately prelapsarian and (post)colonial figurations of the child. She recalls – or imagines recalling – a sense of proximity growing up with the servants' children: 'I spoke like one of them before I learned to speak like this' (7).

> At the feet of an old man I have drunk in a myth of a past when beast and man and master lived a common life as innocent as the stars in the sky, and I am far from laughing. How am I to endure the ache of whatever it is that is lost without a dream of a pristine age, tinged perhaps with the violet of melancholy, and a myth of expulsion to interpret my ache to me? (7)

In this passage, the loss of childhood is intertwined with the loss of the myth of a shared point of origin, a sense of nostalgia for 'a common life', although,

---

1 There is no mention of the temporal setting in the novel *In the Heart of the Country*. However, Coetzee's unrealized 1981 screenplay 'In the Heart of the Country' (*Two Screenplays*, UCT Press, 2014) situates the beginning of the story at 'circa 1910', and the last part in 'the mid-1930's' (28).

of course, this myth is itself based on a hierarchy of 'man and master'. But in the here and now of her narrative, Magda no longer speaks 'like one of them'; instead, distance and difference to 'the brown folk' is evoked through the image of the other as child: '*I live neither alone nor in society but as it were among children ... Reading the brown folk I grope, as they grope reading me*' (8; emphasis added). In Magda's present, the childhood proximity to the farm's servants has been lost; instead, they are '*children*' in their otherness, and both sides 'grope' in vain to overcome the gap of (post)colonial difference. Crucially, Magda's consideration of the servant girl Klein-Anna prompts the former to look back at herself: 'If she is a child, what am I?' (31). At a later point in the text, Magda has trouble reconciling the idea of the innocent child with her own image: 'How can I believe this creature was ever a child, how can I believe she was born of humankind?' (41). Here and elsewhere in Coetzee, the idea of the child draws out ambiguities in the construction of both the self, the other and the self-other relation.

These brief excerpts from *In the Heart of the Country* are emblematic of the complex relation between the self, the other and the child in Coetzee. In fact, it is striking how often child figures feature in encounters between self and (post)colonial other in Coetzee's work, and in this chapter I ask what insights into the ethics of Coetzee's writing might be gained from this observation. Noting the entanglement of ideas of the child with (post)colonial discourses, and remembering also the child's relation to the idea of the self (as discussed in the introduction), I draw attention to how reminders of the child's constructedness surface in the staging of self-other encounters in Coetzee's novels. I observe Coetzee's often ironic treatment of the child, and seek to understand what implications the ambiguity surrounding the child – an ambiguity that reflects both the constructedness of the idea of the child and its resonance with specific historical discourses – might have for the broader critical conversation on the ethics of the other in Coetzee.

I particularly wish to explore how the undecidability of the child in Coetzee always seems to point back to the *self* – of the protagonist, and of the reader. In this context, it is worthwhile thinking about how the ethical force of irony is derived from the way it generates uncertainty in the reader. Claire Colebrook points out the distinction between stable and unstable irony; the former reinforcing shared norms and values, presupposing the idea of a 'social and political life as primarily reciprocal, common, and operating from a basis of agreement'; the latter ethical precisely through its undecidability and its challenge of 'just how shared, common and stable our conventions and assumptions are' (2004; 16, 18). She distinguishes between irony as the simultaneous expression of paradoxical or contradictory ideas (as Socratic irony is often understood), and irony with no intention of a particular meaning – an irony that '[retreats] from the difference and conflict of political life' (a stance often attributed to the Romantic poets) (70). In Coetzee, the ethics of irony lies in the uncertainty produced in the reader, who suspects (but cannot conclusively know) that Coetzee does not mean what he says, yet cannot determine exactly what he means instead, or if the point is in fact the coexistence of contradictory perspectives; there is, as Derek Attridge puts it, a 'permanent possibility of irony' (2004a, 7). In Coetzee's figurations of the child, he occasionally seems to authentically embrace that which he treats ironically, reminding the reader never to allow a sometimes playful tone to obscure an unremitting serious attitude. If irony is, as Claire Colebrook puts it, the act of displaying a certain belief 'in order to show its limits and fragility', Coetzee certainly brings us to the limits of the belief in the child, but, significantly, without ever abandoning that belief (2004, 5). As I show in this chapter, Coetzee's ironic treatment of the child serves both to problematize meaning attributed to the child in fictional representations and ethically to propose the idea of a stable common ground signposted by the child. I understand Coetzee's ironic questioning of fundamental assumptions related to the child not as a retreat from sociopolitical realities – although he does not commit to any particular position, Coetzee is decidedly attuned to the world – but as a continuous endeavour towards a tenable ethical attitude.

Discussions on ethics and politics in Coetzee criticism have conventionally tended to revolve around Coetzee's choice not to engage directly with politics, often as a source of contention. This was especially the case in South Africa during apartheid and in its immediate aftermath, when critical voices – taking issue with early poststructuralist readings of Coetzee's work and deeming Coetzee's preoccupation with language and discourse insufficient, irresponsible even, in the face of South African sociopolitical realities – denounced Coetzee for avoiding representations of the racially oppressed and for not taking an explicit political stand in and outside of his fiction.

Meanwhile, others defended Coetzee's careful approach to questions of authority, complicity and responsibility as an ethically valuable if less overt way of approaching the pressing dilemmas of South African society and history through literature. Influential instances of this argument are David Attwell's coining of 'situational metafiction' as a synthesizing concept to describe the complex relationship between Coetzee's self-reflexive texts and South African history and society; Derek Attridge locating a Derridean ethics of hospitality to the other in Coetzee's work; and Carrol Clarkson bringing together the ethical with the linguistic in her exploration of how 'countervoices' are raised in Coetzee's fiction. In a more recent intervention, Jarad Zimbler shows how Coetzee's prose through its very style 'constitutes the meaning of his fictions', and compellingly argues that Coetzee's style, unlike what has sometimes been assumed, orients his fiction towards – not away from – the world (2014, 202). For Zimbler, as for other critics working in this vein, reflexivity in Coetzee is not a comment on the inescapability of language and linguistic mediation, but a way of engaging with discourses of power.

Against this background – and similarly recognizing Coetzee's ethics as turned towards the world that exceeds the text, and his work as conducive to different readings in different historical moments – my readings in this chapter show how the figure of the child bridges the reflexivity and the historicity of Coetzee's narratives. On the one hand, recurring allusions to the constructedness of the child – as well as the subversions of such constructions – are manifestations of precisely the self-conscious engagement with different types of discourse that inspired early poststructuralist readings of Coetzee's work. I argue here that Coetzee's playful yet persistent attention to coexisting and mutually contesting constructions of the child undermines the authority of his narrators by making visible their position within certain dominant discourses; at the same time, it underlines his narrating figures' varying degrees of limited knowledge about the other and, equally, their unstable conceptions of the self. On the other hand, the child's constructedness is itself a reflection of its situatedness in concrete historical contexts, and Coetzee's persistent subversion of conventional ideas of the child in stagings of self-other encounters serves to highlight the historical contingencies that saturate the content of each narrative. In this process,

I suggest, the destabilization of Western ideas of the child also provides space for the voice of the historically specific other more forcefully than is sometimes acknowledged.

Noticing how Coetzee's figuring of the child and responses to the child undermines his focalizers' tendencies both to universalize and to 'other', I ask whether the ethical potency of the child in his fiction might not be exactly this: its role as a site of difference *and* sameness, interrupting the boundary between self and other. It is worth making the point here that the adult-child relationship is a special configuration of self and other, in that, as Karin Lesnik-Oberstein observes, 'whereas most self-other relationships are based on ostensible differentiation of self from other, every adult has, in some sense or other, been a child' (1994, 34). So, while the adult encounter with the child is always characterized by a certain distance due to the child's perceived unknowability, it also incites a form of uncanny recognition. (These connections are obviously further complicated in the case of individual parent-child relationships, where the sameness/difference of the child to the self are calibrated in particular ways.) In my readings of encounters featuring the child as (post)colonial other in Coetzee, I show how both gestures – both distancing and recognition – provoke the projection of abstract assumptions onto the child that are subsequently overturned, thereby drawing attention to the instability of the focalizer's understanding of self and other. In other words, the self-other relation is troubled both by the assumption that the child is other to the self and by the assumption that it is not. What I am curious about is what the ethical potential might be of this zone of indeterminacy between self and other that the child figure seems to evoke.

It is worth clarifying that Coetzee's child figures themselves are rarely explicitly presented as ambiguous. Instead, the indeterminacy of the idea of the child in Coetzee is often achieved through contradictory moments in the narration, and through children's participation in multiple discourses. Frequently, the irony is dramatized within the realm of the focalizer's consciousness, through successions of disparate reflections on or inconsistent affective responses to the child. The mostly one-dimensional characterization of Coetzee's child figures means that encounters with the child are often shown as responses to a projected idea rather than as interactions with a singular other.

I look here at fictions set in recognizable moments produced by (post)colonial South African history, the early exploration stage of Dutch settler colonialism in the eighteenth century ('The Narrative of Jacobus Coetzee'), the violent years of the apartheid States of Emergency of the late 1980s (*Age of Iron*), and (briefly) the early post-apartheid years of the late 1990s (*Disgrace*). Embedded in these narratives are a number of self-other encounters figuring the child. In such moments, child figures frequently emerge as 'doubly' other; both child – as opposed to adult, not parent – and stranger to the focalizing subject. Significantly, the ironic foregrounding of the idea of the child works directly to animate the ethical interrogations at the heart of each text; for example, in *Dusklands*, the instability of the idea of the child undermines the authority of the narrator; in *Age of Iron*, the unheard history of the 'other' child and the foregrounding of Mrs Curren's (at least partial) failure to hear that other story creates ethical tension; and in episodes in each of the novels, encounters with the child – or the idea of the child – demonstrate the ethical consequences of elusive intersections between self and other. Although the different passages emphasize different constructions of the child, they have in common that child figurations accentuate the texts' self-reflexive gestures; most strikingly, as I have already suggested, through the use of irony. As I noted earlier, it is noticeable that Coetzee virtually always uses irony when invoking constructions of the child.[2] My readings show how irony in relation to the child is put to work in different ways in different episodes; sometimes the joke is unmistakably on the focalizer and his or her implication in a certain discourse, sometimes it is less clear to what extent the focalizer is aware and critical of his or her own position in relation to different discourses – and equally unclear what type of response is elicited from the implied reader. Clearly, the ironic uncertainties implicit in the child figure's overdetermination contribute to its ethical force.

---

2 Another example: In Coetzee's essay 'The Burden of Consciousness in Africa', he comments on how the biographical film on Eugène Marais, *The Guest*, uses the figure of a child in order for its subject to appear 'good', as 'popular wisdom has it that a child can smell goodness as a lion can smell fear'. It is not without irony that Coetzee notes the film's gestures to portray Marais as a Romantic Genius and to allow him 'access to the true and deep of childhood' (*DP* 119–20).

The savage-as-child-as-self

A reading of Coetzee's first novel, *Dusklands*, confirms that Coetzee has been paying attention to the child as a construct at the heart of various discourses of power since the outset of his writerly career. I am interested here in a sequence of disturbing encounters with the child in the second novella, 'The Narrative of Jacobus Coetzee'. This tale of the Dutch settler Jacobus Coetzee's expeditions across the Orange River and his violent encounters with Namaqua villagers consists of several texts, supposedly translated from Afrikaans and Dutch by one 'J.M. Coetzee': the first-person narrative *Relaas van Jacobus Coetzee* relating two expeditions into Namaqualand, an afterword by 'J.M. Coetzee's' father, the scholar S. J. Coetzee (also the editor of Jacobus Coetzee's narrative) and the 'official deposition' by their ancestor Jacobus Coetzee, dated 1760. The constructedness of the texts is made obvious by the discrepancies between them as well as through the attention to inauthentic presentations of historical 'truths'.[3] The text's J. M. Coetzee's translated version of the narrative reveals violence concealed in S. J. Coetzee's original account (judging by the afterword), and, as my reading will show, exposes moments of openness to and fear of the sameness to be found in the other, in both cases provoked by encounters with the figure of the child. The idea of the child is figured in the parodic mode that characterizes *Dusklands* in its entirety, with its repetition of colonial discourse; in fact, the child is at the very core of the parody.[4] As Marek Pawlicki (2013) observes, 'creating myths and claiming universal significance for them' runs as a common thread through the two *Dusklands* novellas. And the central myth, in the narrative of Jacobus Coetzee, is the foundational story of colonial discourse – the idea of the savage-as-child in need of civilization and discipline.

---

3 For a detailed review of the various inconsistencies between the texts (and their inaccuracies in relation to Jacobus Coetzee's historically authentic account), see Attwell (1993, 44–58). For an account of self-reflexive gestures and historical mediations in the texts, see Marek Pawlicki (2013).
4 Linda Hutcheon defines parody as 'repetition with critical distance that allows ironic signalling of difference at the very heart of similarity', arguing that parody signals both continuities and discontinuities with the past (1988, 26). For a discussion of how *Dusklands*' two novellas enact Coetzee's simultaneous complicity with and distancing from colonial discourse, see Attwell's chapter 'The Labyrinth of My History' (1993, 35–69).

The notion of the (post)colonial other as child is a figure of thought that dates back to the eighteenth century. In a study of how assumptions about innocence, imagination, nature and primitivism inherent in the Romantic figure of the child engendered new ways of thinking in the period, Ann Rowland (2012) observes that 'the ideas associated with childhood that emerged in the Romantic period, and the rhetoric and images that gave them shape, became foundational to the dominant cultural and historical paradigms of the nineteenth and twentieth centuries and thus to how for a significant period of time, we have explained the world' (10). Central among the cultural paradigms that emerged out of the Enlightenment and the Romantic idea of the child was recapitulation theory, according to which the life span of the individual reflects the history of mankind as a whole. According to this formula, the development of the growing child reflects the gradual civilizing of the 'savage' in a removed time or place; and, in a circular logic, 'savages were made developmentally equivalent to children, who were made developmentally equivalent to savages figured as children' (Castañeda 2002, 26).[5] In combination with the period's elevated view of the child, the idea that the pre-literate child and savage shared the need for civilization formed a strangely benevolent justification of British imperialism; Jo-Ann Wallace argues that the child-savage analogy paved the way for the 'parent-child logic of imperial expansion' (1994, 175). Similarly, Ashis Nandy (1987) traces 'much of the pull of the ideology of colonialism and much of the power of the idea of modernity' to 'the evolutionary implications of the concept of the child in the Western worldview' (57).

In other words, the idea of the child, as Jo-Ann Wallace puts it, '[made] thinkable' colonial imperialism (1994, 171).[6] The co-emergence of developmentalism, recapitulation theory and new educational theories in the late nineteenth century provided imperialist discourse with compelling analogies between child and savage, both to-be-developed/civilized – and in so doing undermined the

---

[5] Castañeda traces how nineteenth-century developmentalism took as its point of departure the child's potential to grow, figuring the child as the embodiment of human difference across a range of scientific discourses such as biology, anthropology and psychology. She argues that child's value in and for these discourses 'lies in its figuration as a body that can precisely figure forth such a wide range of differences' (2002, 45). See also *The Cult of Childhood* by George Boas (1966), for an account of the relationship between primitivism and the child in the eighteenth century.
[6] Wallace's argument refers to nineteenth-century English colonial imperialism.

boundary between self and other.⁷ The child analogy in colonial discourse makes visible the ambivalent (if consistently condescending) attitudes towards the 'savage' at the time; the child/savage sometimes 'innocent' and sometimes 'bad'; evoking at once well-intentioned missionary enthusiasm and imperialist racism.⁸ The journeys of Jacobus Coetzee, it should be noted, are set in the mid-eighteenth century before the emergence of this discourse (just before the publication in 1762 of Rousseau's *Émile*, which was to underpin later thinking on the intersection between child, education and imperialism), but such anachronisms only serve to draw attention to the fact that the editor 'S.J. Coetzee' and the translator 'J.M. Coetzee' have interfered with their ancestor's account.

The colonial investment in the figure of the child is made visible throughout Jacobus Coetzee's narration, marked also by the Calvinist ideas of the Dutch colonial community. He describes how he 'restore[s] order' among his Namaqua servants 'with a firm but fair hand' and how the servants see him 'as their father' (*DL* 64). The ambiguous colonial identity of being at once 'the father and the oppressor' as Homi Bhabha has it, is soon made apparent when the fatherly tone alternates with the brutal disciplining of servants (1994, 135).⁹ Scattered throughout the narrative are also pseudoscientific statements reinforcing both the idea of the indigenous-as-child-as-primitive and the point of the all-knowing colonizer constantly fitting the other into his own model of the world. Jacobus Coetzee refers to the Namaqua as 'barbarians, children of nature' and presents the Khoisan as feral with their 'inborn knowledge of the veld and wild animals', emphasizing the importance of 'taming' them 'very young, not older than seven or eight' (60, 65, 76).

---

7 A tangent: Coetzee quotes Ernst Haeckel's 'biogenetic law' that 'ontogeny recapitulates phylogeny' in his essay 'Four Notes on Rugby', reflecting that the child's propensity to gradually move from free to rule-based play is analogous to a historical change, where games with variable rules in older societies were gradually replaced by codified games (*DP* 125).
8 A good example of how literature of the time makes use of the child figure is the Scottish writer J. M. Ballantyne's novel for young boys *The Settler and the Savage* (1877), set in the Cape of the 1820s. Finding indigenous 'childlike' customs at once 'quaint' and 'ludicrous', Ballantyne imagines 'the savage' as a bad child: 'a very infant in everything except physical force and wickedness. To put him on an equality with civilized whites is equivalent to granting, in England, the franchise to boys.' See Robert Giddings (1991, 55–60).
9 Bhabha is quoting Macaulay's 1841 essay on Warren Hastings, the first governor of India, but a similar ambiguity can be transposed to Dutch colonial discourse in South Africa, at least as it is rendered in *Dusklands*.

Attwell describes Jacobus Coetzee's patronizing narration as a 'fiction of self-assertion' that is eventually undermined, noting also its 'categorical emphasis on difference' (1993, 48). Certainly, the insistent trope of the savage-as-child is distinctly othering. However, already on the very first page, the universal image of the playing child offers a glimpse of common ground: 'Our children play with servants' children and who is to say who copies whom? In hard times how can differences be maintained?' (*DL* 57). In these questions lie not only the colonizer's preoccupation with maintaining difference, but also an opening for connection, a hint at an insight into the constructed relation between self and other; an interruption from within the colonial discourse of the child. The same opening comes across also in Jacobus Coetzee's later musings about self-other oppositions as 'little comedies of man and man, prospector and guide, benefactor and beneficiary, victim and assassin, teacher and pupil, father and child' (*DL* 81). Such interceptions featuring the child and ironically highlighting the constructedness – 'little comedies' – of othering boundaries, serve to create uncertainty in the reader regarding the position of the narrator, who seems to propose both proximity and distance between the self and the Namaqua other. This tension between sameness and distance is, of course, the very hallmark of colonial discourse, in which violence towards the other is, ultimately, a defence against intimacy. In his Jerusalem Prize acceptance speech, Coetzee reflects on apartheid in terms of the 'denial of an unacknowledgeable desire to embrace Africa … and fear of being embraced in return by Africa' (*DP* 97).

Notice how while the idea of a certain common origin between self and other is evoked through childhood (recall also Magda's fragmented memories of playing with the servants' children), the divergence from such proximity is figured through adulthood, as 'S.J. Coetzee' also indicates in his afterword: 'Thus Coetzee on his farm laid the foundations for another of those durable relations in which farmer and servant dance in slow parallel through time, the farmer's son and the servant's son playing *dolosse* together in the yard, graduating with adulthood into the more austere relation of master and servant' (*DL* 115).

The idea of the child disrupts the self-assertive tone of Jacobus Coetzee's discourse once again in the encounter with an unknown group of Namaquas, when he is momentarily confused by not being able to discern if the strangers are adults or children: 'Was I dealing with adults? I wondered' (67). The point of not knowing whether or not the other is a child has a disorienting effect; the other appears suddenly opaque and indistinguishable and no longer has quite so firm a position within the self's frame of reference. This inability to distinguish between adult and child has similar distancing effects in 'The Vietnam Project', when Eugene Dawn studies a woman in one of his photographs, 'possibly even a child, though one is usually wrong about the ages of Vietnamese', and in *Boyhood*, when young John reflects that 'with Coloured people in general, and with the people of the Karoo in particular, he simply does not know when they cease to be children and become men and women' (*DL* 13, *B* 86).

Clearly, figurations of child and savage work in mutually reinforcing ways, adding to their discursive power. In several instances, Jacobus Coetzee refers to *adult* Namaquas as disobedient children in need of guidance – for example when he threatens to carry back a 'report' about his hosts as 'envious children [squabbling] over gifts', priding himself in the 'schoolmasterly threat' he has just wielded, thinking about how 'Hottentots show only the most perfunctory reverence for authority', and considering them as 'children of nature' (70, 72, 76). Namaqua *children*, on the other hand, he sees consistently as savages – 'predatory juveniles' and 'troops of odious chattering hand-clapping boys' – not considering their childish ways in terms of just that – childishness (71, 76). This linguistic distinction works to maintain distance to the Namaqua; viewing the *other* as *child* maintains the hierarchy where the self is superior, whereas viewing the *other child* as *savage* takes place when this sense of superiority is threatened, forestalling the emergence of the child as a site of sameness.

Jacobus Coetzee's view of the other child as savage is at the centre of what I read as the defining disruption to his discourse, in which the voice of the other speaks unexpectedly. The episode leading up to this interruption – explicitly foregrounded, in fact, as 'the interruption' in the below quote – takes place when Jacobus Coetzee first ventures out from the Namaqua hut where he has been quarantined and attended to after falling ill. Seeking some privacy to deal with an aching abscess, he goes upstream from the village, punctures the boil that is paining him, relieves his bowels in the stream and washes himself:

> It was during the postlude, while I was dipping my buttocks in the running water and enjoying the cool, that *the interruption* came. Boys, those

> detestable boys who had lost no chance to taunt the stranger in their midst, raced screeching out of the undergrowth from which they had been spying on me and whipped my clothes from the bank where they lay. Shocked out of my idyll I stood straddle-legged in the water like a sheep while they pranced up and down waving my trousers, daring me to recover them. (*DL* 89; emphasis added)

Beyond the situational irony here, with the supposedly civilized Jacobus Coetzee eliminating waste in the stream that serves as drinking water, the great irony presents itself in the reversal between savage and civilized in his reaction to the children. Rather than understanding the incident as an instance of playfulness, Jacobus Coetzee reads the 'detestable', 'screeching' children as malevolent and savage, responding with a shocking act of violence:

> Roaring like a lion and enveloped in spray like Aphrodite I fell upon them. My claws raked welts of skin and flesh from their fleeing backs. A massive fist thundered one to the ground. Jehovah I fell upon his back, and while his little playmates scattered in the bushes and regrouped, I ground his face on the stones, wrenched him upright, kicked him down (with the ball of my foot, lest I break a toe), wrenched him up, kicked him down, and so on, shouting the while in the foulest Hottentot I could summon conjurations to his mates to come back and fight like men. This was imprudent. First one and then the whole pack returned. Clinging on my back, dragging at my arms and legs, they bore me to the ground. I screamed with rage, snapped my teeth, and heaved erect with a mouth full of hair and a human ear. (*DL* 90)

There is an interesting movement here that sees Jacobus Coetzee shift between the opposing poles of savage and child. When Jacobus Coetzee for an instant sees himself as a savage – a 'lion' with raking 'claws' – he surprisingly refers to the children as children, 'little playmates'. However, as soon as he himself feels vulnerable, the children appear to him as a 'pack' again. When, following the intervention of adult villagers, the fight eventually culminates with the defeat and humiliation of Jacobus Coetzee, he reverts, remarkably, into child-like behaviour, screaming 'let me go home, I want to go home, I want to go home!'; then invoking a strangely regressive image: 'I withdrew', he recounts, 'inside myself ... in my womb of ice' (91).

This ironic reversal, in which the self is experienced alternately as savage and child, creates an undesirable common ground with the other. This is also signalled in an earlier sequence of passages, when a (possibly delirious) Jacobus Coetzee experiences a child straying into his hut:

> It had no nose or ears and both upper and lower foreteeth jutted horizontally from its mouth. Patches of skin had peeled from its face, hands, and legs, revealing a pink inner self in poor imitation of European colouring. (*DL* 83)

The bizarre figure of the monstrous child's 'pink inner self' suggests an uncanny and unwelcome proximity between Jacobus Coetzee and the other (and recalls Eugene Dawn's experience of a 'hideous mongol boy' inside (39)).[10] Indeed, the threat of sameness reappears on the following page, again through the figure of the child, when Jacobus Coetzee fears being reduced 'to infant weakness' by his illness; in other words, the idea of the child at his core threatens to disturb the colonial discourse that serves to maintain difference (84). On the following page, however, order is restored and the fear of sameness reduced by the reference to the idea of a 'higher humanity' not available to the 'Hottentot' (85). But the ethical implication of the encounter with the child is unequivocal: contained in difference is a common nature rooted in the body.

Such episodes, in which Jacobus Coetzee fears sameness in encounters with the child, constitute disruptions to his discourse. However, the most salient intrusion on Jacobus Coetzee's narrative – conspicuously delineated on the page with pauses before and after – consists in the voice that questions him about his behaviour towards the children by the stream after the event. Set off from the rest of the text, the voice seems to appear to the reader not from within Jacobus Coetzee's discourse – in fact, this is the one character that is not pictured through his gaze – rather, it seems to originate from outside the boundaries of Jacobus's colonial worldview (within which servants say 'yes master' and tribe members are reduced to primitive chanting):

> The ear I had bitten off was not forgotten. 'Go. Leave us. We cannot give you refuge any longer.'
>
> 'That is all I want. To go.'
>
> 'Have you no children of your own? Do you not know how to play with children? You have mutilated this child!'

---

10 For a reading of Eugene Dawn's 'child-parasite' in 'The Vietnam Project', see Attwell (1993, 54).

'It was not my fault.'

'Of course it was your fault! You are mad, we can no longer have you here. You are not sick any more. You must go.' (*DL* 91)

In its insistent tone, its relative sanity and its appeal to a supposedly universal condemnation of violence towards children, this voice interrupts the othering imperialist idea of child-as-savage-as-child. Here, we are offered a glimpse of an other embracing the idea of the innocent child to be protected – dismantling any notion that the innocent child might be a purely Western construct, and assuming instead a common ground between equal adults in relation to the child. Through this interruption, the entire foundation for Jacobus Coetzee's discourse is called into question; notably not, here, by the self-reflexive gestures of the rest of the narrative, but by the voice of the other.[11]

When, after this episode, Jacobus Coetzee leaves the Namaqua village, he persists in trying to subsume the other into his own frame of reference: 'I continued with my exploration of the Hottentots, trying to find a place for them in my history' (97). Yet the encounter with the children – and with the righteous voice questioning his conduct with the children – means that this endeavour is no longer as straightforward as it was before. Jacobus Coetzee's conception of self comes across as muddled, notably in terms of both child/adult and self/other. He fluctuates between schoolmasterly adult pleased to have 'taught them [the Namaqua children] a lesson', and an infant-like state in which he swaddles himself in blankets and dreams of 'a slow torrent of milk, warm and balmy, poured out of the sky down [his] eager throat' (96). In the relation between 'civilized' self and 'savage' other, he experiences a 'blurring of boundaries', questioning the very meaning of savagery and ironically turning it back on himself: 'Even I knew more about savagery than they' (98).

Let us briefly consider *Disgrace* here, as it presents an interesting inversion of 'The Narrative of Jacobus Coetzee' with regard to how 'savage' encounters with the other child trouble self-other boundaries. David Lurie has two

---

11 Mike Marais reads the episode of violence against the Khoi child as an example of Coetzee's conveying an 'understanding of history as a realm characterized by irresponsibility to the other' (2009, 27). He sees this use of the child-metaphor also in *Waiting for the Barbarians*, where the child signifies 'what history has corrupted, defaced, effaced, rendered invisible'; the history of Empire thus 'both the violation and the loss of the child'; history as a 'realm of abandonment, of parental irresponsibility' (27). In my reading, the child is significant through its *presence* in the encounter with the other, rather than its absence.

central encounters with the 'other' child: first, the series of confrontations with Pollux, the boy who has participated in the rape of Lurie's daughter Lucy, and second, the product of that first encounter, Lucy's unborn child. Let us consider Pollux to begin with. When, after the event of the rape, Lurie first hears of the boy's name, he is exasperated to find that it falls not outside of but *within* his own frame of reference: 'Not Mncedisi? Not Nqabayakhe? Nothing unpronounceable, just Pollux?' (*D* 200). Carrol Clarkson observes how 'Pollux' 'does not guarantee an alienating distance from the 'we Westerners' that Lurie would hold apart'; as in 'The Narrative of Jacobus Coetzee', the other child is not quite other enough to uphold the self-other demarcation that Lurie erects in his mind in response to the violent rape (2009, 109).[12] The relation is further complicated when Lurie subsequently catches Pollux spying on Lucy through the bathroom window, and in a fit of rage attacks the boy:

> The flat of his hand catches the boy in the face. '*You swine!*' he shouts, and strikes him a second time, so that he staggers. '*You filthy swine!*' … The word still rings in the air: *Swine!* Never has he felt such elemental rage. He would like to give the boy what he deserves: a sound thrashing. Phrases that all his life he has avoided seem suddenly just and right: *Teach him a lesson, Show him his place.* So this is what it is like, he thinks! This is what it is like to be a savage! He gives the boy a good, solid kick, so that he sprawls sideways. Pollux! What a name! (*D* 206; emphasis in original)

As Clarkson notes, Lurie is 'at once racist colonial settler and savage attacker' in this scene (2009, 110). Unlike Jacobus Coetzee who feels savage *like* the Namaqua children when he '[falls] upon' them and in that movement suddenly sees the children as innocent 'little playmates', Lurie's attack on Pollux causes him to feel other to himself in two senses: *both* savage *like* Pollux, *and even more other* to Pollux than before, as a consequence of the settler-colonial attitude that up to this point has been alien to Lurie: '*Teach him a lesson, Show him his place.*' However, as with Jacobus Coetzee whose own 'savagery' causes him to temporarily see the Namaqua children with new eyes, Lurie looks momentarily at Pollux *as a child* after having attacked him. He sees 'snot …

---

12 For an extended discussion on the ethical dynamics that are produced by Pollux's name in *Disgrace*, see also Attwell (2009). For another useful reading of Lurie's mirroring himself in Pollux, see Sandra D. Shattuck (2009).

running from [the boy's] nostrils' and notices that he 'seems on the point of crying'; he sees Lucy treat the boy as a child, saying, 'Come, let us go and wash it', and how the boy, childlike, 'sucks in the snot and tears, shakes his head' (207). In the aftermath of this incident, Lurie has conflicting emotions, he 'condemns himself', fully aware that he has 'taught no one a lesson – certainly not the boy', but he also notes that 'something about Pollux sends him into a rage', knowing that, if provoked, he is liable 'to strike him again' (208–9). The violent interactions with the child have prompted Lurie to ethically look at himself with new eyes: 'He is not, it would seem, in control of himself', and he is 'too old to change', it is 'too late' for him 'to be a good person' as he later tells Lucy (209, 216).

Lucy's unborn child is also 'other', in that it will be, as Lurie puts it, 'a child of this earth'; however, through its mixed lineage, it also epitomizes the dissolution of the self-other boundary (216). Like Pollux, but in a different way, this child, too, provokes an ethical change in Lurie that is beyond his control, as Lurie discovers when he asks Lucy if she loves the child-to-be 'yet'. The implication is, to his own surprise, that he *takes for granted* the impending love for the child: 'Though the words are his, from his mouth, they startle him' (216). From this moment on, the unborn child's effect on Lurie's outlook is profound: whereas on his first visit to the farm earlier in the novel, he unemotionally noted 'five hectares of land, most of it arable', 'a wire fence and clumps of nasturtiums and geraniums … dust and gravel' (59), the same vantage point now appears as a highly Romantic image in which

> from the last hillcrest the farm opens out before him: the old house, solid as ever, the stables, Petrus's new house, the old dam on which he can make out specks that must be the ducks and larger specks that must be the wild geese, Lucy's visitors from afar.
>
> At this distance the flowerbeds are solid blocks of colour: magenta, carnelian, ash-blue. A season of blooming. The bees must be in their seventh heaven. (*D* 216)

The bees and the flowerbeds lead Lurie to reflections on his own gift to 'a line of existences', and he finds himself thinking of becoming a grandfather: 'Who would have thought it! … He must have a look again at Victor Hugo, poet of grandfatherhood' (217–18). It seems likely that this new perspective, prompted by the advent of the child that has, at least to an extent, made self-other boundaries irrelevant, is what enables Lurie shortly after to 'no longer [have] difficulty in calling [the compassionate killing of dogs] by its proper name: love' (219).

In both 'The Narrative of Jacobus Coetzee' and *Disgrace*, then, the series of disruptions involving the 'other' child serve to destabilize boundaries between self and other. There are important differences, however. In *Dusklands*, the effect of the ironically rendered child encounters is unequivocally to undermine the authoritarian discourse on which the narrative is founded. In *Disgrace*, Lurie's violent encounter with Pollux and his affective reversal in relation to his unborn grandchild emerge rather as moments of ethical uncertainty, in which savagery and love are both closer at hand than was first apparent.

Children of iron

Like *Dusklands* and *Disgrace*, *Age of Iron* centrally features ethically suggestive encounters with children across South African ethnic divides. Like *Dusklands*, *Age of Iron* ironically foregrounds constructed child figures and – at least partially – undermines the discourse in which they are located; and as in *Disgrace*, encounters with 'other' children in *Age of Iron* lead to uncertainty and ethical reflection for the protagonist. The novel is set in distinct streets of Cape Town in 1986 during a State of Emergency pronounced by the apartheid regime to tighten its grip on the country; a period of upheaval and violence in a land where, as Coetzee said in his Jerusalem Prize Acceptance speech around the same time, 'the serfs are in open rebellion and the masters are in disarray' (*DP* 96).

Formally, the narrative takes the shape of a letter that the retired Classics professor Mrs Curren starts writing to her self-exiled daughter – who has vowed not to return before the perpetrators of apartheid are 'hanging by their heels from the lampposts' – after having found out that the cancer that she is suffering from is terminal (75). The epistolary form is prompted, it would seem, not only by the absence of the daughter, but also by the circumstance that Mrs Curren, from her privileged white position, cannot really speak about the dire realities and suffering of black South Africans – about what Coetzee refers to as the '*crudity* of life in South Africa' (*DP* 99; emphasis in original).[13] Thus the letter serves a double purpose for the dying protagonist, as a way to 'feel [her] way closer' to her out-of-reach child and as a form of soul-searching that processes the sociopolitical realities she can neither fully grasp nor authentically engage with in actual human encounters. Poignantly, she asks:

> And I? Where is my heart in all of this? My only child is thousands of miles away, safe; soon I will be smoke and ash; so what is it to me that a time has come when childhood is despised, when children school each other never to smile, never to cry, to raise fists in the air like hammers? Is it truly a time out of time, heaved up out of the earth, misbegotten, monstrous? (*AI* 50)

This letter – approaching a confession in its introspectiveness – addresses, through memories of lost childhood and accounts of children-who-are-not-children, the remains of the idea of childhood itself.

A letter culminating with the death of its subject obviously raises questions about its authenticity. Also, bearing in mind the fundamental dilemma addressed in 'Confession and Double Thoughts', the 'helplessness of confession before the desire of the self to construct its own truth', the confessional nature of the letter in itself causes us to doubt Mrs Curren's account (*DP* 279). Despite these reservations, Mrs Curren's narrative – unlike that of Jacobus Coetzee, where the fundamental premise is that his story is part of a colonial mythology and reflects a colonial outlook – carries an affective power that lends it a sense of authenticity; Mrs Curren is clearly trying to be true to her own values. Certainly, Mrs Curren is deeply implicated in the racial injustice that marks South Africa; yet her ethical reflexivity provokes the reader's sympathy to her perspective. In Coetzee's early notes on *Age of Iron*, he writes, 'It [the novel] must be about innocence. Historical innocence. How my mother, belonging to her generation in SA, was nevertheless innocent', and continues to say, 'Which means tackling the abstract question and taking a "difficult" position

---

13 Johan Geertsema approaches irony in *Age of Iron* precisely in terms of addressing that which cannot be said:

> To speak that which cannot be spoken requires, perhaps demands, irony. Such irony must be understood, however, as an irony beyond or against understanding. It is an irony which is not able to aid understanding (nor, indeed, does it seek to), and which therefore does *not* make possible speaking that (about) which cannot be spoken, but offers possibilities and examines avenues relating to enunciation. It offers provisionality, not relativity, and thus opens the *possibility* of coming to terms with history. (1997, 89; emphasis in original)

on it' (Attwell 2015, 168). This 'difficult position', as I read it, is precisely about protecting the idea of innocence, even as violent realities seem to render it irrelevant. For while the narrative traces the parallel movement of Mrs Curren's gradual awakening to the magnitude of black suffering around her, largely figured through encounters with children, and her corresponding gradual loss of authority and gradually declining belief in the idea of the innocent child, it nevertheless seems to incorporate remnants of this belief into a new more complex position. I trace below the ironies evident in the staging of this parallel awakening to the real and refusal to let go of the ideal, and find an ethics in the attempt to negotiate these two ultimately irreconcilable positions.

As an aside, it is worth recalling from Chapter 1 how Coetzee addresses innocence as a 'foundational fiction' in the essay 'Taking Offense' (published six years after *Age of Iron*), stating categorically that 'children are not, *qua* children, innocent' (*GO* 14). Coetzee writes that 'affronts to the innocence of our children ... are attacks not upon our essential being but upon constructs', adding that 'this is not to say that ... the outrage with which we respond to them is not real, in the sense of not being sincerely felt' (14). These ideas are visibly at work already in *Age of Iron*; the novel shows precisely how affronts to the idea of innocence generates 'real' and 'felt' outrage in response. Indeed, the insistent embrace of the idea of the child, inevitably abstract and constructed though it may be, signifies nothing less than an attachment to the value of human life.

Age of Iron speaks to the moment in South African history when youngsters led the resistance against apartheid in the streets. Saul Dubow recounts how in the mid-1980s

> militant youths attacked township police and officials collaborating with the 'system' ... Sometimes youngsters used the rough justice of neighbourhood 'people's courts' to settle disputes or impose sanctions. From 1985, a gruesome method emerged to kill collaborators and those accused of being *impimpi* (informers). Tyres filled with petrol were put around such people and set alight, a practice known as 'necklacing'.
>
> ... From 1984 school boycotts became the rule rather than the exception, as slogans like 'liberation now, education later' gained in popularity ... There were calls to make 1986 'a year of no schooling'. (2014, 234–5)

In 1986, 'affronts to the innocence of … children' were thus very much a political reality, and through its dogged focus on the child, *Age of Iron* keeps probing the consequences of innocence as an ideal. In fact, Mrs Curren's views about the child-as-innocent are as central – and often as incongruously presented – to this narrative as the colonialist idea of the savage-as-child is to 'The Narrative of Jacobus Coetzee'. The attention to the child in *Age of Iron* is especially striking through the excessive use of child imagery. Consider the conspicuous repetitions and rhetorical richness of the following passage:

> It is the roaming gangs I fear, the sullen-mouthed boys, rapacious as sharks, on whom the first shade of the prison house is already beginning to close. Children scorning childhood, the time of wonder, the growing time of the soul. Their souls, their organs of wonder, stunted, petrified. And on the other side of the great divide their white cousins soul-stunted too, spinning themselves tighter and tighter into their sleepy cocoons. Swimming lessons, riding lessons, ballet lessons; cricket on the lawn; lives passed within walled gardens guarded by bulldogs; children of paradise, blond, innocent, shining with angelic light, soft as *putti*. Their residence the limbo of the unborn, their innocence the innocence of bee grubs, plump and white, drenched in honey, absorbing sweetness through their soft skins. Slumbrous their souls, bliss-filled, abstracted. (*AI* 7)

'Childhood, the time of wonder, the growing time of the soul', 'children of paradise, blond, innocent, shining with angelic light' and so on – in their stylistic exuberance, these images all serve to reinforce universalizing Romantic notions of childhood in an almost parodic manner; although the passage at the same time points unequivocally towards a divided social reality. Effectively, Mrs Curren's self-consciously cynical musings about illusions of childhood innocence at this early point in the novel serve to highlight the unsustainability of her perspective. (We might recall how Coetzee, apropos *Age of Iron*, emphasizes the right to have a say also for 'those who speak from a totally untenable historical position' (*DP* 250).) Yet, while the rhetorical opulence suggests irony, we cannot exclude the possibility that the figure of children whose innocence is 'the innocence of bee grubs' marks what is in fact a sincere longing for obsolete values of the past. Either way, the ambiguity surrounding the innocent child in the above passage and elsewhere in the novel never cancels out the reader's sympathy for the protagonist.

It is still early in the novel when Mrs Curren, with her – as she comes to regard it – ineffectual liberal humanist outlook, realizes that she must count herself to the latter 'slumbrous souls'. Indeed, while provoked by encounters with actual, oppressed children as the story proceeds, Mrs Curren's reflections on the child remain largely Romantically introspective; for instance, her narrative is sprinkled with Wordsworthian allusions. Her thoughts wander to memories of her own lost childhood, 'days of charm and sorrow and mystery too! Days of innocence!' (24); she anchors her personal history in a childhood story of her mother's; and in her dreams she is a child again. Certainly, Mrs Curren is preoccupied to the point of obsession with the idea of the child; her account virtually abounds in child imagery – the words 'child', 'children' and 'childhood' appear 172 times (in a novel of 198 pages). Significantly, the many, often surprising, references to the child create an at once ironically distancing and affectively immersive effect. When a rock is thrown through the front screen of her car during a night-time visit to infernal scenes of violence in the burning township Guguletu, she notes that it is 'big as a child's head' and a few pages later observes that it has left a hole 'big enough for a child to climb through' (104, 118). She repeatedly laments the loss of childhood innocence; her own and that of an age when 'childhood is despised, when children school each other never to smile, never to cry, to raise fists in the air like hammers' – a society where goodness has no agency (50). Her gradual awakening from her 'bed of childhood slumber' to the violent realities outside her safe house provokes moments in which she views herself as a helpless child; her voice 'a child's voice' from an 'old person's throat'; her powerless arms 'a child's arms'; the wavering of the illusion of the innocent child also the loss of her own authority and agency (109, 51). Paradoxically, then, while Mrs Curren is nostalgic for lost childlike innocence, she is also disapproving towards what she considers to be childish, irresponsible features of her adult self.

Ironically, however, while Mrs Curren, like J. C. of *Diary of a Bad Year*, approves of children in the abstract, this sentiment does not extend unconditionally to actual children. When her housekeeper Florence's 15-year-old son Bheki moves into her garage to escape township violence, Mrs Curren is distinctly annoyed; his presence seems to disturb her whole being; the sound of his bouncing a tennis ball is 'maddening', a 'remorseless thudding' (38). In contrast, when Florence's toddler daughters Hope and Beauty play with a dog in the garden, Mrs Curren welcomes the barking and the 'shrieks of pleasure': 'Such noise! Such excitement!' (38). Indeed, the girls' allegorical names seem to resonate with Mrs Curren's romanticized idea of the child – although later in the novel, when reality intrudes, she reflects despondently: 'Hope and Beauty. It was like living in an allegory' (90).[14] Mrs Curren's discomfort increases with the appearance of Bheki's friend in her backyard; the 'scraping and thudding' of the music they are playing 'even worse than the tennis ball' (45). She wants to clasp her hands over her ears to shut out the 'inhuman' and 'wearying' noise of the boys, and tells Florence that she 'can't have strangers walking in and out' (47).

Mrs Curren's double standards vis-à-vis the actual children reflect her difficulties in reconciling their two-sided significance to her; they are, on the one hand, cherished universal symbols of innocence, on the other hand, unwelcome bearers of particular historical violence threatening that same innocence. Her marked hostility towards Bheki and his friend early in the novel becomes all the more conspicuous considering her openness to the derelict vagrant Verceuil, who arrives at her doorstep and is invited to stay. Perhaps this inconsistency can be understood through her reflection that Verceuil has 'an air of childlessness about him. Of having no children in the world but also of having no childhood in his past' (11). With his 'air of childlessness', Verceuil is shielded, in Mrs Curren's mind, from the tension between innocence and politics, allowing her to focus on the ethics of the face-to-face encounter, and, hence, to welcome him unconditionally.

In contrast, Mrs Curren's encounter with Bheki's sullen friend John suggests an ethics based rather on the suffering body as a common ground – the recognition of the self in the child.[15] (We are reminded of Coetzee's remark on the body as the ethical standard that runs through his fiction: 'Whatever else, the body is not "that which is not" and the proof that it *is* is the pain it feels' (*DP* 249).) When Bheki and John are injured in an incident trying to evade the police on a bicycle, it is Mrs Curren's instinctive association between the blood streaming from John's head and the memory of her own daughter's

---

14 While the names Hope and Beauty are allegorical, they are also realistic South African female names.
15 See Sam Durrant's Lacanian reading of moments in *Age of Iron* in which the experience of the encounter with the real body of the other takes over when the capacity to grasp within language fails (Durrant 2006, 125).

blood following a childhood accident that prompts her to intervene and stop the bleeding: 'It was blood, nothing more, blood like yours and mine' (63). However, coupled with this feeling of sameness is a momentarily paralyzing feeling of otherness: 'Yet never before had I seen anything so scarlet and so black ... I stared at it, fascinated, afraid, drawn into a veritable stupor of staring.' Mrs Curren relates to her daughter why, despite the uncanny feeling of otherness evoked by the boy's blood, she felt compelled to act:

> Because blood is one: a pool of life dispersed among us in separate existences, but belonging by nature together: lent, not given: held in common, in trust, to be preserved: seeming to live in us, but only seeming, for in truth we live in it. (63–4)

As with Jacobus Coetzee, the concomitant feeling of sameness and otherness evoked by the 'other' child's body is a source of discomfort for Mrs Curren; although, in her case, this discomfort forms the basis for ethical action. However, and disturbingly, her afterthought suggests that her ethics is not unconditional; the boy is strange to her and embodies a range of contradictions that cannot be contained in her idea of the innocent child; she 'would rather [she had] spent [herself] on someone else':

> I did not like him. I do not like him. I look into my heart and nowhere do I find any trace of feeling for him. As there are people to whom one spontaneously warms, so there are people to whom one is, from the first, cold. That is all. This boy is not like Bheki. He has no charm. There is something *stupid* about him, something deliberately stupid, obstructive, intractable. He is one of those boys whose voices deepen too early, who by the age of twelve have left childhood behind and turned *brutal, knowing*. A simplified person, *simplified* in every way: *swifter, nimbler,* more tireless than real people, without doubts or *scruples*, without *humor, ruthless, innocent*. While he lay in the street, while I thought he was dying, I did what I could for him. But, to be candid, I would rather I had spent myself on someone else. (78–9; emphasis added)

Note how the assonance divides Mrs Curren's description of the boy into opposing poles: to her, he is at once 'stupid' and 'knowing'; he is 'brutal' and 'ruthless', without 'scruples' and without 'humor' – but also 'simplified', 'swifter', and 'nimbler' than real people and, finally, 'innocent'. The emphatic tone of the passage along with the jumble of connotations draw attention to the degree of affect and frustration that the boy provokes in Mrs Curren; he seems to annoy her as he complicates the idea of the innocent child.[16] The irony is evident in Mrs Curren's inconsistent responses to this child; this mixture of strong and indeterminate feeling produces a residual of uncertainty.

However, the child figure doesn't just point to ironies and inconsistencies in Mrs Curren's ethics. It also makes visible the gap between her Western frame of reference – Classics professor that she is – and the sociopolitical realities in Cape Town in 1986, of which her knowledge is clearly insufficient. Failing to grasp the actual here and now, she attributes her own inadequate perspectives to the events around her, as she tries to process the state of affairs in the black townships where children spearhead the resistance, and where, in her domestic Florence's words, 'there are no more mothers and fathers' (39). During an extended exchange with Florence who is ironing in the kitchen, Mrs Curren questions what she understands as parental abdication before children whose 'hearts are turning to stone', asking: 'Are you going to blame them on the whites and then turn your back?' (50)

> 'No', said Florence. 'That is not true. I do not turn my back on my children.' She folded the sheet crosswise and lengthwise, crosswise and lengthwise, the corners falling together neatly, decisively. 'These are good children, they are like iron, we are proud of them.' On the board, she spread the first of the pillow slips. I waited for her to say more. But there was no more. She was not interested in debating with me. (50)

Florence's speech (much like the voice reproving Jacobus Coetzee in *Dusklands*) is highlighted by the pauses surrounding it, the silent folding of sheets and the silent continued ironing; a strong voice that refuses to be incorporated into or deal with Mrs Curren's way of thinking. However, Mrs Curren – who can only see the destruction of parental authority and innocent children losing their way – fails to hear the historically specific resonance of

---

16   It is worth reflecting on how John's stupidity is linked to his *resistance*. Rita Barnard makes the important point that 'in Coetzee's fiction stupidity is never inherent or inert: it is a chosen or imposed condition and one with psychological, political and ethical resonances. In the case of characters like Michael K, or Friday, or the young comrade John, ignorance is resistance: an active passion to ignore' (2014, 35). I will return in Chapter 4 to another resisting child figure, David in *The Childhood of Jesus*, to discuss how such perceived 'stupidity' can be understood in terms of Agamben's idea of impotentiality.

Florence's response. Instead, she, both innocent and ignorant, subsumes the idea of 'children of iron' to her own inherited discourse; her mind wanders off, making connections that have little bearing on what Florence actually means.

> Children of iron, I thought. Florence herself, too, not unlike iron. The age of iron. After which comes the age of bronze. How long, how long before the softer ages return in their cycle, the age of clay, the age of earth? A Spartan matron, iron-hearted, bearing warrior sons for the nation. 'We are proud of them.' We. Come home either with your shield or on your shield. (50)

First, Mrs Curren thinks of the 'age of iron', the idea of decline through the ages (or, more problematically, the races) of man described in Hesiod's *Works and Days* and later in Ovid and Virgil, the fall from an original Golden Age to the present.[17] It makes sense that this downward movement through the ages, modelled on the individual life cycle, might reflect the loss of childhood innocence that troubles Mrs Curren.[18]

Certainly there is an irony in how far removed Mrs Curren's thoughts are from the person actually in front of her, when she proceeds to associate Florence with the 'iron-hearted' 'Spartan matron', depicted in Rousseau's *Émile* and referring to the Spartan ideal where the destruction of the family was a necessary price to pay for worthy citizenship.[19] Of course, Florence has nothing to do with this unsentimental Spartan 'we', she is neither unloving nor are her children alienated from or sacrificed by their community. On the contrary, if what she says is considered in the light of an intertext other than those that appear to Mrs Curren (but that were available to the South African reader at the time of the novel's publication), the picture becomes a different one. It seems likely that the contextually relevant allusion that Florence is evoking with the image of children 'like iron' is neither Hesiod nor Ovid or Rousseau, but the exiled South African poet Mazisi Kunene, more specifically

---

17 It is understandable that Mrs Curren might liken the state of chaos and injustice of South Africa in 1987 to Hesiod's age of iron where: 'Nor will father be to children nor children to father, nor guest to host or comrade to comrade, nor will a brother be friendly as in former times. Soon they will cease to respect their ageing parents … Law and decency will be in fists' (2008, ll. 181–91).
18 'Age of iron' refers to the *present* age in the novel, but following Bheki's death, Mrs Curren thinks also about the 'age of iron waiting to *return*' (126; emphasis added).
19 David Attwell proposes that Coetzee deliberately inscribes distance to black Africa in his work; that he 'subjects Africa as sign to a process of occultation so that it becomes a source of aesthetic power' (2009, 71).

his poem 'The Rise of the Angry Generation', first published in 1982, and then republished in 1986 by Coetzee in the anthology *A Land Apart* (coedited with André Brink). The poem recounts how 'the shells of childhood are scattered' and how 'a vast space' is opened for 'the merciless talons of the new generation':

> They who are not deterred by false tears
> Who do not turn away from the fire
> *They are the children of iron*
> They are the fearless bees of the night
> They are the wrath of the volcanic mountain
> They are the abiding anger of the Ancestral Forefathers
>
> (Kunene 1986; emphasis added)[20]

In Kunene's poem, the 'children of iron' are closely linked to the 'abiding anger of the Ancestral Forefathers' – the image thus one of continuity between past, present and future; ancestral roots empowering the generation to come. Kunene's poem speaks to the post-1976 (the year of the Soweto uprising) moment in South Africa when youths led the resistance in the streets; apartheid itself undermining childhood, in other words. But although it laments the present, the poem, like others in the collection in which it was originally published, is essentially optimistic and future-oriented, placing its trust in the 'angry' generation, just as Florence places trust in her son.[21]

This orientation towards the future is radically different, of course, from Mrs Curren's looking backwards for authority (or comfort perhaps), as she does when she anchors all her thinking in the classics; and as she does when she thinks nostalgically back to the times when John would have been an innocent garden boy instead of a resistance fighter. So when Mrs Curren asks: 'What kind of parents will they become who were taught that the time of parents is over? Can parents be recreated once the idea of parents has been destroyed within us?' – she misses the future-oriented strength of an alternative idea of continuity (49–50). Although Florence denies turning her back on her children, Mrs Curren

---

20 The poem, originally written in Zulu, was translated by its author.
21 Another strong intertext featuring Guguletu children at the forefront of township uprisings is Maria Tholo's *Diary of Maria Tholo* (1980), an extract of which was also anthologized by Coetzee in *A Land Apart*. Thanks to Hedley Twidle for alerting me to this.

cannot embrace the idea of authority being granted to the 'rising generation' not as a way of giving up, but as a way of passing responsibility forward. As Kunene's poem – which, while it is protest poetry addressing a very specific time and place, is also the product of African, in this case Zulu, tradition – shows, this is not merely a response to the state of emergency, but also reflects fundamentally different ideas of continuity between generations. I will return in more detail in Chapter 3 to the ways in which the child in Coetzee generates complex responses to the relation between the past, the present and the future.

The question remains to what extent Mrs Curren, in her universalizing thoughts and gestures, actually grasps cultural difference. She clearly does not see her own views of the child as culturally contingent, relentlessly returning to her universalizing ideals in the face of violence. In an encounter with Mr Thabane, a teacher and figure of authority in Guguletu, she again draws seemingly far-removed conclusions after not properly hearing the voice of the other regarding the child – this time after Bheki's death. Indeed, Thabane says as much when Mrs Curren questions the children's violence: 'we must stand back for them, for the youth. We stand back but we stand behind them. *That is what you cannot understand, because you are too far away*' (150; emphasis added).[22] And Mrs Curren doesn't prove him wrong, when she in her response resorts to images from other times and places:

> 'I am far away, certainly', I said, 'far away and tiny. Nevertheless, I fear I know comradeship all too well. The Germans had comradeship, and the Japanese, and the Spartans. Shaka's impis too, I am sure. Comradeship is nothing but a mystique of death, of killing and dying ... It is just another of those icy, exclusive, death-driven male constructions. That is my opinion.' (150)

It seems jarringly out of place to enter into an academic discussion about 'exclusive, death-driven male constructions' when children are dying in the townships. Here and elsewhere, the narrative extends authority to Thabane, who, like Florence and unlike Mrs Curren, does not lean on abstractions but is firmly grounded in the sociopolitical conditions determining the violence. Yet, while Mrs Curren herself acknowledges here how removed she is from the particulars of the present, 'far away and tiny', she *nevertheless* insists on

---

22 The novel, needless to say, does not extend any sympathy towards violence – and Coetzee has said emphatically 'I am unable to, or refuse to, conceive of a liberating violence' (*DP* 337).

the relevance of universal lessons to be learned from. And crucially, the ironic treatment of the child in the narrative both undermines her authority and – by continuing to elicit the reader's sympathy to her perspective – grants her its remainder.

Ethics of indeterminacy

In this chapter I have traced ethical implications of different mobilizations of the 'other' child in Coetzee. I have shown how the patronizing and pseudoscientific tone of colonial discourse parodied in 'The Narrative of Jacobus Coetzee' is punctured momentarily by episodes centred on encounters with children, in which the totalizing nature of that discourse is disrupted by an anxious intimation of sameness (the child/savage within). The concurrent mobilization of universalizing and exoticizing gestures in relation to the child, then, serves to destabilize both the identity of the colonizer self (less certain than it first seemed) and the perception of the (no longer quite so) other. In *Disgrace*, David Lurie's violent encounters with Pollux, and his anticipated encounter with his unborn grandchild, in different ways prompt him to look back at his self with new eyes – as capable of both savagery and love. In *Age of Iron*, the abundant rhetorical focus on the innocent child – contrasted with the parallel presentation of the violent sociopolitical experiences of the 'real' child – paradoxically serves both as challenge to and reminder of the foundation of liberal humanist discourse. The child imagery in the novel creates a distance between the reader and Mrs Curren, who comes across as naïve at best in her inadequate understanding of sociopolitical realities. Yet, while exposing the limits of Mrs Curren's perspective, the irony never completely eradicates the strength of her apparent belief in the value of childhood innocence; the ethics of the novel emerges precisely in the not-knowing the appropriate response to Coetzee's simultaneous use of irony and commitment with regard to the child.

Observing the ambiguous responses of Coetzee's adults to Coetzee's children does not merely highlight the child figure's constructedness and position in various discourses. It shows too that not only do we not know the full story of the other; we also do not know the full story of the self and its many potentialities. In thus pointing to the unknowability of both self and other, the child emerges as an uncanny site of indeterminacy in the intersection between self and other, a grey zone of potentialities that opens up an ethics based on sameness *and* difference. By demonstrating the instability of the self in encounters with the other child, Coetzee shows how the ethics of the self-other relationship is inflected by the interplay between different possible versions of the self, on the one hand, and the responsibility towards the 'other', on the other.

I have highlighted in this chapter how the child in episodes figuring (post)colonial self-other encounters in Coetzee emerges as a site of sameness *and* difference, due to alternately universalizing and othering gestures. However, the appropriate way to describe the *politics* that might emerge out of this condition is, perhaps, rather in terms of *neither* sameness *nor* difference; of *indifference*, in other words. In his chapter on the relation between writing and politics in Coetzee, Patrick Hayes traces how in South Africa the debate on how to achieve a good community has been shaped by two competing political ideals, 'both with their roots in distinctively modern concepts of human identity': on the one hand, 'a universalist impulse towards a "politics of equal dignity"', and on the other hand, 'a ... particularist impulse towards a "politics of difference"' (2010, 11).[23] Hayes argues that Coetzee's 'stance as a writer is driven by his appreciation of the necessity for, but inadequacy of' either of these two ideals, suggesting instead that Coetzee's fiction is more responsive to an 'anti-foundational approach' (11, 28). As part of the discussion in Chapter 5, in which I read *The Schooldays of Jesus* in dialogue with Giorgio Agamben, I will suggest that the idea of infancy as a 'nonposition' evinced in Coetzee's late work points precisely towards an 'indifferent' or 'anti-foundational' approach to being together.

I have touched briefly here on how in *Age of Iron* and *Disgrace*, the figure of the child points to Coetzee's preoccupation with continuity between generations. In Chapter 3, I continue this discussion by looking at how the child figure brings to light the complex relations between past, present and future in Coetzee's work.

---

23 Hayes refers to the framework developed by Charles Taylor in *Multiculturalism: Examining the Politics of Recognition* (1994).

3

The child between past and future

In the Magistrate's despondent daydreams towards the end of *Waiting for the Barbarians*, he finds himself unable to imagine a future beyond the oppressive reign of the Empire, his dreams confined to

> becoming an unthinking savage, of taking the cold road back to the capital, of groping my way out to the ruins in the desert, of returning to the confinement of my cell, of seeking out the barbarians and offering myself to them to use as they wish. Without exception, they are dreams of ends: *dreams not of how to live but of how to die*. And everyone, I know, in that walled town sinking now into darkness (I hear the two thin trumpet calls that announce the closing of the gates) is similarly preoccupied. *Everyone but the children!* (*WB* 146; emphasis added)

He 'dreams of ends'; the ends available to him, though, are all bleak options limited to joining the ranks of the Empire, futilely resisting the Empire as its prisoner, escaping the Empire to the desert ruins or handing himself over to the opposing camp, the barbarians among whom he does not belong. Lamenting his entrapment, he can picture freedom only *outside* of history: 'What has made it impossible for us to live in time like fish in water, like birds in air, like children? It is the fault of Empire! Empire has created the time of history' (146).

Caught in the Empire's 'time of history', which might be understood as the determining and oppressive force of the Empire's discourse of history, the Magistrate cannot imagine change *within* 'history', but longs instead in vain for an existence *beyond* human narrative, 'the smooth recurrent spinning time of the cycle of the seasons' (146).[1] To him, the children who 'live in time like

---

1 David Attwell observes how the narrative highlights historical time as 'a construction imposed on formless chronicity' (2009, 86).

fish in water, like birds in air' evoke a simplified life where generations succeed generations as seasons succeed seasons: 'The children never doubt that the great old trees in whose shade they play will stand forever, that one day they will grow to be strong like their fathers, fertile like their mothers, that they will live and prosper and raise their own children and grow old in the place where they were born' (146). As the above passage suggests, such continuity and cyclicity is rendered inconceivable by the Empire's 'time of history', which obstructs the Magistrate's capacity to imagine regeneration.

Throughout the novel, however, the possibility of the birth of the new is held up tentatively to the reader through recurring images of playing children – play, as we know, meaning the creation of something new with what is given. A reading of the scenes featuring children at play suggests that the Magistrate's attitude towards the possibility of the new and unexpected evolves during the course of the novel. Early on, when the Magistrate still identifies as 'a responsible official in the service of the Empire', the playing children in his dream are out of his reach and 'melt away' as he approaches (8, 10). He attributes the transient and ungraspable nature of his visions of children to his own 'bulk' and 'shadowiness', as if he himself carried the weight of the Empire suppressing the possibility of the new (10). In a later dream, the playing children once again 'melt into the air', yet the Magistrate manages to catch a glimpse of a hooded child, only to find its face 'blank, featureless; it is the face of an embryo or a tiny whale; it is not a face at all' (40). The child's face is not recognizable; it is, again, ungraspable and out of reach; not, here, a figure of possibility.

However, the novel's final scene gestures forcefully towards the potentialities of the emergence of the new beyond the limits imaginable in the present. Unlike his daydreams of 'ends', none of which allow for an escape from the confines of the current discourse of history, and unlike his frustrated dreams of ungraspable children-as-alterity, the Magistrate is now confronted with a new beginning in the form of real children at play in the present moment. While he still cannot imagine what the future might bring, his feeling is no longer one of frustration and failure, but one of 'inexplicable' joy:

> In the middle of the square there are children at play building a snowman. Anxious not to alarm them, but *inexplicably joyful*, I approach them across the snow.

> They are not alarmed, they are too busy to cast me a glance. They have completed the great round body, now they are rolling a ball for the head.
>
> 'Someone fetch things for the mouth and nose and eyes', says the child who is their leader.
>
> It strikes me that the snowman will need arms too, but *I do not want to interfere.*
>
> They settle the head on the shoulders and fill it out with pebbles for eyes, ears, nose and mouth. One of them crowns it with his cap.
>
> It is not a bad snowman.
>
> *This is not the scene I dreamed of.* Like much else nowadays I leave it feeling stupid, like a man who lost his way long ago but presses on along a road that may lead nowhere. (170; emphasis added)

We observe how the Magistrate approaches the children slowly, not wishing to 'interfere' with their play, making sure to leave room for the new that is emerging. Importantly, the scene exceeds what the Magistrate previously could imagine – 'This is not the scene I dreamed of.' The Magistrate's view of the future, then, has evolved from 'dreaming of ends' to a position where a new beginning appears not only as a possibility, but also as a source of hope; of joy, even. In a 1982 interview with Folke Rhedin, Coetzee reflects on the Magistrate's difficult historical position and his lack of viable choices; he cannot turn a blind eye to the reality of imperial life once he has seen it for what it is, but nor can he, an 'old man set in his ways', choose the barbarian way of life (7). However, Coetzee points out that

> there is a very strong presence of children in that book and *there is no saying* – although the book doesn't deal directly with it – *what those children might do* and what sort of life they might lead. They might be able to make choices that he [the Magistrate] finds impossible. (Coetzee and Rhedin 1984, 7; emphasis added)

What Coetzee is suggesting here is that the children in the novel point to *something new that cannot be anticipated.*

I take this final scene from *Waiting for the Barbarians* as my cue to think about how the possibility of the new is intimated through the child in Coetzee's work. What interests me in particular is how the appearance of the new in this scene is *worldly,* in the sense that the children's building of the snowman is a figure of presence and embodiment. This worldliness helps us catch sight of the fact that Coetzee's poetics are structured not just by the responsibility to an alterity beyond language – as figured by the ungraspable children in the dreams, or for that matter, by the radically other barbarians that are being *waited for* – but also by responsibility towards a common social world that is already there. Also, the scene suggests that the emergence of the new is something for which one *as part of the world* needs to assume responsibility: this is why the Magistrate takes care not to 'interfere' with the building of the snowman, and, as I will argue, this is also why Coetzee's characters are so often torn between their desire to safeguard the 'old', on the one hand, and their responsibility to allow the 'new' to emerge, on the other.

It is in view of such moments of ambivalence that this chapter will consider how the child invites us to think about new beginnings and the responsibility for the world, looking specifically at episodes in which Coetzee's protagonists find themselves at a point where continuity between the past and the future is at stake and a source of anxiety, on a historical and/or a personal level – the two often coincide in Coetzee's fiction. This predicament is often the product of fraught historicopolitical junctures in South African history that are either presented recognizably as in *Age of Iron* and *Disgrace*, or that find an analogy in a different place and time, such as the Russian context of *The Master of Petersburg*, or, indeed, the unspecific setting of *Waiting for the Barbarians*. In other instances, the severing of time is not as obviously politically inflected, for example, in the case of Paul Rayment's solitary existence in *Slow Man* or the sequestered afterlife-like world of *The Childhood of Jesus*. In each of these cases, I explore how the child makes visible the tension between the past and the future in the text.

To help my thinking about these matters, I enlist Hannah Arendt's concept of *natality* – the distinctive and always latent human capacity of introducing something new into the human world, exceeding and transforming what was already there. I also engage Arendt's related reflections on education, which along with the concept of natality offer a valuable way of approaching Coetzee's dramatizations of the precarious task of moving in the gap between the old and the new. Although Arendt never explicitly defines natality, she coins the term to describe man's unique capacity for beginning – rooted in the fact of human birth and replicated in (political) action and in the life of the mind. Each person, by virtue of being born, is a newcomer who can create a new beginning in the world. Natality serves as a central inspiration to Arendt's political and philosophical thought, and is first expressed in the concluding paragraph of *The Origins of Totalitarianism* (1951), where the freedom inherent in the human capacity for new beginnings is offered as an image of hope against the background of the dark history of twentieth-century totalitarianism:

> But there remains also the truth that every end in history necessarily contains a new beginning; this beginning is the promise, the only 'message' which the end can ever produce. Beginning, before it becomes a historical event, is the supreme capacity of man; politically, it is identical with man's freedom. *Initium ut esset homo creatus est* – 'that a beginning be made man was created' said Augustine. This beginning is guaranteed by each new birth; it is indeed every man. (Arendt 2017, 629)[2]

Arendt's thinking on natality emerges in part as a reaction against the long-standing preoccupation in Western philosophy with death as a determinant of human life. She writes that 'the life span of man running toward death would inevitably carry everything human to ruin and destruction if it were not for the faculty of interrupting it and beginning something new', declaring, crucially, that humans 'are not born in order to die but in order to begin' (Arendt 1998, 246). The Magistrate, as we recall, dreams 'not of how to live but of how to die', but, we also remember, this determinism is interrupted, ultimately, by children at play (*WB* 146). In fact, it is not just the Empire's determinist 'time of history' but equally the Magistrate's longing for cyclical time – living 'like fish in water, like birds in air, like children' – that is disrupted by the playing children (146). As Rosalyn Diprose and Ewa Ziarek point out, 'the temporal gap that prevents determinism of the linear time of political life also interrupts the cyclical time of biological determinism' (2013, 113).

The force of natality lies in its potential to interrupt the social world with the creation of something radically new and unforeseen; something that exceeds and, with its concretization through action, changes what was there before.

---

2 Arendt is citing Augustine's *The City of God (De Civitate Dei)*, Book 12, chapter 20.

To Arendt, humans are natals, not mortals, and in her political theory this translates into a focus on the *vita activa*, the life of action, rather than the *vita contemplativa*, the life of contemplation, that marks the condition of being towards death (a predicament that we recognize not only in the Magistrate but in many of Coetzee's protagonists). The possibility of action, in turn, is rooted not only in the condition of natality, but also in *plurality*, the distinctive human condition of being among others 'through which the human world is constantly invaded by strangers, *newcomers whose actions and reactions cannot be foreseen* by those who are already there and are going to leave in a short while' (Arendt 2006, 61; emphasis added). Natality, then, is concerned with the introduction of something new *into a shared human history* – which is a notion radically different from the natural cyclical movement of eternal return, the idea of being 'like fish in water, like birds in air' that the Magistrate momentarily imagines as an escape *from* history. The playing children in *Waiting for the Barbarians* manifest such introduction of the new into the world; they are, in Arendt's terms, 'newcomers whose actions … cannot be foreseen.'

Natality as the entry of the new into the world is, of course, a way of understanding the 'miracle' of literary creation, captured here by the character Elizabeth Costello's son John: 'Out of the dark emerging, out of nowhere: first not there, then there, like a newborn child, heart working, brain working, all the processes of that intricate electrochemical labyrinth working. A miracle' (*EC* 27). However, the existence of the world into which the new inserts itself, perpetuated through natality as an ever-growing web of narratives, is equally miraculous in Arendt's account. This condition is illuminated, remarkably, by Coetzee, when he has Elizabeth Costello say in her lecture 'The Future of the Novel' that

> there is something miraculous about the past that the future lacks. What is miraculous about the past is that we have succeeded – God knows how – in making thousands and millions of individual fictions, fictions created by individual human beings, lock well enough into one another to give us what looks like a common past, a shared story. (*EC* 38)

For Costello here, as for Arendt, it is the plurality in the 'thousands and millions of individual fictions' that constitutes the 'shared story' that is miraculous.[3] Natality, to Arendt, is 'the miracle that saves the world, the realm of human affairs, from its normal, "natural" ruin' (1998, 247). Importantly, Arendt's description of natality as a 'miracle' is not to be taken as an allusion to transcendence, but as an embrace of the world into which the new is inserted. Arendt, who is a thoroughly secular thinker, emphasizes that it is through and among humans that the miracle occurs; although, interestingly, she finds the greatest expression of 'faith in and hope for the world' in 'the few words with which the Gospels announced their "glad tidings": "A child has been born unto us"' (247). Susannah Young-ah Gottlieb points out that Arendt mistakenly – deliberately or not – attributes 'a child has been born unto us' to the Gospels, when in fact the phrase appears not in the 'otherworldly spirit' of the New Testament but in the 'worldliness' of Isaiah (9.6) in the Old Testament (Young-ah Gottlieb 2003, 136–7). Regardless of the origins of this misattribution, the phrase 'unto us' shows how Arendt's idea of natality is directed towards the renewal of a common social world. As Young-ah Gottlieb observes, to Arendt the important thing is that 'the *world* is saved – not souls from the world'; the 'salvation' in natality 'has nothing to do with any effort to transcend the conditions in which human beings find themselves … The child appears as a representative of the world and an antidote to ruin' (Young-ah Gottlieb 2003, 137; emphasis in original). As I will argue, this care for the *world* is a distinctive feature also in Coetzee.

Natality and the event

It should be apparent by now how Arendt's concept of natality prefigures Derek Attridge's notion of the *event* (derived from Derrida) in his ethics of reading.[4] Like natality – the human capacity for radical and unforeseen novelty – the event, in Attridge's formulation, is characterized by 'innovation and unpredictability' that breaks the cycle of repetition; and like natality, the

---

3 Elizabeth Costello would probably not approve of being likened to Hannah Arendt. In *The Lives of Animals*, the character 'Dean Arendt' is one of Costello's interlocutors who fails to understand her reasoning on the zones of indistinction between human and non-human animals (*LA* 44).
4 As Diprose and Ziarek observe: 'Since Arendt wrote her political philosophy, Jacques Derrida has elaborated her idea of the disclosure and welcome of natality into a political ontology of hospitality, although with reference to the philosophy of Emmanuel Levinas rather than Arendt' (2017, 237).

event cannot be reduced to or understood within the frameworks that precede it, yet it arises from within those frameworks: 'it is often through the old that otherness makes itself felt' (2004b, 13; 20). Like Arendt, Attridge sees the event as a 'miracle' in the sense that it arises from outside the realm of what is possible within a particular explanatory framework (2004b, 135).[5] Attridge explores how, over and over again, Coetzee's fictions stage and call for a responsiveness to the event; they exemplify 'the value (but also the risk) of openness to the moment and to the future, of the perhaps and the wherever' (2004a, 64).

However, while 'event' and 'natality' overlap in significant ways, the concept of natality is productive in that it captures the tension *between past and future* in Coetzee's work in a way that the event does not. For unlike the event, the concept of natality, as I have outlined above, highlights *both* a responsibility towards that which is to come (the new), *and* a responsibility towards that which is already there (the world).[6] Beyond the event, the idea of natality, then, highlights for us the existence of a human world that is dependent on the continuing appearance of the new, and the way in which that world is itself the condition for the new to be brought into existence.[7] As I will show, in Coetzee, the anxious negotiation between these two responsibilities surfaces particularly in episodes revolving around education and transmission between generations.

Furthermore, the concept of natality is valuable beyond the event not only in how it takes into account the world in its past, present, and future incarnations, but also in how it situates itself explicitly in relation to *mortality*. Coetzee's characters – like the Magistrate who 'dreams of ends' – are often preoccupied with their own mortality; consider, for example, Mrs Curren, David Lurie, Dostoevsky, and Paul Rayment, all of whom are concerned with,

---

5 Attridge clarifies that otherness, in his understanding, is not an 'absolute alterity', it 'does not come from outer space' (2004b, 30).
6 Attridge *mentions* responsibility towards the past when he writes that Coetzee's fiction 'opens the possibility of an ethics of unique acts, rooted always in the here and now, yet acknowledging a deep responsibility to the otherness of elsewhere, *of the past*, and of the future' (2004a, 8; emphasis added). However, his *readings* focus rather on the responsibility towards the (post)colonial other and the event of the unforeseeable future or of the reading of the literary work.
7 Let me note here, parenthetically, that while it is the world of *humans* that is explored in this chapter in the context of education and transmissibility (certainly Arendt's focus is on the *human being's* distinctive capacity for beginning), this should not eclipse the fact that the relation between human and non-human animals is a central and enduring concern in Coetzee's work. The concept of the event, which does not exclude the non-human other, is closer than natality to Coetzee in this respect.

as Mrs Curren and David Lurie both put it, their 'lines' '[running] out' (*WB* 146; *AI* 195; *D* 199). As Jan Wilm puts it, Coetzee's texts

> may be seen to explore the philosophical idea that death is strung through the fiber of life rather than a mere closing of the brackets at the end, and that all of life is given both its magnitude and its inconsequence by the final bookend looming uncertainly yet certainly in the distance. (2016, 196)

Yet disturbing these characters' orientation towards their own death, there are always openings towards the new, as figurative 'countervoices' of children generate dialogical tensions in the narratives. For the Magistrate, the children at play are intimations of new beginnings; for Paul Rayment, the appearance of the children Drago and Ljuba in his isolated life incite the desire for being with others and a hope for continuity; for David Lurie, his daughter Lucy's unborn child paradoxically catalyses both thoughts of finitude and unprecedented openness to the new; for Mrs. Curren, the township boys John and Bheki and her distant grandsons similarly signal both beginnings and endings. In each of these cases, the child's figuring of the possibility of the new *interrupts* and *complicates* the adult character's solitary and contemplative mode of being-towards-death. Thus, these children are reminders not only of the capacity for new beginnings, but also of human plurality, the exchanges between different perspectives that are inherent in natality.[8]

Worrying about the child

I have suggested that, like the Magistrate, several of Coetzee's characters are preoccupied with death and troubled by their failure to imagine the birth of the new; I am thinking particularly of Mrs Curren, David Lurie, Dostoevsky, and Paul Rayment. For each of these characters, the child is, at first glance, less a figure of hope than a mark of failed continuity, as it prompts (in some cases) their preoccupation with their 'cut-offness' from the past, and (in each case)

---

8 In other words, when Coetzee's adult characters are disturbed in their being-towards-death by the appearance of children, this is a manifestation both of spatial and temporal disruption. As Patricia Bowen-Moore points out, 'the most obvious of natality's features has to do with its temporal and spatial appearance: a life begins at a definite moment in time and appears in the world at a particular place' (1989, 13).

their frustration in relation to a future that they cannot imagine. However, in each case, the child also introduces the possibility of the new. In other words, the child represents 'both the promise of and resistance to continuity' as Ala Alryyes puts it in his account of the child's foundational role in the symbolic constructions of novelistic and national discourses (2001, 15).

Slow Man offers an illustrative example of the tension between the past and the future that is contained in the desire for continuity, particularly through the central character Paul Rayment's encounters with his caregiver Marijana Jokić's son Drago. The narrative's point of departure is a bicycle accident – inflicted on Rayment by the careless young driver Wayne Blight – as a consequence of which Rayment has his leg amputated. Left with a stump where his leg used to be, Rayment feels unhomed in his body, in language, and in the world; the accident reminds him of his divorce, his childlessness, and his estrangement from both the France of his childhood and the Adelaide of his adulthood. Rayment's estrangement from the world catalyses a personal crisis in which he despairs of his missing link to the next generation: 'childlessness looks to him like madness, a herd madness, even a sin' (34). (Note that Rayment's predicament, characterized by both 'inwardness' and 'estrangement from the past', recalls the condition of 'worldlessness' that, as Zakin writes, distinguishes the 'modern condition' for Arendt (2017, 123).) Comically, Rayment's desire for continuity prompts him to consider the possibility to 'locate (but how?) some wayward orphan, some Wayne Blight in embryo, and put in an offer to adopt him' (45).

Rayment's desire for a child is reinforced by his first encounter with Drago, provoking a surprising surge of affect:

> As he speaks he is aware of the boy watching his lips, brushing aside the word-strings as if they were cobwebs, tuning his ear to the intention. His respect for the boy is growing, growing by leaps and bounds. No ordinary boy, this one! The envy of gods he must be. *The Ballad of Drago Jokić*. (*SM* 70)

As the passage shows, and as Rayment himself notes, the encounter with Drago brings about '*heightened emotion*' (71; emphasis in original). Rayment finds himself '[hungering] suddenly and urgently for motherhood. Hungry enough to steal another's child: it is as mad as that' (73). He self-consciously interrogates Marijana 'as casually as he can' about Drago, and despite himself – 'even as he speaks he feels the recklessness of what he is saying, but he cannot stop himself' – offers to sponsor the boy's education (74–5). I read this gesture, in which Rayment lets go of any conventional restraint, as ultimately about finding a sense of belonging in time through the child; indeed, Elizabeth Costello attributes Rayment's affective response to the Jokić children to the fact that 'they are at home in the world. It is, to them, a good place' (87). So when Rayment later writes to Miroslav Jokić, Drago's father, *'can you find a place in your hearth and in your home, in your heart and home, for a godfather? .... will you in principle open your home to me?'* it is to find a figurative home for himself through a new beginning (224; emphasis in original).

Interestingly, the child in *Slow Man* offers not only the prospect of continuity through new beginnings, but also the retroactive construction of continuity with the past. This is staged in two episodes centering on Rayment's collection of photographs of early Australian miners. In the first scene, Rayment shows Drago the prints and is overcome by emotion as he articulates to the boy the idea of a common Australian history: *'Our record, yours and mine',* he thinks – deeply ironic, of course, since it isn't their history at all. Yet by establishing this link between himself, 'the little boy from Lourdes' and the child, 'Drago, son of Dubrovnik', Rayment approaches the sense of continuity he lacks (177; emphasis in original). Later, it transpires that Drago has made a copy of one of the prints, inserting his own grandfather among the faces; literally constructing a continuity with an Australian past.

In these ways, then, the child becomes a central vehicle for continuity with the past and the future in *Slow Man*. However, Paul Rayment's exchanges with Drago also draw attention to the former's *misgivings* about the new:

'Do you hate things if they are new, Mr Rayment?' says Drago out of the blue.

'No. Why do you say that?'

...

'I'll give you a straight answer, Drago, but not at the cost of being laughed at. I have been overtaken by time, by history. The flat, and everything in it, has been overtaken. There is nothing strange in that – in being overtaken by time. It will happen to you too, if you live long enough. Now tell me: what is this conversation really about? Is it about a computer that doesn't match up to your standards?'

> Drago stares at him in shocked puzzlement. And indeed he surprises himself. Why such sharp words? What has the poor boy done to deserve them? *Do you hate things if they are new?* A fair enough question to an old man. What is there to be cross about? (178–9; emphasis in original)

Paul Rayment's agitated rebuttal to Drago's question, surprising even to himself in its intensity of affect, illustrates the ambivalence that lies in longing for a link to the world of the next generation (as opposed to being 'overtaken by time, by history'), and at the same time being repelled by the new. One might say that while Rayment acknowledges the need for and inevitability of new beginnings, he is not particularly hospitable to the unknown. However, his attitude changes over the course of the novel, as he is repeatedly *surprised* in his encounters with Drago, who repeatedly disproves Rayment's prejudices about the next generation. In the novel's penultimate scene, Rayment – again to his surprise – is presented with a recumbent bicycle that Drago has built for him, a sign of care where he had anticipated indifference. Embracing the 'blush of shame, starting at his ears and creeping forward over his face', Rayment is markedly humbled by his failure to imagine the unexpected gesture and makes a point of being open to the moment (254).

What the strong presence of the child establishes in *Slow Man*, in the end, seems to be what Rayment's metafictional creator and uninvited houseguest Elizabeth Costello says here: '*Through our children we become the servants of time*' (182; emphasis added). I mentioned this moment in Chapter 1 as one of several instances in Coetzee where an apparently ironic formulation about the child appears to be seriously intended. 'She believes what she is saying, it would seem', Rayment reflects, and I think that it would not be unjust for Coetzee's reader to draw a similar conclusion (182). This brings us back to Arendt and natality, because what Costello (and, I venture, Coetzee) is saying here is that the child – the arrival of the new – requires us to take responsibility for the world.

Getting beyond death

Paul Rayment is not alone in his worries about the child – for characters in other Coetzee novels, the anxiety about the future is often of both a public and a private nature. Characters such as Mrs Curren, David Lurie, and Dostoevsky are conflicted about societal upheavals where the new stands against the old; their political concerns mirror their apprehensions about the future also on a personal level with regard to their children: Mrs Curren and David Lurie are both estranged from their daughters and Dostoevsky has lost his son.[9] Although this book is not primarily concerned with biographical facts, it is worth noting that such parallel public and private concerns have been pressing also for Coetzee himself over the years. So just as Coetzee's stagings of 'cut-offness' in several instances reflect evolving political circumstances in South Africa, they are also traces of the deeply personal; hence the inexorable intertwining in the novels of the uncertain future of the nation and the tenuous link to the next generation. Attwell observes from his archival research how Coetzee's anxieties about the future at the time leading up the writing of *Disgrace* were 'personal as much as they were political, because they had to do with being an ageing parent and imagining one's children and *their* future' (2015, 224; emphasis in original). Coetzee's personal circumstances, including the tragic death of his son Nicolas, Attwell writes, 'would have challenged his sense of continuity with future generations'.[10] What I would like to note especially, here, though, is the following passage that Attwell cites from the notebook in which *Disgrace* was conceived. In his notes, Coetzee writes that the character-to-be David Lurie

> consistently takes the line, Nothing matters, soon I will be dead anyway. In other words, he cannot see beyond his death. Somehow he (I too!) must *get beyond that*. Hence, of course, the daughter, the only way in which he (I too!) can conceive of the future. (Attwell 2015, 224–5; emphasis added)

What I am concerned with here is precisely how Coetzee's characters manage to 'get beyond' their death, to conceive instead of the future in terms of

---

9 For an account of filial relations in Coetzee's work from *Dusklands* to *Summertime*, see Dooley's chapter 'Parents and Children' (2010).
10 Attwell also observes how Coetzee, when he set out to write *Waiting for the Barbarians*, having tried 'to imagine South Africa in the aftermath of a revolutionary war', found himself unable to complete such a narrative, instead writing a novel about 'failing to imagine a future' (2015, 106). Tracing the manuscript revisions for *Waiting for the Barbarians*, Attwell shows how the novel was born out of Coetzee's 'efforts to imagine a future after apartheid', writing of 'a society in a state of paranoia, seemingly on the edge of dissolution' (2014, 214–15). Equally, Attwell finds 'much of Coetzee' in *Slow Man*, including 'the sense of being cut off from one's past and from the future' (2015, 243).

beginnings. Key to this, it seems, is that the failure to imagine the future is overcome by the reimagining of the unimaginable new in terms of openness and possibility.

Also in the finished novel David Lurie struggles to imagine his daughter 'Lucy's future, his future, the future of the land as a whole', dismissing it all as 'a matter of indifference' (*D* 107). Despite his failure to imagine the future, however, he tries to enable it to be born. A professor of English-cum-Communications at the Cape Technical University where his ideals of *bildung* are no longer in demand, Lurie seems prepared to accept his position as a 'hangover from the past'; he seems to *want* to acknowledge the new, although it at times appears not only unfamiliar but also undesirable (40). In several instances Lurie reflects on Lucy's choices with what – signposted by conspicuous exclamation marks – reads as contrived enthusiasm: 'A solid woman, embedded in her new life. Good! If this is to be what he leaves behind – this daughter, this woman – then he does not have to be ashamed'; 'Making her own life. Coming out of his shadow. Good! He approves!' (62, 89).

But although Lurie forcefully tells himself that he approves of his daughter's 'coming out of his shadow', he seems to view her situation as an end rather than a new beginning. Time and again, he wonders silently at her choices, and tries, albeit weakly, to convince her to reconsider her resolve to live alone in the rough and bare realities of the rural Eastern Cape. When the violent rape at the centre of the novel results in '*the child*', the unborn child in Lucy's womb, Lurie's feeble faith in the new dissolves temporarily (199, emphasis in original). He conceives of the unborn child as a figure of the *end*, lamenting: 'A father without the sense to have a son: is this how it is all going to end, is this how his line is going to run out, like water dribbling into the earth?' (199). The break between past and future that runs through the novel provokes a sense of resignation and disorientation, captured by Lurie's comment to Bev Shaw at the Animal Welfare Clinic where he helps out: 'I don't know what the question is any more. Between Lucy's generation and mine a curtain seems to have fallen' (210). However, this is only part of the story; importantly, the unborn child *also* directs Lurie towards the future. Lurie attends to his tasks at the dog clinic with renewed energy, and also finds inspiration for the opera he is composing:

> Twice a day he feeds the animals; he cleans out their pens and occasionally talks to them; otherwise he reads or dozes or, when he has the premises to himself, picks out on Lucy's banjo the music he will give to Teresa Guiccioli.
> Until the child is born, this will be his life. (*D* 211–12)

Here the child is not an end point, but a new beginning; after 'the child is born' his life will not be 'this', but something new. Indeed, through the child, the novel gestures towards a renewed faith in continuity, as Lurie imagines himself a grandfather: 'He must have a look again at Victor Hugo, poet of grandfatherhood. There may be things to learn' (218).

Like David Lurie, Mrs Curren in *Age of Iron* is troubled by endings and the idea of her line '[running] out', her biological grandsons in America too distant – born, after all, into a different 'world' – to constitute a link to the future (195). Her anxiety of having to 'die without a child', as she puts it, is dramatized repeatedly throughout the novel, up to this poignant passage on the penultimate page (139):

> Last night, growing terribly cold, I tried to call you up to say good-bye. But you would not come. I whispered your name. 'My daughter, my child', I whispered into the darkness; but all that appeared to me was a photograph: a picture of you, not you. Severed, I thought: that line severed too. Now there is nothing to hold me …
> I am going to release you soon from this rope of words. (197)

We are given, here, the image of Mrs Curren's letter to her estranged daughter as a 'rope of words'; as ineffectual in its bid to span the gap between a lost past, an unfamiliar present, and an unforeseeable future as in its attempt to stretch across the spatial distance – the Atlantic Ocean – separating mother and daughter. The figure of a rope between past and future recurs in Coetzee's work as an image epitomizing the yearning for continuity between generations. In *The Master of Petersburg*, the bereaved Dostoevsky 'feels the cord of love that goes from his heart to his [dead] son's as physically as if it were a rope' (*MP* 23). Mrs Curren's image of a 'severed' string between generations reappears also in the early pages of *The Childhood of Jesus*, when the boy David and his guardian Simón have just arrived to Novilla, bearing no memories of their past:

> 'And what is your mama's name?'

> The boy casts him an interrogative glance.
>
> 'He doesn't know her by name', he says. 'He had a letter with him when he boarded the boat, but it was lost.'
>
> 'The string broke', says the boy.
>
> 'The letter was in a pouch', he explains, 'which was hanging around his neck on a string. The string broke and the letter was lost. There was a hunt for it all over the ship. That was how David and I met. But the letter was never found.' (*CJ* 27)

Just as in *Age of Iron*, the reference here is to a letter from a parent to a child; the former unlikely to reach the future, the latter lost from the past. (In fact, the figure of a rope in time, 'from land to land', between this life and the next, resurfaces in *The Schooldays of Jesus* as well (206–7).) In David's case, the broken string speaks of the irretrievable memory of a family; in Mrs Curren's case, the 'rope of words' of an individual soul thrown out into a void likewise comes across as fragile and futile.[11] Parenthetically, the image of 'the string [that] broke', is not just a figure for these private stories, but also calls attention to the idea of *transmissibility* in a broader sense, recalling, especially for the reader familiar with South African literature, the vulnerability of a collective history and its potential inability to reach into the future.[12]

Amor mundi and transmissibility

As I have observed, the birth of the new is often figured in Coetzee as inconceivable (although, as I have also argued, *actual* children in the fictions repeatedly interrupt this tendency) – a cause of frustration and anxiety.

---

11 This fragility becomes especially clear when set against the more communitarian narrative that can be traced in the parallel black world in *Age of Iron*. The novel seems to suggest that it is Western individualism that produces this cut-offness, by juxtaposing Mrs Curren's alienation against the continuity implied in the coming of the 'children of iron'. Eckard Smuts's dissertation chapter 3.3 '*Age of Iron* and the Question of Voice' (2014) has a useful discussion on the rejection of Western individualism in *Age of Iron*.

12 'The Broken String' is the title of a much-quoted Bushman/San poem, originally sung in lament for a rainmaker killed in the 1860s by Afrikaner farmers and later narrated by Dia!kwain and transcribed (Chapman 2003, 26). According to Michael Chapman, the image of the broken string can be taken to refer to the state of drought imposed on the entire community following the death of the rainmaker. In this it reflects, of course, a sense of loss at a severed link to the past, a collective feeling shared among those once listening to the song.

Consider, for example, Magda in *In the Heart of the Country*, who cannot imagine being able to bring something new into the world – or, indeed, belonging to the world herself: 'There is no act that I know of that will liberate me into the world. There is no act I know of that will bring the world into me' (*HC* 10). Seeing no escape from the oppressive burden of colonial history (much like the Magistrate), Magda laments: 'Labouring under my father's weight I struggle to give life to a world but seem to engender only death' (11). Crucially, the novel links Magda's inability to imagine a future to her isolation from a social world, past and present. Her world lacks interaction with others – she is stuck in a 'monologue of the self' – and, equally, it lacks the continuity with the past that would enable renewal (17). Wistfully, Magda imagines a bygone era's schoolmistress inspiring 'cheerful submission to the wisdom of the past' and rendering the children of the desert 'heirs of all the ages':

> Someone must have built and stocked a schoolhouse, and advertised for a schoolmistress in the *Weekly Adviser* or the *Colonial Gazette*, and met her train, and installed her in the guestroom, and paid her stipend, in order that the children of the desert should not grow up barbarian but be heirs of all the ages … But where has it all gone now, this cheerful submission to the wisdom of the past? … where has all the humane learning gone? (*HC* 50)

Magda herself, however, has never 'had a tutor', and with no teacher figure to serve as guide to the world, she has, to her own mind, grown up 'barbarian' rather than 'heir to all the ages' (21). Being 'heir to all the ages', we might infer, is *the key to being able to bring something new into the world*. What the novel invites us to think about, I propose, is that Magda's predicament of struggling to 'give life to a world' is not only the effect of the lack of reciprocity with the 'brown folk' discussed in Chapter 2, but also largely comes down to a failure of transmission between generations, as the oppressive determinism of a patriarchal discourse (Magda is 'labouring under [her] father's weight') has eliminated the potential for renewal (8, 11).

Arendt's essay 'The Crisis in Education' in *Between Past and Future* helpfully addresses the role of education in the difficult balancing act of moving in the gap between the old and the new. Describing newness as both a threat and a promise, Arendt understands the task of education to be the protection of 'the child against the world, the world against the child, the new against the old, the old against the new' (2006, 188). She argues that educators have the responsibility to teach children 'what the world is like', in order for children to be able to introduce something new into the common human world (192). Patricia Bowen-Moore explains how the basis for Arendt's theory of education is 'natality guided by the attitude of *amor mundi*', love for the world, an attitude that 'entails the hope that the world of human plurality will not only continue in time but will also continue to anticipate and to welcome newcomers into its communal experiences' (1989, 35; 19). Arendt argues that education can forego neither authority nor leaving room for the new:

> Our hope always hangs on the new which every generation brings; but precisely because we can base our hope only on this, we destroy everything if we so try to control the new that we, the old, can dictate how it will look. *Exactly for the sake of what is new and revolutionary in every child, education must be conservative; it must preserve this newness and introduce it as a new thing into an old world*, which, however revolutionary its actions may be, is always, from the standpoint of the next generation, superannuated and close to destruction. (2006, 189; emphasis added)

In other words, *in order for* the new to be introduced, education must turn towards the old. Arendt writes of education that it 'is the point at which we decide whether we love the world enough to assume responsibility for it and by the same token save it from that ruin, which, except for renewal, except for the coming of the new and young, would be inevitable' (2006, 193). Unquestionably, the Magistrate embodies the attitude of *amor mundi*, demonstrating that he 'loves the world enough to assume responsibility for it', when he approaches the playing children carefully, 'anxious not to alarm them', and, crucially, without *interfering* with their creation of the new (WB 170). Arendt comes very close to Coetzee, I believe, in her thinking on education, which Emily Zakin describes as the rejection of both 'an exalted past infused with glory and an idealistic future that equates the new with progress', suggesting that Arendt 'confronts the threats to human community when new beginnings are no longer contextualized by durable inheritances' (2017, 120). I will return to how *amor mundi* appears in scenes of education in Coetzee's fiction, but first I turn my attention to the special category of temporality that helps us understand why moving between the old and the new is particularly precarious in certain moments in South African history.

The interregnum, freedom, and writing

Interestingly, the perceived responsibility to relinquish authority to an unknown future seems more fraught with anxiety for Coetzee's characters than the relinquishment of authority in the encounter with the (post)colonial other. Unlike the case of encounters with the (post)colonial other described in Chapter 2, where often playful allusions to the child figure's indeterminacy provoke ethical reflection, the subject's struggle to find a position between the old and the new is dramatized without ambiguities regarding the construction of the child as such. The subject's ambivalent relation to history – history as the passing of time – is marked in the narratives by the double connotations carried by the child – both continuity and new beginnings – but with an urgency that is rarely tempered by irony. In these instances, the child instead evokes an ethics as it calls into question the authority of the self in relation to time, creating a tension, but also a productive relationship, between the desire for continuity (personal and cultural), on the one hand, and the felt duty to accept – and ultimately to embrace – the unknowability of the future, on the other.

One reason for the particular relevance of thinking of Coetzee's work in terms of natality is that natality hinges on, in the words of Diprose and Ziarek, '*the opening of a gap in the potential continuity between past and future, a hiatus between no longer and not yet*' (2013, 113; emphasis in original). Consider, for example, how *Age of Iron* approaches the possibility of beginning something new. As we saw in Chapter 2, for a large part of the novel the figure of the child – the innocent child – above all marks the stability of the *past* in Mrs Curren's mind, and the *failure* of that past to reach into the future. To Mrs Curren, the presence of a small child named Hope is more a cause for cynicism than faith in the future: 'Hope and Beauty. It was like living in an allegory' (*AI* 90). Indeed, Mrs Curren's predicament reflects the 'impasse' described by Andrew van der Vlies in *Present Imperfect*, an 'affective and temporal displacement, a feeling otherwise, an enduring of something (some condition) other than that for which one has hoped', although, poignantly, Van der Vlies is writing about the post-apartheid South Africa that Mrs Curren cannot yet foresee (2017, 14). The impasse, for Mrs Curren, lies in her gradual awakening to the insight that her views on childhood, politics, and education are if not, to her mind, obsolete, then *unwanted* and thus irrelevant; she must relinquish authority to a future that she can neither envisage nor place hope in.

Mrs Curren's position – in Coetzee's words, a 'totally untenable historical position' – needs to be understood in terms of the period in which *Age of Iron* is written and set (*DP* 250). This time in South African history been referred to by Nadine Gordimer and others as the *interregnum*, a period of political transition when, in Antonio Gramsci's words, 'the old is dying and the new cannot be born.'[13] In fact, already the title of *Age of Iron* alerts us to the prominence in the novel of the idea of an 'age', signifying a time preceded and superseded by something radically different. As Martin Jay argues in his piece 'Historical Explanation and the Event', 'understanding events is always apprehending them on a horizon of meaning that they have opened themselves' (2011, 567).[14] In the interregnum, the implication is, society has broken with the old but the event has not yet opened new history within which the moment can be understood. It is striking how, in this situation, Mrs Curren shows not resignation but *amor mundi*, an unrelenting love for the world. This care for the world assumes different shapes: Classicist professor that she is, she clings to the classics for their explanatory power and anchoring potential; yet her care for the world is also manifested, ultimately, in her privileging of John and Bheki, 'the two boys whose lives have brushed [hers]' – and who mark the emergence of the new in her world – over her grandsons, the distant 'seed planted in the American snows' (*AI* 195). Put differently, she is trying to show the new generation the world as (she believes) it is, but at the same time she is allowing that world to be interrupted in order for it not to be ruined.

The *interregnum* is also the temporal horizon of *The Master of Petersburg*. As with *Age of Iron* and *Disgrace*, the novel presents the character Dostoevsky's anxiety in relation to the severed link to the next generation: he feels that with the news of his son Pavel's death 'he has been tugged out of

---

13 The full quote from 'Crisis of Authority' in Gramsci's *Prison Notebooks* (~1930) is: 'The crisis consists precisely in the fact that the old is dying and the new cannot be born; in this interregnum a great variety of morbid symptoms appear.'
14 Jay is quoting Claude Romano's *L'Événement et le Monde* (1998) translated as *Event and the World* by Shane Mackinlay (New York: Fordham University Press, 2009), 152.

human time' (2). In the novel, the character Dostoevsky is preoccupied with trying but failing to understand the political world view of the generation to which Pavel belonged; as Attridge has shown, the novel manifests an ethics of hospitality in how Dostoevsky's impossible desire to grasp Pavel's life and death coincides with his waiting for the inspiration to write. The character Dostoevsky 'must answer to what he does not expect', but, as Attridge observes, being 'wholly responsive to the new, the other, doing justice to it every time, is impossible', as the new cannot always be identified as such (*MP* 80; Attridge 2004a, 123). However, in my reading the creative tension in the novel arises not only from the anticipation of the ungraspable new, but also from the negotiation between past and future, the generational conflict that Dostoevsky thinks of as the pitting of 'children against those who are not children' (*MP* 63). The trench between the old and the new is reinforced by the noticeable use of colons in the text, for example: 'Fathers and sons: foes: foes to the death' and 'A war: the old against the young, the young against the old' (239, 247). In contrast to Dostoevsky, who, like Mrs Curren, is frustrated by the 'sickness of [his] age' with 'young people turning their backs on their parents', the police officer Maximov suggests that the conflict is itself a matter of tradition and continuity: 'Perhaps it is just the old matter of fathers and sons after all, such as we always have had', adding that 'perhaps the wisest course would be the simplest: to dig in and outlast them – wait for them to grow up' (137, 45).

However, waiting for the arrival of the future – and, by analogy, for the lost child Pavel – will not release Dostoevsky as a writer; instead, it is *in* the interregnum that the new will be born. When, in the novel's final chapter he 'unpacks the writing-case, sets out his materials', it is 'no longer a matter of listening for the lost child calling from the dark stream'; 'ultimately it will not be given to him to bring the dead boy back to life' (*MP* 235, 237–8). Remarkably, the limbo position in which the child cannot be reached in the past or in the future – a limbo mirrored by the political landscape in which the old is no longer relevant and the new has not yet been born – emerges as its own inversion, a site of *freedom and possibility where writing can take place*. The condition of simultaneous irresponsibility and responsibility implied in this position is staged through Dostoevsky's alternating responses to the blurred imaginary 'figure' that appears across his writing table, the meaning of which he cannot grasp:

> From the figure he feels nothing, nothing at all. Or rather, he feels around it a field of indifference tremendous in its force, like a cloak of darkness. Is that why he cannot find the name – not because the name is hidden but because the figure is indifferent to all names, all words, anything that might be said about it?
>
> The force is so strong that he feels it pressing out upon him, wave upon silent wave. (*MP* 238)

The 'indifference' of the figure prompts Dostoevsky to abandon his waiting, and to ask himself: 'Has he misunderstood from the beginning? Is he required … to put aside all that he himself is, all he has become, down to his very features, and *become as a babe again*?' (240; emphasis added).[15] The implication of the writer needing to *be irresponsible like a child in order to write* becomes more clear in a passage in the text that he proceeds to write: 'History is coming to an end; the old account-books will soon be thrown in the fire; *in this dead time between old and new, all things are permitted*' (244; emphasis added). In this understanding, the creative impulse arises at a point in time when existing explanatory models are insufficient; not because there is meaning lurking behind the corner, but because of the freedom inherent in an inexplicable present moment. The reason for this is that natality, the human capacity to create something new, is not guided by any determinate direction.

Interestingly, in his correspondence with Paul Auster in *Here and Now*, Coetzee returns to this idea of the interregnum – the moment of not knowing the outcome – as a glimpse of freedom: 'I keep thinking that it is only in those all too brief interregnums, when one power has been overthrown and the next has yet to install itself, that people have a true taste of liberty' (221). (Coetzee echoes Arendt's conclusion to *The Origins of Totalitarianism* (2017), where she writes that 'beginning, before it becomes a historical event, is the supreme capacity of man; politically, it is identical with man's freedom' (629).) In his final letter to Paul Auster, writing on the day after the end of the Battle of

---

15 I will return in Chapters 4 and 5 to how Giorgio Agamben's notion of *infancy* helps us understand this 'indifference' to meaning not as nihilistic, but as an emancipatory way of approaching the world – and literature.

Tripoli in August 2011, Coetzee (much like the character Maximov above) muses on the inevitability of the new joining the old:

> Perhaps that is what revolutions are really about, perhaps that is all one should expect from them: a week or two of freedom, of exulting in one's strength and beauty (and of being loved by all the girls), before the gray old men reassert their grip and life is returned to normal.
>
> The world keeps throwing up its surprises. We keep learning. (Coetzee and Auster 2013, 247–8)

Coetzee gives voice to a certain scepticism here, when he notes that 'perhaps all one should expect' from revolutions – the revolution, of course, being the epitome of historical innovation – is that, eventually, 'life is returned to normal'. Yet, observe how the final line contradicts the preceding paragraph, leaving a combined feeling of the inevitability of repetition and an always remaining opening towards the new: the 'gray old men' will 'reassert their grip', *but at the same time*, the world 'keeps throwing up its surprises'. Ultimately, then, and despite the reservation in the first clauses, Coetzee here conveys the openness to the possibilities inherent in natality that is, I believe, always latent in his novels.

Pedagogy and play

I have suggested that Coetzee's novels enact the attitude that Arendt calls *amor mundi* in their insistence on the simultaneous importance of continuity with the past and need to grant authority to the unforeseeable new. Along with the preoccupation with death and finitude, there is always a simultaneous orientation towards the new that, due to the pervasive presence of children, cannot be ignored. In the novels, this results in a tug of war of sorts, as protagonists navigate the tension that arises in the discontinuity between a lost past and an uncertain future – although, on balance, Coetzee seems inclined towards Elizabeth Costello's position that 'there must be some limit to the burden of remembering that we impose on our children and grandchildren. They will have a world of their own, of which we should be less and less part' (*EC* 20). As discussed, Arendt identifies *education* as the 'point at which we decide whether we love the world enough to assume responsibility for it and by the same token save it from that ruin, which ... except for the coming of the new and young, would be inevitable' (2006, 193). Unsurprisingly, educational moments in Coetzee's novels stand out as scenes highlighting the straddling of gaps between past and future; indeed, Coetzee returns time and again to the dynamics of pedagogy in and outside of his fiction.

Himself a teacher, Coetzee tends to stage the perspective of the educator rather than that of the student. An exception is the account in *Boyhood* of the young John's school years, which assumes the school boy's viewpoint. The young John, it should be said, is far from revolutionary in his view of the future, set rather on '[staying] on at school, moving up through the ranks', disliking when 'now and then, a teacher's ignorance is exposed', and wishing to 'protect his teachers if he could' (33–4, 108). Admittedly, John 'does not want to have a father', and, in order not to follow in his father's footsteps, he briefly revolts against the idea of liking Shakespeare (43). In this case too, though, the authority of tradition outweighs resistance: 'If his father likes Shakespeare then Shakespeare must be bad, he decides. Nevertheless, he begins to read Shakespeare, in the yellowing edition with the tattered edges that his father inherited and that may be worth lots of money because it is old, trying to discover why people say Shakespeare is great' (104). *Boyhood*'s ending reinforces the import placed on cultural continuity. On the final page, John and his mother are being given a lift back to town by the undertaker after the funeral of John's great-aunt Annie, a schoolteacher. 'She taught for over forty years', says John's mother. 'Then she left some good behind', says the undertaker: 'A noble profession, teaching' (166). John, Aunt Annie's godson and favourite, is left with the implicit legacy of books and stories about the past to tell, wondering how he will shoulder the burden. Certainly, ending the book with this particular episode imprints on the reader the importance of establishing continuity between the past and the future through the telling of stories, or the transmission of culture.

However, while a certain measure of cultural continuity is presented as desirable in Coetzee, the reality is of course that the intended learner is not always receptive to being guided by tradition. Recall David Lurie's exasperation at 'the range of ignorance of his students, Post-Christian, posthistorical, postliterate, they might as well have been hatched from eggs yesterday'; Mrs

Curren and her fruitless attempts to reach the resisting township boys John and Bheki is another example (*D* 32). In the novels, Coetzee's 'teacher' focalizers are typically figured as frustrated by the resistance – sometimes understood as ignorance – of the other-to-be-educated. Judging from his comments on pedagogy and play in interviews and essays, Coetzee himself appears to endorse such resistance. In *The Good Story*, Coetzee reflects on the obscure nature of certain students' 'stubborn resistance' and 'refusal to accept the teacher's critical authority', but also on the inverse but equally puzzling 'slavish' following of the teacher of other students (166). Relatedly, Coetzee asks:

> Why, in the professional literature, is there so little psychological or indeed political analysis of what goes on in the classroom? (I say political because the task facing the teacher from the first day is that of establishing his/her authority; while for at least some of the children the great if unarticulated task is that of subverting an authority whose legitimacy is not obvious to them). (*GS* 163)

Coetzee suggests that ultimately, for real education to take place, the teacher 'has to be resisted, followed, resisted and followed, transcended, and left behind' (169). The implication, here, is that the teacher must both assume responsibility for the world as it is and leave room for the birth of the new. Coetzee's repeated revisiting of this topic suggests the difficulty in striking the right balance and, relatedly, the creative potency in the tension between past and future.

Intimately related to education and the creation of the new is, of course, the notion of *play*. In my introduction, I cited Coetzee's remark that writing fiction, to him, is 'playing with possibilities', and, as I have argued, a key feature of Coetzee's poetics is precisely such a sense of 'irresponsibility' and experimentation (*DP* 246). Relatedly, it is striking how Coetzee emphasizes and elevates the activity of child's play in different remarks over the years.[16] In

---

16 In Coetzee criticism, the question of play is addressed in Patrick Hayes's *J.M. Coetzee and the Novel: Writing and Politics after Beckett* (2010), part of which is dedicated to an exploration of the playfulness of Coetzee's work in relation to the novelistic form. The concept of play is mainly discussed in two places: the chapter on *Age of Iron*, which Hayes places in dialogue with Coetzee's 1992 essay 'Erasmus: Madness and Rivalry' and with *Don Quixote*, demonstrating the novel's 'jocoserious play with rules and boundaries' (Hayes 2010, 133); and the chapter on *Michael K*, which is read in dialogue with Derrida's notion of *playing the law*. Also, Christian Moser has a chapter titled 'Social Order and Transcendence: J. M. Coetzee's Poetics of Play' in the volume *The Intellectual Landscape in the Works of J.M. Coetzee* (2018).

a conversation with Joanna Scott (1997), Coetzee calls play 'one of the defining characteristics of human beings', pointing to 'creative play – inventing games rather than just playing games' as something 'very precious, one of the most precious things about childhood.' Also, speaking to David Attwell, Coetzee explicitly addresses the idea of play as the creation of the new:

> Game-construction, which we associate with yet-to-be-socialized children, seems to me an essentially higher activity than socialized play, as typified by sport. It is a curious fact that older children and adults do not invent games with the facility of young children, and indeed rarely show any desire to do so. If the arts constitute a higher activity than physical culture, it is surely for the reason that they continue to vary the forms and rules of the games they play. (*DP* 104)

Of course, varying 'the forms and rules' of games might be understood as analogous to giving birth to the new in a broader cultural sense; indeed, the playing child's act of creating something new and unforeseen that exceeds existing boundaries brings natality to mind. Patricia Bowen-Moore finds in child's play a 'mirror experience of natality in that it reflects the child's ability to exercise beginnings' (1989, 33). Unlike natality, which to Arendt is linked to political action, play takes place in the private rather than the public sphere. Child's play, writes Bowen-Moore, introduces the child to 'the element of the arbitrary and the unpredictable inherent in all beginnings', and is 'a creative adaptation of the capacity for novelty' through which the child experiments with the human capacity to begin (33, 35).

However, while Coetzee recurrently highlights the value of creative or free play, he also expresses concern about play being disregarded. Further along in the aforementioned interview with Joanna Scott, Coetzee observes: 'I'm not aware that anyone talks much about play nowadays. A pity.' While this seems a doubtful statement, it does suggest certain misgivings about the space accorded in society to play – and, perhaps, by analogy to the conditions through which the new can appear in the public sphere. This scepticism is apparent also in the essay 'Four Notes on Rugby' (1978) to which the interview harks back. In the essay, Coetzee notes how in schools, sport (which he equates with conforming to existing rules) is privileged over free play: 'From long before adolescence the child is put under pressure to leave the open air of games and live under the umbrella of the codes' (*DP* 125). Expanding the argument to make a connection between child's play and culture at large, he emphasizes as seemingly inevitable the point at which the perpetuation of the old prevails over the creation of the new: 'The child who submits to the code and plays the game is … reenacting a profoundly important moment of culture: the moment at which the Oedipal compromise is made, the moment at which the knee is bent to government' (*DP* 125). More recently, similar concerns resurface in Coetzee's exchanges with Arabella Kurtz in *The Good Story*, when Coetzee reflects on rational discourse and symbolic play as alternative ways for the child to learn to deal with the world, saying that he would 'be sorry to see bright young souls turned into exemplary reasoning machines' (2015, 156).

In the fiction, the educational conflict between free play and the adherence to rules appears, for example, in *Summertime*. In one of the 'undated fragments' near the end of the novel, the character John Coetzee (whom we are invited to read as Coetzee the writer), who 'has been reading here and there on educational theory', juxtaposes two traditions: the Dutch Calvinist teachers of his early childhood and their emphasis on *forming* the child 'as a craftsman forms a clay pot' – educators that he had resisted as a child 'as he resists them now' – against the child-centred Montessori and Rudolf Steiner schools of thinking that, he realizes in hindsight, influenced his mother's parenting (252–4). This is a topic that he expects to return to, writing, in a note-to-self: '*To be developed: his own, home-grown theory of education*' (255; emphasis in original).

While *The Childhood of Jesus* is perhaps not the 'home-grown theory of education' foreshadowed in *Summertime*, the trajectories of its protagonist-educator certainly amplify the character John's reflections – as well as, indeed, the experiences of *Boyhood*'s school boy. The novel revolves very much around 'moments of culture' such as those described in 'Four Notes on Rugby', in which the central adult and child, Simón and David, sometimes do and sometimes do not 'submit to the code and play the game'. The novel thematizes, through its formal and thematic attention to pedagogy and play, the widespread prevalence of – essentially fictional – rules in all walks of life, and the strange paradox between, on the one hand, the ready acceptance of such rules, and, on the other hand, the desire to resist them (or at least render them comprehensible). I will return in greater detail to *The Childhood of Jesus* in Chapter 4, but would like to observe at this point that although the world of Novilla is new to Simón who – he too cut off from the past – has no memories in which to anchor the present, he instinctively assumes responsibility for its (sometimes inexplicable) customs vis-à-vis the child, guarding and transmitting the order of things – embodying, thus, *amor mundi*, a love for the world:

> He takes the boy to a football match, and pays at the turnstile.
>
> 'Why do we have to pay?' asks the boy. 'We didn't have to pay before.'
>
> 'This is the championship game, the last game of the season. At the end of the game the winners get cake and wine. Someone has to collect money to buy the cake and the wine. Unless the baker gets money for his cake, he won't be able to buy the flour and sugar and butter for the next cake. That's the rule: if you want to eat cake then you have to pay for it. And the same goes for wine.'
>
> 'Why?'
>
> 'Why? The answer to all your *Why?* questions, past, present and future, is: *Because that is the way the world is*. The world was not made for our convenience, my young friend. It is up to us to fit in.'
>
> The boy opens his mouth to reply. Swiftly he presses a finger to his lips. 'No', he says. 'No more questions. Be quiet and watch the football.' (*CJ* 169)

As the plot progresses, the reader follows Simón in his internal tug of war between asserting authority and leaving room for the new, in his quest to arrange the boy's education. However, the novel goes beyond the replication of the tension between continuity and the emergence of the new that is the focus of my discussion here. In fact, as I will argue, it eventually does away with the anxiety inherent in this tension, to embrace, instead, its uncertainty; this is the subject of Chapter 4.

From natality to infancy

I started this chapter suggesting that in *Waiting for the Barbarians* the possibility of the birth of the new is held up insistently to the reader through recurring images of playing children, culminating with the final scene where the Magistrate experiences 'inexplicable joy' at the sight, unexpected to him, of children building a snowman. Let me return here to the very final lines of the novel: 'This is not the scene I dreamed of. Like much else nowadays I leave it feeling stupid, like a man who lost his way long ago but presses on along a road that may lead nowhere' (170). Notice how the Magistrate's newborn faith in the possibilities inherent in natality *coincides* with 'feeling stupid' and not having a particular end in view, like someone who 'presses on along a road that may lead nowhere'.[17] It is striking how this 'feeling stupid' resembles the human state that Giorgio Agamben describes as *infancy* or the experience of the *impotentiality* of study. In ending on this note, *Waiting for the Barbarians* foreshadows *The Childhood of Jesus* and its reimagining of the relation to history, where uncertainty about the future is no longer a source of anxiety.

---

17 Sam Durrant reads this final line as 'explicitly anti-redemptive', but, in accordance with my argument on impotentiality that will be developed through the following two chapters, I read this moment in the opposite way, as a gesture towards the possibility of redemption (2003, 49).

4

Childish behaviour: The poetics of study

'I can read, only I don't want to' (146). These are the words of David, the young child around whom the plot revolves in *The Childhood of Jesus*. I take them as my starting point when approaching this bewildering text, which in its refusal to confine itself to a consistent interpretation has continued to confound its readers since its publication in 2013. Emblematic of the novel's reception, Jennifer Rutherford and Anthony Uhlmann point out in their introduction to the essay collection *J.M. Coetzee's The Childhood of Jesus: The Ethics of Ideas and Things* that the novel 'is built around paradox and seemingly deliberately points its readers in several directions at once' (2017, 3). How, then, are we to understand the presence in this novel of this child, somewhat reminiscent of Herman Melville's Bartleby in his preferring not to? In this chapter, I trace how *The Childhood of Jesus*, which thematically concerns a child resisting learning to read 'by the book', through its various circularities and inconsistencies in pursuing this theme forces the reader (at least this one) to recognize herself as a resisting child. In fact, I will argue that the child's withholding of potential is intimately linked to the novel's thematic focus on education and the idea of a quest. Reading *The Childhood of Jesus* in dialogue with Giorgio Agamben's meditations on infancy, impotentiality, and the messianic, I find in the novel's oscillating rhythm and quest-like form a poetics of *study*, inviting, I suggest, a mode of reading characterized by irresponsibility – significantly different, thus, from the ethics of hospitality that has dominated the postmillennial reception of Coetzee's work. Importantly, it is the child that points us towards this emergent poetics.

In my introduction, I cited Coetzee's pivotal remark on the '*feel*' of writing fiction as 'one of freedom, of irresponsibility, or better, of responsibility toward something that has not yet emerged, that lies somewhere at the end of the road'

(*DP* 246). As I observed, critics such as Derek Attridge and Mike Marais choose to emphasize only the later part of this statement, and, as I also described, Marais finds a key metaphor for this other yet-to-emerge in the figure of the lost child. For example, Marais reads the hooded child in the Magistrate's dreams in *Waiting for the Barbarians* as 'other than history, beyond the domain of the same'; *Michael K*'s K as 'still to be born'; *Foe*'s Friday as a 'child waiting to be born'; Verceuil and Mrs Curren's alienated daughter in *Age of Iron* as 'the invisible child'; Dostoevsky's deceased son Pavel, and 'potentially, at least, every being' as 'the lost child' in *The Master of Petersburg*; Melanie Isaacs in *Disgrace* as the abandoned 'child that is not phenomenally apparent' but to whom David Lurie must respond responsibly (Marais 2009, 27, 51, 82, 121, 138, 167). These are all persuasive readings; indeed, throughout Coetzee's work, there is an insistent suggestion of an ethics based on the hospitality to an at least not-quite-graspable other. Like Marais, Attridge convincingly argues that such stagings of openness to alterity translate into analogous ethical demands on the reader; reading *The Master of Petersburg*, for example, he closely links the novel's 'intractable questions of waiting, of expectation, of hospitality, of giving oneself to the future, to the other' to the reader's responsibility to try to 'do justice to the real originality of a new novel' (2004a, 122). Attridge observes that Levinas and Derrida 'link the future indissociably to ethics, responsibility and alterity', crucially placing the idea of being open to that *which is to come in the future* at the centre of his ethics of reading (98).

However, this chapter will demonstrate that the responsibility towards the other that is yet to arrive only *partially* accounts for Coetzee's poetics. (It should be noted that *The Childhood of Jesus* was itself yet-to-arrive at the time of Attridge's and Marais's respective interventions.) Coetzee speaks about writing as *at once* 'irresponsibility' and 'responsibility', and I propose that by paying careful attention to the stubborn child in *The Childhood of Jesus*, as well as to the *responses* to that child elicited from central characters and the reader, we are brought closer to an understanding of the feeling 'of freedom, of irresponsibility' that Coetzee offers as an equally important aspect of writing. As I will argue, it is particularly the novel's mobilization of the child's *resistance to learning* – drawing our attention to the indeterminate state of *infancy*, and relatedly, to the idea of *study* as a restless oscillation between activity and passivity, between clarity and obscurity – and the way that the novel takes the form of a quest, that together point to what I choose to call a poetics of study, to evoke Agamben's understanding of the term which I will elucidate over the coming pages. Importantly, this poetics of study, brought to the forefront by the child figure, both explains and embraces the sometimes frustrated feeling of being pointed 'in several directions at once' that *The Childhood of Jesus* appears to produce in its readers. Indeed, the diversity of the essays that are included in the aforementioned edited volume *J.M. Coetzee's The Childhood of Jesus: The Ethics of Ideas and Things* serves as testimony to the wide array of formal and thematic concerns raised by the novel.

Interestingly, an ethics of hospitality is foregrounded thematically in the early pages of *The Childhood of Jesus*. The novel casts the reader along with its protagonists, the teacher-character Simón and the 5- or 6-year-old boy David – the former the self-appointed guardian of the latter following a voyage at sea where the child has been separated from his parents – into the markedly vague setting of Novilla. When Simón takes it upon himself to find David's lost mother, following the strange conviction that he will recognize her when he sees her (despite never having seen her before and not knowing her name), he mirrors the reader's anticipation of a meaning that has not yet been grasped. So, at the outset, the novel stages Simón *waiting* for the arrival of the unknown mother-to-be:

> *I am girding my loins*, he tells himself. *I am girding my loins for the next chapter in this enterprise.* By the next chapter he means the quest for the boy's mother, the quest that he does not yet know where to commence. *I am concentrating my energies; I am making plans.* (*CJ* 52; emphasis in original)

In this '*girding* [of] *loins*', anticipating '*the next chapter*', we recognize the formula of hospitality to the unexpected outlined by Attridge. We might also note, however, that this moment of anticipation coincides with David's incessant and seemingly pointless game of '[roaming] along the washing lines … winding himself like a cocoon in drying bedsheets, then gyrating and unwinding himself' (*CJ* 52). It is, Simón notes, 'a game he [David] never seems to tire of'. At the time, Simón questions the boy's game; yet, significantly, he takes his cue from the child and stops to press his face into a sheet the next time he passes the courtyard, relishing the new sensation. Perhaps we might read this as a starting point for Simón's being open to all thought's possibilities in the present moment rather than waiting and '*girding* [his] *loins for the next chapter*', in his subsequent winding and unwinding himself along the interminable paths of study.

When Simón eventually encounters Inés, the woman whom he will persuade to assume the role of David's mother, what he demands of her is – literally – unconditional hospitality to the other:

> Please believe me – please take it on faith – this is not a simple matter. The boy is without mother. What that means I cannot explain to you because I cannot explain it to myself. Yet I promise you, if you will simply say Yes, without forethought, without afterthought, all will become clear to you, as clear as day, or so I believe. Therefore: will you accept this child as yours? (75)

Notice here how, when Simón says 'if you will simply say Yes, without forethought, without afterthought', his words are uncannily similar to Derrida's:

> Let us say yes *to who or what turns up*, before any determination, before any anticipation, before any *identification*, whether or not it has to do with a foreigner, an immigrant, an invited guest, or an unexpected visitor, whether or not the new arrival is the citizen of another country, a human, animal, or divine creature, a living or dead thing, male or female. (2000, 77; emphasis in original)

In this way, then, the idea of an ethics of hospitality – of being unconditionally open to an other, or a meaning, that is yet to arrive – is explicitly evoked in *The Childhood of Jesus*.

From waiting to 'pressing on'

However, while *The Childhood of Jesus* echoes earlier moments in Coetzee's fiction of holding out for a particular meaning or belief – or, 'the other' – to arrive; the novel at the same time discourages the very idea of waiting. Instead, it compels the reader towards an intensity of thought, to actively follow Simón in the latter's attempts to navigate and make sense of the bland yet enigmatic Novilla, with its rules lacking in logic, its food lacking in spices and its people lacking in passion; it is unclear whether we are dealing with a utopia, a dystopia, or something else. Time and time again signs in the landscape appear to be clues to something that has been lost – 'They strike a town named Laguna Verde (why? – there is no lagoon)' (*CJ* 261). Wandering around Novilla, Simón deciphers signs but cannot pin down their meaning; his bewilderment alternates with fleeting moments of recognition, inciting in him a constant shuttling between activity and passivity.

This sense of disorientation is replicated in the experience of reading the novel, most notably through its treatment of language. The following scene is a good example:

> They are on the bus, heading out of the city into the countryside. Though there are several other passengers, the boy is not shy to sing. In his clear young voice he chants:
>
> *Wer reitet so spät durch Dampf und Wind?*
>
> *Er ist der Vater mit seinem Kind;*
>
> *Er halt den Knaben in dem Arm,*
>
> *Er füttert ihn Zucker, er küsst ihm warm.*
>
> 'That's all. It's English. Can I learn English? I don't want to speak Spanish any more. I hate Spanish.'
>
> 'You speak very good Spanish. You sing beautifully too. Maybe you will be a singer when you grow up.'
>
> 'No. I'm going to be a magician in a circus. What does it mean, *Wer reitet so?*'
>
> 'I don't know. I don't speak English.' (66–7; emphasis in original)[1]

So, Goethe's 'Erlkönig', sung in German, is presented as English; while the dialogue that we recognize as English purportedly takes place in 'very good Spanish'. The novel continues to destabilize the reader's sense of recognition in this way, causing the reader to alternately follow and withdraw from the narrative. In the same way, while Simón strives to understand and adhere to Novillan order, he also withdraws from it, like a child asking *Why?*, and then wondering to himself: 'Why is he continually asking himself questions instead of just living, like everyone else?' (57).

---

1 Coetzee has distorted the original lines of Goethe's poem; the original fourth line reads 'Er faßt ihn sicher, er hält ihn warm', thus 'He holds him safe, he keeps him warm' and not, as David sings, 'He feeds him sugar, he kisses him warm.'

As the child's schooling is placed firmly at the centre of the plot, Simón's trouble orienting himself among Novillan topographies and bureaucracy is paralleled by a similar frustration in his more abstract quest into the world of educational philosophy. Initially of the opinion that the child 'needs to face up to the real world', he later changes his mind (168):

> There are two schools of thought, Eugenio, on the upbringing of children. One says that we should shape them like clay, forming them into virtuous citizens. The other says that we are children only once, that a happy childhood is the foundation of a happy later life. Inés belongs to the latter school; and, because she is his mother, because the bonds between a child and his mother are sacred, I follow her. Therefore no, I do not believe that more of the discipline of the schoolroom will be good for David. (251)

Yet Simón is reluctant to assume any definitive stance, and the reader is prompted to follow him in his inconclusive explorations of tensions that have marked educational thought since Plato's *Republic*: essentially, the need for forming young citizens to meet predetermined ends set against the merits of learning through free play. These divides are not entirely clear-cut, of course, and throughout the novel Simón oscillates uncertainly between these poles, reluctant to commit firmly to a specific pedagogical regime.

Indeed, constantly present in Coetzee's writing on education, in *The Childhood of Jesus* and elsewhere, is the tension between authority and continuity, on the one hand, and resistance and renewal, on the other. (As discussed in Chapter 3, such a dynamic is described by Arendt in 'The Crisis of Education'.) In its engagement with different schools of educational thought, the novel echoes questions about pedagogy and play that Coetzee has been asking throughout his writerly career, in and outside of the fiction. The reader of *The Childhood of Jesus* is sent off in different directions in the exploration of these fundamental tensions in educational philosophy, actively trying but inevitably failing to locate the novel's (and Simón's) stance on pedagogy, authority, and resistance. Conflicting ideas on how the child should be educated are tested in Simón's own reflections and in his exchanges with Inés, Elena, and his co-workers at the dock, but the narrative consciousness does not invite us to privilege one over the other.

The novel's inconclusiveness mirrors the inadequate maps Simón is provided with at various points; Novillan officials give directions to Simón to help him find his way around Novilla, but they are unclear sketches on scraps of paper; he loses time by setting out on tracks that turn out to be the wrong ones, and the countryside is void of recognizable signs: 'Now and again they see birds in flight, but too far away and too high in the sky for him to be sure what kind they are' (67). The reader's incessant process of reflection – the testing and rejection of ideas – echoes the rhythm of Simón's following of obscure traces in the landscape of the novel, not least the arrival at an unforeseen dead end:

> They press on. But either he has misread the map or the map itself is at fault, for after rising sharply and then plunging as steeply, the track terminates without warning at a brick wall and a rusty gate overgrown with ivy. Beside the gate is a weather-beaten painted sign. He pushes aside the ivy. '*La Residencia*', he reads.
> 'What is a *residencia*?' asks the boy.
> 'A *residencia* is a house, a grand one. But this particular *residencia* may be nothing but a ruin.' (68)

Crucially, Simón is figured, here and elsewhere in the novel, as '[pressing] on', rather than as waiting for an epiphany as earlier Coetzee protagonists often seem to do. But how are we to understand the '[misreading]' of maps, tracks terminating 'without warning', encounters with something that may actually be something else than what it appeared to be? How are we to understand, as Jennifer Rutherford puts it so well, 'the way *The Childhood of Jesus* glimmers and flashes with ideas, as if the entire lexicon of Western philosophy lies under the surface' (2017, 59)? Indeed, how are we to understand the novel's cultivation of an unsettled reader? Even for a Coetzee novel, the reception of *The Childhood of Jesus* has been remarkably inconclusive.

I propose that this 'pressing on', and the appearance of new opportunities for thought at each turn, staged in *The Childhood of Jesus* and also reflected in my own experience of reading the novel, can productively be described as a poetics of *study*, a notion I derive from Giorgio Agamben's (very brief) reflection on study in his *Idea of Prose* (1995). As I show below, Agamben's thought on study – bringing together his foundational thinking on *infancy* and *potentiality* – offers a highly fruitful yet surprisingly unexplored point of entry to both ethical and aesthetic aspects of Coetzee's work, and, not least, to our reading of the Bartleby-like child David.

The incessant shuttling of study

The understanding of study that underlies my discussion draws on Tyson E. Lewis's rich extrapolation of Giorgio Agamben's work on potentiality in his *On Study: Giorgio Agamben and Educational Potentiality* (2013), in which Lewis sets what he refers to as 'an educationally profane life without end' against the standardizing imperatives of the learning society in which 'potentiality [is reduced to] a "not yet" that actualizes itself in a "must be"' (2013, 8, 15).[2] Relatedly, we might take note of Coetzee's concerns with the increasing instrumentality of higher education: 'All over the world … universities have been coming under pressure to turn themselves into training schools equipping young people with the skills required by a modern economy' (2014, xi). Reading Agamben on potentiality, Lewis proposes a philosophy of education predicated not on fulfilling one's 'true potentiality' according to prevailing educational logic, but rather on embracing the ontological indeterminacy of the human, where freedom, and, indeed, redemption, lie precisely in the unfulfilled of each moment; the moment of 'I can, I cannot' in which 'the contingency of a life to be *rather than* what it is' may be recognized (Lewis 2013, 11; emphasis in original). Acknowledging that Agamben himself makes only a 'passing gesture' towards education in his writing (11), Lewis argues that Agamben's 'emphasis on the connections between study, im-potentiality, messianic time … and freedom' invites us to 'think through the ontological, temporal, spatial, aesthetic, and political dimensions of study' (2013, 15).[3] As I will show, the connections between study, impotentiality, and messianic time, together with Agamben's related concept of infancy – in fact, Agamben's thinking on (im)potentiality might be understood as a broader and deeper

---

2 A second book on Agamben and education was published in November 2018: Igor Jasinski's *Giorgio Agamben: Education without Ends* (Springer).
3 Lewis cleverly suggests that education might be thought of as the '*unthought* potentiality' of Agamben's own thinking (2013, 11, emphasis in original).

account of the ideas originally articulated within his concept of infancy – help make visible the poetics of *The Childhood of Jesus*. Here is Agamben on study:

> Study, in effect, is per se interminable. Those who are acquainted with long hours spent roaming among books, when every fragment, every codex, every initial encountered seems to open a new path, immediately left aside at the next encounter, or who have experienced the labyrinthine allusiveness of that 'law of good neighbours' whereby Warburg arranged his library, know that not only can study have no rightful end, but [sic] does not even desire one.
>
> ... The scholar ... is always 'stupid'. But if on the one hand he is astonished and absorbed, if study is thus essentially a suffering and an undergoing, the messianic legacy it contains drives him, on the other hand, incessantly toward closure. This ... shuttling between bewilderment and lucidity, discovery and loss, between agent and patient, is the rhythm of study. (1995, 64)

There are several points to be made here (aside from noting the image of the scholar as 'stupid', an image that may well spark recognition in bewildered readers of *The Childhood of Jesus*). The idea of study as a process of roaming along ever new paths, desiring 'no rightful end', resonates with the multiplicity of ideas evoked by the novel as well as its inconclusive structure; its final pages featuring the main characters setting off on a journey with no destination: 'let us keep going and see what comes up' (*CJ* 261). Moreover, and as discussed above, this is a novel that repeatedly sends not only its protagonists but also its *reader* off on unresolved quests in different directions, following the 'labyrinthine allusiveness' of obsolete signs, incomplete maps, and tentative philosophical ideas. It is conspicuous how *The Childhood of Jesus* rather than striving for unity embraces its own disarray, and the reader, just like Simón, must soon abandon any desire for wholeness. Simón shuttles restlessly 'between bewilderment and lucidity' as he approaches both Novilla and the more abstract realm of educational philosophy, following signs and gestures that could be interpreted in different ways, going back and forth, often uncertain in his response to what he encounters. A similar oscillation is experienced by the reader, who, in the absence of any reference to recognizable particulars in the irreality of Novilla, has no more knowledge of the novel's world than its protagonist; there is no dramatic irony to rely on for meaning. Significantly, the rhythm thus achieved is markedly more restless, active, and inquisitive than the mood of *waiting* that characterizes many of Coetzee's earlier novels.

Grasping the potentialities of the present

A helpful way of understanding the essential difference between an ethics of reading based on Derrida's thinking on unconditional hospitality and one based on Agamben's concept of study is to briefly explore the two thinkers' respective conceptions of the messianic. In *Specters of Marx*, Derrida explains 'undetermined mesianic [sic] hope' as the 'eschatological relation to the to-come of an event … of an alterity that cannot be anticipated'; this mode of anticipation clearly ties the messianic to the future (2006, 81). Agamben's understanding of messianic time, on the other hand, is focused not on the 'to-come' but on the present. It can be traced back to Walter Benjamin's idea of weak messianic power as postulated in his 'Theses on the Philosophy of History': Benjamin critiques 'homogenous empty time', which he associates with 'the historical progress of mankind', privileging instead 'time filled by the presence of the now [*Jetztzeit*]'; stating, significantly, that in each instant, each generation is endowed with the power to redeem past generations, by recognizing images of the past as concerns of the present as the 'true picture of the past flits by' (1999, 253, 247). As Leland de la Durantaye explains,

> To many, 'messianic time' suggests indeterminate waiting for the Messiah to come, redeem mankind, and complete human history. For Agamben, however, 'messianic time' means, as it did for Benjamin, the very opposite. This messianic time is not one of apocalypse, but of immediacy … For Agamben, Benjamin's messianism, like his own, is an attempt *to grasp the potentialities of our present situation*. (2009, 376; emphasis added)

In this philosophical junction, *The Childhood of Jesus* tends towards Agamben's '[grasping] the potentialities of our present situation', rather than towards Derrida's 'to-come'; this, as I have argued above, is the foundation of the novel's poetics of study, and of the ethics of reading through which it might be approached – or 'studied', as it were.

Interestingly, these respective conceptions of the messianic surface in an exchange between Simón and his co-worker Eugenio, the latter apparently espousing what Benjamin discounted as 'empty homogenous time', when he says that 'history has no manifestations in the present. History is merely a pattern we see in what has passed. It has no power to reach into the present' (*CJ* 116). However, Simón's vision is radically different: 'I am not trying to save you. There is nothing special about me … But I have not let go of the idea of history, the idea of change without beginning or end. Ideas cannot be washed out of us, not even by time. Ideas are everywhere' (114–15). Remarkably, in saying that 'ideas are everywhere', Simón seems to propose a view of time and history strikingly reminiscent of Agamben's (and Benjamin's) idea of messianic time as something that can be redeemed in each moment. Indeed, perhaps it is in this idea of the messianic that we might locate an important answer to Robert B. Pippin's frustrated question: '*Why* are so many of the events and dialogue we read about in the novel always already a reflection of or an echo of or an allusion to some literary or philosophical text?' (2017, 28; emphasis in original).⁴

Simón, as he himself makes clear, does not set out to be a saviour. Significantly, he is not a prophet of something to come either; his idea of history is one of 'change without beginning or end'. In fact, rather than a saviour or a prophet, Simón comes across as the 'apostle of uncertainty', which, according to Lewis, becomes the role of the teacher when education is viewed as a quest without a determined road: 'In Agamben's description of the messianic, the apostle – as opposed to the prophet – is *uncertain*, constantly searching for a language to express his or her message' (Lewis 2013, 103; emphasis added). Helpfully, Lewis draws a direct line between Agamben's conception of messianic time and study, when he suggests that the messianic can be found in 'the temporality of perpetual study where the student holds judgment in suspension in order to touch the im-potentiality of thought itself' (107). In the poetics of study evinced in *The Childhood of Jesus*, the figure of the uncertain apostle is apt also

---

4   Pippin offers his own answer to his question, suggesting that the novel's conspicuous intertextuality points *not* towards the 'postmodern' inescapability of the play of language (the idea that there is nothing *hors texte*) but towards 'just the opposite': 'It is *in* the interanimated world of thought and letters that whatever reality worth knowing is always to be found' (30). Although Pippin's concerns are different than mine and he does not explicitly engage with these notions, it seems to me that he, too, finds in *The Childhood of Jesus* the elevation of the potentialities latent in the present moment.

when considering the reader making sense of the work, perpetually engaging in different possibilities for reflection.

In *The Childhood of Jesus*, the *presence* of the child is the key to the mobilization of this privileging of the present over the future that is the 'temporality of perpetual study'. For Simón's 'urge to act' (recalling Agamben's words on study quoted earlier) is set off by the presence of the child, but brought to a standstill – a state of *waiting* – when the child is removed from his presence. In a sequence during which the child is kept away from Simón by Inés, he is absorbed by his loss of vocation and falls into passivity: 'he had one great task, and that task is discharged … There is nothing left to build his life around' (*CJ* 90). Instead of pursuing different ideas, he '[drifts] about, killing time' (91). The link between the child and grasping the potentialities of the present is addressed explicitly in the novel by Simón's friend Elena, who says: 'Instead of waiting to be transfigured, why not try to be like a child again?' (143). Being like a child, the implication goes, is living in the present rather than awaiting what is to come (or desiring a vocation, a 'great task'). We are reminded, of course, of the Gospel's teaching that only by becoming like a child can one enter the kingdom of heaven (Mt. 18.3). In Chapter 5, I will return specifically to how the redemptive aspect of being like a child is brought forth in *The Schooldays of Jesus*.

Impotentiality and the curious state of infancy

In Agamben's work, these ideas of indeterminacy, openness, and immediacy cluster around the notion of *infancy*, which helps us locate the interrelatedness between the child and the state of 'study' as I have described it so far. In the short essay 'The Idea of Infancy' in *Idea of Prose*, Agamben imagines a 'neotenic infant', who, in the fashion of the peculiar axolotl salamander who prolongs its larval state throughout its lifespan, retains its malleability and the potential 'not to' develop as it grows into adulthood:[5]

---

5 This strange creature is featured in Julio Cortázar's short story 'Axolotl'.

The neotenic infant ... would find himself in the condition of being able to pay attention precisely to what has not been written, to somatic possibilities that are arbitrary and uncodified; in his infantile totipotency, he would be ecstatically overwhelmed, cast out of himself, not like other living beings into a specific adventure or environment, but for the first time into a *world*. He would truly be listening to being. His voice still free from any genetic prescription, and having absolutely nothing to say or express, sole animal of his kind, he could, like Adam, *name* things in his language. In naming, man is tied to infancy, he is for ever linked to an openness that transcends every specific destiny and every genetic calling. (1995, 96–7; emphasis in original)

To Agamben, then, infancy signifies a condition – not restricted to a certain developmental stage in the individual's life – of infinite and sustained openness and curiosity in which language is available but specific discourse not yet undertaken; an openness not directed towards an unknown other to come (à la Attridge), but simply as an indeterminate state. It is clear that Agamben conceives of infancy as a desirable state of strength ('infantile totipotency' – the obstinate child David springs to mind!) and freedom (a 'voice ... free from ... prescription'); importantly, this is a state available to the adult as well. In 'pay[ing] attention precisely to what has not been written', the individual can access the arbitrariness of the world; its possibility of being otherwise than it is. Importantly, the indeterminacy inherent in infancy, according to Agamben, is what distinguishes humans from other living beings, in that the latter, so to speak, are born into a specific and predetermined role, '*they can only do this or that*' (Agamben 1999b, 182; emphasis in original). As Elizabeth Costello puts it in 'Poets and Animals', 'when we see the salmon fighting for its life, we say, it is just programmed to fight'; whereas, on the other hand, 'man is different. Man understands the dance as the other dancers do not' (*EC* 99).[6] In other words, the human, unlike non-human animals, is not compelled to follow a certain preprogrammed genetic code, but, 'for ever linked to an openness that

---

6 A beautiful image of human infancy is found also in the New Testament: 'The foxes have holes, the birds of the air have nests. But the son of man hath not where to lay his head' (Mt. 8.20). Pippin notes two instances (pp. 187 and 231) in *The Childhood of Jesus* in which Simón alludes to the idea of having no place 'to lay your head'. Pippin reads this as a reminder of the fact that humans are 'ontological gypsies, restlessly wandering through various historical epochs ... yearning always for more than they have, with no final resting place', and suggests that Novilla appears to be a 'warning' about the possibility of a state of indifference that might arise, should such human yearning and restlessness cease (2017, 16–17).

transcends every specific destiny', can choose to actualize or not-actualize any given potential (Agamben 1995, 97).

In his essay on infancy, Agamben writes that 'somewhere inside of us, the careless neotenic child continues his royal game', proposing that it is the play of this inner child that 'keeps ajar for us that never setting openness' (1995, 98). Importantly, it is in this eternal latent potential inherent in infancy that Agamben locates the messianic. What Agamben suggests here – and what we see staged in *The Childhood of Jesus* through the child David's instants of 'infantile totipotency' and in his resistance to learning by the book – is a perception of the messianic as the possibility of experiencing the world *otherwise than* how it has hitherto been described or experienced. Here, the intersection between study and infancy becomes clear; the 'never setting openness' that the child 'inside of us' gives access to is also the hallmark of a 'study that has no rightful end' (as Agamben has it in his essay on study). In other words, through perpetual study, the scholar (or the reader of *The Childhood of Jesus*) inhabits a state of infancy.

It is striking, especially in educational moments in the novel, how *The Childhood of Jesus* embraces the idea of *impotentiality* (which is fundamentally linked to infancy in Agamben's thought).[7] Let us dwell for a moment on this concept and on how it relates to education. When conceptualizing impotentiality, Agamben makes use of Aristotle's distinction between generic and existing potentiality. To Aristotle, *generic* potentiality refers to, for example, the child's potential to learn something in order to become something other – for example, learning to swim. *Existing* potentiality, on the other hand, belongs to someone who already has a certain knowledge or ability, and who on the basis of this 'having' can choose whether or not to actualize this potential. A poet, for example, can choose to write or not write (or, as *The Childhood of Jesus* shows, a child who is able to read can read or not read): 'It is a potentiality that is not simply the potential to do this or that thing but potential to not-do, potential not to pass into actuality' (Agamben 1999b, 179–80). Educational discourse traditionally focuses on the actualization of a generic potentiality; in other words the possibility, inevitability – or duty, even – for the child to learn something in order to become this or that. Wary of predetermined ends,

---

7 For a useful elucidation of the interrelatedness of Agamben's concepts of infancy, potentiality, and the messianic, see Vloeberghs (2007).

Agamben instead picks up the idea of existing or negative potentiality, always containing within itself the capability of impotentiality. For Agamben, it is within the '*abyss of human impotentiality*' that freedom can be found: 'To be free is not simply to have the power to do this or that thing, nor is it simply to have the power to refuse to do this or that thing. To be free is ... *to be capable of one's own impotentiality*' (1999b, 182–3; emphasis in original).

In presenting Novilla as a learning society of sorts, *The Childhood of Jesus* caricatures the idea of constant self-improvement with a certain prototype in view. Crowds of Novillans congregate at edifying evening classes with titles such as 'Life Drawing' and 'Philosophy and Everyday Life'. As Simón notes: 'No wonder the city is like a morgue after dark! Everyone is here at the Institute, improving themself. Everyone is busy becoming a better citizen, a better person. Everyone save he' (121). Simón is not interested in learning about 'chairs and their chairness' and does not believe in learning about the human body by drawing models at the Institute, but the notion of aspiring towards certain prototypes permeates other aspects of Novilla too (122). Indeed, initially Simón himself is intent precisely on teaching David to do 'this or that thing', to actualize his potential. Football, linked in the novel to maturity, progress, and order, is a useful motif for thinking about the necessity of actualizing potential. 'He has to start sometime', Simón's co-worker Alonso remarks when inviting David to come along to a football match (which he does, reluctantly): and when the children later join a football game in the park, 'though they are really too young', they are figured as 'dutifully ... [surging] back and forth with the other players', the game clearly a chore, the very opposite of freedom (23, 58). This contrasts with the image of the children '[racing] ahead', 'glowing with health', 'flushed, sweaty, bursting with life' when they are free and unconstrained (54, 55, 65). Simón similarly asserts the necessity of actualizing potential when trying to convince David to practise chess: 'If one is blessed with a talent, one has a duty not to hide it', he tells the resisting boy (43). At this moment, early in the novel, it would seem that the child's choice to preserve his potentiality *not* to play chess goes against not only the spirit of Novilla, but also Simón's own beliefs, for at the outset he very much approaches the child as a 'not yet' to be fulfilled.

An interesting example of how the novel sets up the link between the child and impotentiality is David's collection of disused objects: 'pebbles, pine cones, withered flowers, bones, shells, bits of crockery and old metal' (167). Simón dismisses such objects as 'rubbish' and urges the child to 'throw out that mess', but the child refuses, insisting that the objects are his 'museum' (167). In *State of Exception*, Agamben writes about rendering the law inoperative as a path towards a new form of being in relation to power: 'One day humanity will play with law *just as children play with disused objects*, not in order to restore them to their canonical use but *to free them* from it for good … This liberation is the task of study, or play' (2005a, 64; emphasis added). This chapter is not about Agamben's political thought; however, the deactivation of the law is a political analogy in Agamben's thinking to the redemptive linguistic condition of infancy, which is, as I have outlined, the experience of the impotentiality (or 'inoperative' potentiality) of language. This connection makes visible how David's collection of 'deactivated' objects is, in fact, an embrace of impotentiality.

In a series of defining episodes, Simón attempts to educate his young charge, who proves singularly unwilling to accept basic laws of letters and numbers. 'Naming numbers isn't the same as being clever with numbers', Simón points out to the know-it-all child who claims 'I can name them all' (149–50). But David stubbornly defends his own outlook where the stars are numbers, where numbers are places that you can visit, and where people risk falling in the gaps between numbers or between the pages of a book.[8] It is difficult not to read David's frame of mind, in these moments, as instances of infancy; instances of actively embracing a state of radical openness in the figurative interval between being exposed to language and employing it in speech.

Significantly, these moments of freedom speak to Simón too. Overwhelmed time and time again by David's doggedness, Simón is cast between wanting to lead his student towards learning in the fashion of an ancient Greek pedagogue, and simply stopping before the child in moments of awe:

> Why is it that this child, so clever, so ready to make his way in the world, refuses to understand?
>
> …

---

8 Vincent Pecora reads David's fear of 'falling through the cracks' of language as a reminder of 'both the ubiquity and the arbitrariness of detention', and associates this arbitrariness with Agamben's notion of 'bare life' (2015, 121–2).

> For the first time it occurs to him that this may be not just a clever child … but something else, something for which at this moment he lacks the word. He reaches out and gives the boy a light shake. 'That's enough', he says. 'That's enough counting.'
>
> The boy gives a start. His eyes open, his face loses its rapt, distant look, and contorts. 'Don't touch me!' he screams in a strange high-pitched voice. 'You are making me forget! Why do you make me forget? I hate you!' (*CJ* 150–1)

Two things stand out in this passage. The first is Simón's incomprehension at David's '[refusal] to understand'. Simón repeatedly asks himself why the child resists instruction. 'For real reading', Simón tells the boy, 'you have to submit to what is written on the page … You have to stop being a baby' (165). But David wants to read his own way, and in his fully comprehending yet not complying, he appears as opaque to Simón as Herman Melville's protagonist in 'Bartleby, the Scrivener' does to his employer. (In terms of his resemblance to Bartleby, David has an important precursor in Michael K, who is equally ungraspable and immune to society's expectations.)[9] If Simón is merely bemused here, he will, just like Bartleby's employer, gradually become increasingly frustrated, as will, eventually, the educational authorities and David's school teacher, Señor León. As the latter puts it:

> The boy David is not stupid. He is not handicapped. On the contrary, he is both gifted and intelligent. But he will not accept direction and he will not learn. I devoted many hours to him … trying to coax into him the elements of reading, writing, and arithmetic. He made no progress. He grasped nothing. Or rather, he pretended to grasp nothing. I say *pretended* because in fact he could already read and write by the time he came to school. (*CJ* 229; emphasis in original)

What Señor León and other representatives of the learning society find so difficult to comprehend, is the idea of the freedom of impotentiality – of understanding our 'potential to not-do' (Agamben 1999b, 180).

---

9 Several critics have noted Michael K's affinities with Melville's Bartleby; see Mills (2006), Chesney (2007), Monticelli (2016), and Wilm (2016). Wilm notes that Coetzee in his composition diary when writing *Life and Times of Michael K* in 1982 refers explicitly to Bartleby: 'Michaels is like that man in New York who said, "I prefer not to"' (2016, 162 n. 22).

Embracing uncertainty

The second point worth noting in the above passage is the 'something else' that Simón thinks that he can detect in the child, which seems to strike a vague chord of recognition – it is 'something for which *at this moment* he lacks the word' (151; emphasis added). In the child's dramatic resistance to being made to forget, we are reminded that Simón, too, has 'the memory of having a memory' (98). This reminder of an infantile state of linguistic openness is repeated in a later exchange between David and Simón:

> He looks into the boy's eyes. For the briefest of moments he sees something there. He has no name for it. *It is like* – that is what occurs to him in the moment. Like a fish that wriggles loose as you try to grasp it. But not like a fish – no, like *like a fish*. Or like *like like a fish*. On and on. Then the moment is over, and he is simply standing in silence, staring. (186–7; emphasis in original)

This moment, in which the idea of 'something … like *like like a fish*' – strangely catalysed by Simón seeing David seeing – evokes a series of slightly different perspectives, recalls, again, the earlier discussion of infancy as an ever-present state of openness and indeterminacy. We understand that, also in Simón, the adult, 'the careless neotenic child continues his royal game' (Agamben 1995, 98). Importantly, this moment also mirrors the constant emergence to the *reader* of different intertextual and philosophical allusions in the novel.

As Simón continues in his endeavour to educate the boy, it becomes increasingly evident that this process is not about the child actualizing his potential; rather, it is about the adult becoming aware of his own impotentiality, or, in other words, of the world's potential to be otherwise than it is (and, analogously, of the novel's potential to be read in different ways). Perhaps we might locate here a way of understanding Coetzee's words at the Witwatersrand graduation ceremony that it is 'good for [the] soul, to be with small children', as the embracing of the state of openness and experimentation associated with infancy.

Other teaching episodes, too, show Simón supporting the openness of the child: When Simón undertakes to teach the boy to read, it is with the help of a library copy of *An Illustrated Children's Don Quixote*. Incidentally, this depicted copy of *Don Quixote* fittingly features its protagonists facing a winding road as its first illustration, suggestive of the path of study ahead of its readers (and of the reader of *The Childhood of Jesus* too, as it were). Unsurprisingly, David is greatly taken with the hero of the story, with whom he shares his belief in alternative versions of the real. Although Simón initially tries to dissuade the boy from believing in giants rather than windmills, he gradually adopts a less determined stance, leaving the possibilities of David's thinking open. When David asks whether Benengeli (the fictional Moorish chronicler of the adventures of Don Quixote whom Simón mistakenly believes to be the book's author) lives in the library, Simón doesn't immediately reject the idea: 'I don't think so. It is not impossible, but I would say it is unlikely' (154). In fact, by in this way featuring *Don Quixote*, often seen as the first modern novel, as the text to initiate study with 'no rightful end', *The Childhood of Jesus* seems to be commenting on its own operation as a novel and its participation in a tradition, inviting its readers to engage in study.

When Simón eventually removes the boy from the reach of the – to his mind oppressive – educational authorities, he emerges as, to borrow Lewis's phrase, an 'apostle of uncertainty'. He complains to his co-worker Eugenio about how the school system will not accept 'children who won't obey the rules for addition and subtraction laid down by their class teacher. The man-made rules. Two plus two equalling four and so forth', and insists, instead, on the possibility of an infantile arbitrariness in which 'two and two could just as well equal three or five or ninety-nine if we so decided' (248). In the ensuing discussion, Simón, in the manner of a scholar, seems to be testing alternative ways of thinking, embracing, it would appear, the openness to ontological indeterminacy that he previously tried to counteract in the child.

If Agamben's notion of study enables us to see how *The Childhood of Jesus* points towards infancy and impotentiality as messianic openings in the present, it also helps us understand the quest-like movements in the novel, with Simón constantly pursuing new avenues of thought. 'The Idea of Study' provides several figures of the student, although only one of them tends to be noticed by interpreters of Agamben's work:

> But the latest, most exemplary embodiment of study in our culture is not the great philosopher nor the sainted doctor. It is rather the student, such

as he appears in certain novels of Kafka or Walser. His prototype occurs in Melville's student who sits in a low-ceilinged room 'in all things like a tomb', his elbows on his knees and his head in his hands. And his most extreme exemplar is Bartleby, the scrivener who has ceased to write. (1995, 65)

'Melville's student' here is Clarel, the protagonist of Melville's work of the same name – the theology student who, disillusioned by his loss of belief, sets out on a quest for spiritual meaning. So while Lewis's account of Agamben's idea of study draws heavily on the idea of impotentiality as represented by Bartleby, who comes to mind in our encounter with David, the resisting child, we might also keep in mind this other figure of the scholar setting out on a quest when considering Simón and his undertaking and undergoing the rhythms of study. As I have suggested, the driving force in this novel is the movement of *looking while not knowing what you are looking for*. While, at first glance, this reminds us of the quest for the 'other' (e.g. the lost child), there is an important nuance – this is a quest with no end in view. Agamben reflects on the quest as a preamble to his discussion on infancy: Noting the impossibility of recovering experience in the 'pre-Cartesian' sense, he argues that the quest 'expresses the impossibility of uniting science and experience in a single subject' (2007, 32). Unlike scientific experiment, which is 'the construction of a sure road … to knowledge', the quest, says Agamben, 'is the recognition that the absence of a road … is the only experience possible for man' (33). The 'absence of a road', of course, is also the experience of study. And so it makes sense that, in the novel's final pages, with Simón, Inés, David, and the dog Bolívar escaping from the educational authorities in a Rosinante-like 'old rattletrap' of a car across the mountains, Simón is undeterred by the lack of a map and a clear destination. He simply says 'let us keep going and see what turns up' (261). Because, crucially, like the activity of study itself, *The Childhood of Jesus* not only has no ending, it 'does not even desire one' (Agamben 1995, 64).

Importantly, just as it is a story that desires no end, *The Childhood of Jesus* is also a story that, despite its thematic engagement with the idea of hospitality, never compels its reader to wait for an arrival. Rather, the reader is invited to inhabit a state of impotentiality, pursuing the possibilities of thought that open up in the present moment. This condition approaches, I think, the mode of reading that Jan Wilm calls 'slow reading', which 'does not ask what a text means … it does not primarily wish to get reading over with, but it wants to remain in reading' (Wilm 2016, 45); as well as what Patrick Hayes refers to as a 'creative [interpretative] "anxiety"' generated in the reader by the way in which Coetzee's prose 'brings about an alternative way of apprehending truth in literary narrative' (Hayes 2010, 72–3, 116). Being open to the possibilities of thought available in each moment is, as I have tried to show, a restlessly active state of experimentation, which is quite different from following something presupposed that due to its irreducible otherness can never quite be fathomed or represented. Indeed, this is also how we might understand the back-and-forth rhythm of the novel. Furthermore, *The Childhood of Jesus* does not call for the 'relinquishment of intellectual control' or 'helplessness in the face of what is coming' that Attridge locates in his future-directed ethics of reading; quite the opposite, in fact (Attridge 2004b, 24, 26). After all, when Simón ends up following the child, he embraces his capability of impotentiality, and in so doing remains at the steering wheel, so to speak, simultaneously undergoing *and* undertaking. What *The Childhood of Jesus* does, then, is to gesture towards infancy, towards a state of freedom *before* any particular meaning has been determined. Never surrendering its potentiality to any given actualization – and reminding us of Agamben's words that 'the end to study may never come' – *The Childhood of Jesus* thus offers itself to the reader as an invitation to perpetual study (Agamben 1995, 65).

From childish to childlike

Taking my cue from the Bartleby-like child David, I have argued that *The Childhood of Jesus* evinces a poetics characterized by the endless asking of questions, the movement back and forth between different possibilities and the stubborn withholding of the potential to commit to any given interpretation; a *childish* poetics, no less. I have suggested that this childishness, and the experimentation that it signifies, provides us with a way to understand the feeling 'of freedom, of irresponsibility' that, *along with* 'responsibility', describes Coetzee's poetics also beyond this particular novel (*DP* 246).[10]

---

10 This might be a good moment to remind the reader of my comments in the introduction (p. 11) on how I approach the terms 'childish' and 'childlike'.

Let us turn to Elizabeth Costello making her case before the bench of judges at the gate to the afterlife, where, as we recall, she includes children among 'the invisible' whose 'secretary' she is (although, as she says, she has 'yet to be summoned by a child') (*EC* 203–4). Undoubtedly, the 'special fidelities' of the writer on which Costello attempts to clarify her views are a manifestation of the Derridean/Levinasian ethics of responsibility and hospitality that we have learned to recognize in Coetzee (*EC* 224). However, there is something else at work as well: In her dormitory, Costello reflects, not without frustration, on her situation. Noting how the surroundings, 'the wall, the gate, the sentry', are 'straight out of Kafka', she wonders: 'why it is Kafka in particular who is trundled out for her?' (209). Costello develops her reflection: 'Most of the time she cannot read him without impatience. As he veers between helplessness and lust, between rage and obsequiousness, she too often finds him … simply *childish*' (209; emphasis added). Why Kafka indeed? I would like to think that it is precisely due to the circumstance that such *childish* 'veering', which I have called 'study' above, is an aspect of Costello's (and Coetzee's) poetics; that it is, in fact, the other side of the coin to her ethics of responsibility.

Let me elaborate this point. Costello has obvious problems in articulating her writerly allegiances to the jury at the gate, and, not least, to herself; imagining counterarguments in her mind, she pre-empts interruptions at several points in her statement. Unsuccessfully, she tries to explain how, as a writer, she can be 'clean of belief … capable of holding opinions and prejudices at bay' (200). At one point, one of the judges comes to her aid with a suggestive prompt: 'Negative capability … Is negative capability what you have in mind, what you claim to possess?' (200). 'Yes, if you like', answers Costello. Negative capability, of course, is Keats's term for the human ability to remain in uncertainty, and it is understandable that it might be difficult for Costello to articulate how this condition – which is, as I read it, ultimately a figure of impotentiality, of freedom from determination – might be reconciled with her readiness to be summoned by a 'call' from an unknown yet presupposed other (200).[11] Indeed, Costello's assertion that, as a writer, she 'has to suspend belief', is scorned by a woman at the gate, who claims that such 'unbelief – entertaining

---

11 For an extended discussion of the concept, see Li Ou's *Keats and Negative Capability* (2009).

all possibilities, floating between opposites – is the mark of a leisurely existence' (213). Yet, as I understand Costello, and Coetzee, *her responsibility as a writer necessarily includes this irresponsibility.*

What this chapter has argued, then, is that in Coetzee, responsibility towards the other – in writing and in reading – is paired with an equally vital irresponsibility, both made visible through the figure of the child. To emphasize the *childish* dimension of such a poetics, I have highlighted how notions of infancy and impotentiality gesture towards reading-as-study, which constitutes a significant diversion from the emphasis on hospitality and responsibility in earlier Coetzee novels and their reception. In Chapter 5, I show how *The Schooldays of Jesus* invites us to consider the state of infancy as a model for the adult, suggesting, thus, the redemptive potential in the *childlike*.

5

The redemptive nonposition of infancy

On the last page of *The Schooldays of Jesus*, Simón, undertaking the stumbling steps of his first dance lesson, experiences how the music 'begins to reveal a new structure, point by point, like a crystal growing in the air' (260). A moment later, the novel's final sentences provide not a closing but a beginning to something unknown: 'Arms extended, eyes closed, he shuffles in a slow circle. Over the horizon the first star begins to rise.' These suggestive images – a not-yet-crystallized form in motion and a rising star on the horizon – epitomize the poetics of indeterminacy and openness that the idea of the child intimates in Coetzee's writing, as I have argued throughout this book.

Importantly, in this scene – this lesson – it is Simón the *adult*, not Davíd the child, who is in focus; in fact, throughout the novel we are given reason to believe that it is Simón's 'schooldays' we should be paying attention to rather than the boy's. For although, as in *The Childhood of Jesus*, the plot partly turns around different educational options for Davíd – a series of tutors, academies, and pedagogical regimes are considered – Simón claims to have abdicated from his role as the boy's pedagogical guide: 'I no longer even pretend to advise him', he says (40). Instead, Simón's encounters with Davíd's schooling turn the former's thoughts towards his own soul. When the *Academia de la Danza*, where Davíd is eventually enrolled, is introduced as 'an academy devoted to the training of the soul through music and dance', Simón, who believes himself to be 'not on close terms with his soul', silently repeats to himself '*the training of the soul*'; the words seem significant to his own condition (194, 43; emphasis in original). Similarly, when attending a dance performance at the Academy, he experiences 'a certain radiance in himself', redirecting the focus from the children on stage to his own self (71).

Clearly, *The Schooldays of Jesus*, as indeed much of Coetzee's fiction, is preoccupied with the 'saving' of the soul: Simón's 'soul aches with longing for it knows not what'; he finds himself saying that 'the only way to be saved is to save oneself'; and he refers to himself as, in Davíd's eyes, 'beyond redemption' (194, 227, 258). Importantly, these notions of *soul*, *salvation*, and *redemption* – increasingly present throughout Coetzee's oeuvre – are, despite their spiritual connotations, not unequivocally to be understood in terms of religious belief.[1] In the interview that concludes *Doubling the Point*, Coetzee offers an understanding of 'grace' as the condition 'in which the truth can be told clearly, without blindness' (*DP* 392). While Coetzee's ongoing dialogue with Christianity is apparent in his novels, some critics insist that Coetzee's engagement with the spiritual is strictly secular; the phrase that is often highlighted is Coetzee's remark that, 'no, regrettably, no: I am not a Christian, or not yet' (*DP* 250).[2] For example, observing the frequent references to the 'soul' in Coetzee's work, as well as his characters' 'recurrent concern with "salvation"', Derek Attridge argues that Coetzee's inclination towards terminology from religious discourse is 'without any particular religious belief being implied' (2004a, 180–1). Similarly, Jarad Zimbler writes that the 'spiritual dimension' of Coetzee's work 'does not entail the existence of God or the soul', but 'has to do with the capacity of fiction … to produce the *truth content* of a particular moment' (2014, 197; emphasis added).

Other critics emphasize the affirmative dimension of Coetzee's approach to religion. Martin Woessner makes the case that while Coetzee's novels do not call for 'an end to secularism', they 'seek … to loosen its grip on our thinking; they attempt to keep open a space – the space of the imagination … the space of the possible' (2017, 145). Jack Dudley observes that 'religious questions have increasingly preoccupied Coetzee's fiction', and proposes that Coetzee 'invites us to *reconsider* religion after secularism with openness and curiosity'

---

1 For a discussion of Coetzee's 'postsecular engagement with religion', see Dudley (2017); for a discussion of how Coetzee's engagement with realism is connected to his interest in postsecular themes, see Woessner (2017); and for a discussion on 'secular grace' in Coetzee, see Wiegandt (2018). For an extended discussion of the prominence of 'soul language' in Coetzee's fiction from *Foe* to *Disgrace*, see Zimbler (2014, 152–98). See also Attridge on 'grace' and 'salvation' in Coetzee's work until *Age of Iron* (2004a, 177–81).
2 For discussions of Coetzee's long-running dialogue with and ambivalent relationship to Calvinist doctrine, respectively, see Broggi (2018) and Pecora (2015).

(2017, 111; emphasis added). Noting, for example, David Lurie's reference to and experience of the 'post-Christian condition' in *Disgrace*, Dudley argues that Coetzee, 'rather than leave his characters in final irony or depthless disorientation ... follows the failure of epiphany ... towards more *tentative possibilities for transformation* drawn from a postsecular engagement with religion' (2017, 118; emphasis added). Similarly, Kai Wiegandt presents an affirmative reading of 'the elated grace like moments' in Coetzee's novels and argues that they are 'enabling' and come close to 'religious experience proper' (2018, 70, 73). Such moments, he argues, are instances of 'creatureliness', which Wiegandt understands as 'secularised grace residing in the body's ability to share others' suffering, but also its ability to share the pleasure of being a living body in a world of living beings' (71).[3]

Plainly, whether framed in terms of the 'postsecular' or the 'postreligious', notions of soul, salvation, and redemption lead us to the point where philosophical and theological concerns intersect in Coetzee. As I will show, the idea of the child helps us think carefully about this intersection. Recall how in the introduction I referred to various ways in which the figure of the child has been understood as redemptive in cultural history; think, for example, of Biblical elevations of the child as a model of innocence and freedom from sinful calculation; Romantic ideas of the child as a figure for the possibility of attaining unity with nature or transcendence by way of imaginative capabilities; twentieth-century figurations of the child as a privileged foil to the adult world, whether as a figure of violent rebellion or of harmony and feeling; and postmodern conceptions of the child as a figure of possibility. In earlier chapters, I have mentioned how Coetzee plays with Biblical and Romantic conceptions of the redemptive potential of the child, for example, in *Slow Man* when Elizabeth Costello tells Paul Rayment that he has 'glimpsed something angelic in Drago' and that he should 'learn from [him] while [he]

---

3 Vincent Pecora refers instead to Coetzee's ambivalent relationship to Calvinism, when he makes the case that Coetzee's work (like Beckett's and Mann's), sketches a world that is 'bereft of the grace that would provide redemption for fallen, secular existence' but at the same time 'disturbed constantly ... by the always already foreclosed human desire ... to somehow play a role in determining that redemption' (2015, 166). In this constantly disturbing yet 'always already foreclosed human desire' for 'the grace that would provide redemption', we find, of course, an analogy to the tension in Coetzee's fiction that was discussed in Chapter 1 in terms of the writer's persistent desire for a never-available truth of self.

can', or in *The Childhood of Jesus* when Simón's friend Elena urges him to 'try to be like a child again' rather than 'waiting to be transfigured' (*SM* 182, *CJ* 143). I have also referred repeatedly to Coetzee's words at Wits on how it is 'good for your soul' to be with children and that children are 'never anything but their full human selves', which also seem to evoke the redemptive potential of the child. In each of these cases, however, it is difficult to assess the degree to which Coetzee is serious or ironic, and this is also true in *The Schooldays of Jesus*, where it is far from clear that the mystical rhetoric of the Academy of Dance, with its notions of the child holding the key to a transcendent realm, should be understood as a privileged idea.

Let us return to Simón. Vincent Pecora makes the point that in *The Childhood of Jesus* Simón has 'no greater understanding of what redemption would mean' than Elizabeth Costello does before the gate (2015, 118). However, as I argue in this chapter, the answer to 'what redemption would mean' to Simón *is* intimated especially in the final scene of *Schooldays*, in how it points towards a childlike state that is not transcendent; a redemptive nonposition that, in fact, makes redundant any divisions between 'postsecular' and 'postreligious'. As in Chapter 4, it is Giorgio Agamben's notion of infancy – with its associations with innocence and impotentiality – that will help me develop my argument.

The burdensome search for truth

Like Coetzee's earlier novels, *The Schooldays of Jesus* explores the idea of writing one's way towards truth, towards 'something that has not yet emerged, that lies somewhere at the end of the road' (*DP* 246). Notably, this dynamic is staged through Simón's decision to attend a writing class towards the end of the novel; he hopes that Martina, the teacher of 'Spanish Composition (Elementary)', will listen to him and 'tell him whether his speech – the speech he is trying his best to write down on the page – rings true or whether on the contrary it is one long lie from beginning to end' (181).[4] However, no salvation or comfort is to be

---

4   There are also other references to being 'called' by the other in terms that quite explicitly – and sometimes rather humorously – evoke an ethics of hospitality in the Derridean/Levinasian sense. For example, Simón responds, albeit with irritation, to the condemned Dmitri's 'summons' to come to his aid; he appeals with the words 'we are sometimes called on when we least expect it' to his

had from writing; to borrow Coetzee's remark on confession in Dostoevsky's *The Idiot*, 'no act of will seems able to compel the truth to emerge' (*DP* 287). Instead, the novel sees Simón gradually abandoning his 'strenuous efforts of the intellect' to grasp the mystery of the dancing children at the Academy, which is where Simón intuits that the '*training of the soul*' might take place (207, 43; emphasis in original). In an episode foreshadowing the final scene, Simón, hearing music through an open door, '*tries not to think*, to do nothing that might alarm the timid soul within' (194; emphasis added). As I will show, the idea of infancy helps us understand this notion of holding thought in suspense.

The Schooldays of Jesus thematically foregrounds the child as a figure holding the key to a transcendent state of being through the Academy's rhetoric of how the young child ... still bears deep impresses of a former life' and how the 'souls' of children may be 'guided ... toward that realm' through dance (67–8). Moreover, it is conspicuous how Simón's soul-searching is paralleled by his interest in *purity*, most bizarrely perhaps through his marked attention to the absence or presence of facial hair on the people he encounters. He observes how a shoe shop assistant has 'a moustache so thin it might be drawn on his lip with charcoal', and how the desk clerk at the relocation centre has 'a scraggly beard', and Davíd perceptively charges him with not '[liking]' the seedy Dmitri 'because he has a beard' (50, 57, 47). In contrast, the first detail Simón notices about the enigmatic dance teacher Ana Magdalena Arroyo at the Academy – 'something disquieting about the woman's appearance' – is that she 'has no eyebrows'; he later thinks of her as 'alabaster-pure', and similarly takes note of the clarity of the saintly school assistant Alyosha's face: 'There is no sign that he shaves' (44, 110, 106).

However, Simón's desire for purity – or 'truth' or 'salvation' or 'redemption'; these words surface repeatedly, but exactly *what* he longs for he cannot articulate – is obstructed by the divisions imposed by language on his thinking, a dynamic that we recognize from earlier novels. The fundamental split is the one between reason and passion: Simón accepts 'what people tell him' about

---

writing-class instructor Señora Martina, in a failed bid to make of her his confessor; and, to his frustration, he is told by Señor Arroyo, when trying to grasp the Academy's philosophy, that 'the answer will come when you least expect it. Or else it will not come. That too happens' (160, 182, 199).

his soul being 'dry, deficient, rational', yet harbours the intuition that 'far from lacking in passion, his soul aches with longing for it knows not what' (194). Simón's internal conflict revolves largely around the Academy's elevation of the child as a mystical figure with access to the 'dance of the universe', an idea that at once attracts and frustrates him in its resistance to rational comprehension; he struggles to reconcile 'how an intelligent person like Juan Sebastián Arroyo can talk about stars, numbers, and music in the same breath' (67, 183). A self-professed 'sane, rational person', Simón initially tries to 'make sense' of Arroyo's ideas, then sceptically calls them 'a load of mystical rubbish', only to find himself increasingly unable to dismiss their attraction as he wavers between reason and mysticism in his search for something in which to believe (207, 69, 99). Believing in *something* is crucial: 'His own opinion is that, whether or not there is a beyond, one would drown in despair were there not an idea of a beyond to cling to' (183). One scene sees Simón's inner debate dramatized on the Academy's stage, as the visiting Señor Moreno lectures on the philosopher 'Metros and his intellectual legacy' under the rubric '*Man the Measure of All Things*' (233). Moreno recounts how

> the arrival of Metros marks a turning point in human history: the moment when we collectively gave up the old way of apprehending the world, the unthinking, animal way, when we abandoned as futile the quest to know things in themselves, and began instead to see the world through its metra. (242)

In response to Moreno's image of an Enlightenment ideal laying thought over experience, Arroyo instead puts forward 'music-dance' as 'its own way of apprehending the universe, the human way but also the animal way, the way that prevailed before the coming of Metros' (243). This 'older mode of apprehension', according to Arroyo, involves 'body and mind moving together', and leads to the surfacing of 'archaic memories, memories of a prior existence' accessible specifically to the child (243–4).[5] Arroyo illustrates his point by inviting two children on stage to perform a dance, and Simón, 'though Arroyo's philosophy of dance is as obscure to him as ever' begins to 'glimpse,

---

5   The novel gestures rather overtly towards anthroposophy and eurythmy, the art form developed by Rudolf Steiner to achieve 'visible music'. See, for example, Steiner's *Eurythmy as Visible Music* (1977).

in the dimmest of ways ... what Arroyo means by dancing the numbers', only a moment later to find his body 'too stupid, too stolid' to follow the pattern of the dance (244–5). In this sequence, then, Simón is trying in vain to grasp the meaning or pattern of the dance, but neither his mind nor his body bring him closer to any supposed core.

Let me consider the implications of the presence in *The Schooldays of Jesus* of these irreconcilable ways of viewing the world. Clearly, the divisions in language between conflicting polarities – reason versus passion, 'metra' versus 'older modes of apprehension', mind versus body – are conducive to reflection for Simón, and, presumably, for Coetzee's reader.[6] Indeed, this dynamic, whereby the text exposes the reader to opposing positions without clearly endorsing one or the other, is recurrent in Coetzee's fiction and has been repeatedly remarked upon in critical commentary. For example, Jan Wilm writes that Coetzee's work 'stages neither a simplistic privileging of body over mind nor of mind over body, but ... it choreographs currents between the two and renders an opening out of the one into the other, and vice versa' (2016, 111). Similarly, Patrick Hayes notes how in *Age of Iron* Mrs Curren's universalism is set against a 'politics of difference', and argues that the novel is 'neither asserting' Mrs Curren's position, 'nor suggesting that she should be ignored' (2010, 133). Hayes traces Coetzee's presentation of this unresolved interplay between irreconcilable political positions in *Age of Iron* to the possibility of a 'nonposition' that Coetzee locates and admires in Erasmus's *The Praise of Folly*. Equally, Johan Geertsema observes the juxtaposition of different opinions across the horizontally delineated sections of the pages of *Diary of a Bad Year*, and argues, also in dialogue with Coetzee's engagement with Erasmus, that Coetzee in his inconclusive staging of irreconcilable opinions desires 'an ironic '*non*position' ... the position of folly' (2011, 73–4; emphasis in original). Yet another example is how in *The Lives of Animals* different positions on the relations between human and non-human animals are dramatized through different characters, without, at least visibly, asserting a stance that the text as a whole endorses. In 'The Novel Today', Coetzee explicitly addresses this

---

6 The conflict between Moreno and Arroyo approaches the confrontation that Patrick Hayes notes in *Slow Man* between 'a predominantly utilitarian modernity' and 'the ... demand for spiritual urgency' (2010, 223–4).

possibility of assuming a nonposition that refuses oppositions, claiming the writer's 'freedom to decline – or better, rethink' all those 'oppositions out of which history and the historical disciplines erect themselves' (3).[7] Relatedly, Coetzee's more recent piece 'On Literary Thinking' (2016) refutes what he calls the 'binary thinking' of a digital age in which 'making a sequence of YES-NO decisions is called being free to make choices' (1152). The constraint of such binary thinking is similarly articulated by Mrs Curren in *Age of Iron*:

> It is like being on trial for your life and being allowed only two words, Yes and No. Whenever you take a breath to speak out, you are warned by the judges: 'Yes or No: no speeches.' 'Yes', you say. Yet all the time you feel other words stirring inside you like life in the womb. Not like a child kicking, not yet, but like the very beginnings, like the deep-down stirring of knowledge a woman has when she is pregnant. (145)[8]

Notice how in contrast to the binary 'Yes or No' choice, Mrs Curren senses in the 'deep-down stirring of knowledge' the potentiality of other *as yet unarticulated* possibilities for thought.[9]

For Simón, however, the fundamental division between reason, on the one hand, and longing for something 'beyond', on the other, is *burdensome*, as his fraught responses – anger, curiosity, failure to grasp, dejectedness – to the Academy and its dancing children suggest. (This burden is evoked also in the postscript to *Elizabeth Costello*, figuring a fictional letter from Lady Elizabeth Chandos to Francis Bacon, in which she asks to be saved from the 'affliction' of an existence where mind and body are separated (227–30).) I propose that it is in this burden of division that we might begin to locate the answer to the question that Simón asks himself at one stage: 'Salvation from *what*?' (228; emphasis added).

The point that I am working my way towards is that in *Schooldays*, the idea of the child – much like Erasmus's fool – directs us to a state of freedom outside – or rather, *in relation to* – the arena of politics or language in which

---

7 Recall the discussion in Chapter 2 on how the early Coetzee was criticized for textual idealism as a way of avoiding taking a political stance.
8 Thank you to Aparna Tarc for drawing my attention to this passage.
9 Relatedly, Ileana Şora Dimitriu identifies a 'secular spirituality' in *The Childhood of Jesus*, and suggests that the novel's 'religious impulse lies in the negation of opposites, in a faith based not on dogma … but on a search for the inchoate, unimaginable and "invisible" alternatives to polarities' (2015, 140).

commitments to different positions takes place. My contention, as I have already suggested, is that *The Schooldays of Jesus*, like its precursor, points towards a nonposition that we can productively describe as a state of infancy. However, where in Chapter 4 I observed the implications of infancy in terms of the freedom of impotentiality in an ethics of study and reading, I now direct my focus instead to its redemptive potential. Infancy, I propose, is redemptive not in the sense of being 'truth-directed' (as in accessing a particular origin or arriving at a certain end); but in the sense of moving before all divisions between origins and ends, between the rational and the mystical, between reason and passion, between what can and cannot be said, to a state characterized rather by the pure experience of language *as such*. I will move now to an elaboration of how 'being like a child' might be understood as a relief from the burden of negotiating irreconcilable and ungraspable meanings, indeed, from the burden of meaning itself. Importantly, as I read Coetzee, the redemptive relief to be found in infancy is not to be understood as nihilistic, but simply as a state of freedom, of holding meaning in suspense.

Infancy and language as such

Recall how, on the novel's last page, Simón experiences how the 'little aria begins to reveal a new structure, point by point, like a crystal growing in the air' (260). Notice how Simón's focus here, unlike in previous episodes in which he tries to grasp the 'logic' of the music and the dance, is merely on the *taking place* of the music, and how the music and dance together form a gesture *without meaning*.[10]

As a first step in shedding light on the redemptive implications of this scene, I turn to Agamben's piece 'Notes on Gesture' in *Infancy and History*. In this short

---

10 It seems possible that the last page of *The Schooldays of Jesus* is in conversation with the episode in Hermann Broch's *The Death of Virgil* (1995) that features the dying Virgil experiencing 'the law of music, stated in the crystal, stated through music, but over and above that, expressing the music of the crystal', against the backdrop of 'stars ... circling' (207–8). (In Broch, however, the music is connected to arriving at the word beyond death, whereas in my reading of Coetzee's novel, the unfolding of the music is connected to infancy.) Jean-Luc Godard's rendering in *Soigne ta Droite* of this precise scene from Broch has been read alongside Agamben in the context of a discussion on cinema and gesture, the point being that gesture is the demonstration of mediality (Williams 2015, 27–54).

essay, Agamben considers cinema in terms of the 'freeing of the image in the gesture', likening this phenomenon to what ancient Greek legends expressed as 'statues breaking the fetters that contain them and beginning to move' (2007, 153).[11] (Curiously, in *The Schooldays of Jesus*, Dmitri, the museum attendant, describes how he sets the statues 'free' in the mornings, prompting Simón to think of the former as the 'liberator of the statues' (46–7).) Agamben's discussion of cinema is not my point here, but rather the way in which he posits gesture as a third type of action beyond Aristotle's distinction between *poeisis* (an action that has in view an end beyond itself) and *praxis* (an action that is an end in itself).[12] Gesture, glosses Deborah Levitt, is '"pure praxis" freed from any pre-existing determination (such as life or art) and freed of any *telos*, including any aesthetic one (such as art for art's sake)' (Levitt 2011, 79). Here is Agamben:

> What characterizes gesture is that in it there is neither production nor enactment, but undertaking and supporting ... If dance is gesture, this is ... because it is nothing but the physical tolerance of bodily movements and the display of their mediating nature. *Gesture is the display of mediation: the making visible of a means as such.* It makes apparent the human state of being-in-a-medium and thereby opens up the ethical dimension for human beings. (2007, 154–5; emphasis in original)

Having absorbed this configuration of dance-as-gesture as the '*making visible of a means as such*', we begin to see how Simón's tentative dance steps might be understood precisely in this way; he is neither willing himself towards a certain revelatory end, nor is he dancing for the sake of the intrinsic aesthetic value of the dance. He simply experiences – in Agamben's words, '[undertakes] and [supports]' – the unfolding of the dance as such. Importantly, in so doing, Simón illustrates the emancipatory state of being 'free from any genetic prescription ... having absolutely nothing to say or express' that Agamben calls infancy (1995, 97). Infancy, we remember, can be understood as the experience of the

---

11   Agamben is probably referring to the ancient Greek sculptor Daedalus's statues which were said to be so lifelike that they needed to be shackled in order not to escape. This legend is evoked in Plato's *Meno* dialogue, when Socrates likens Daedalus's statues to true belief (that may get away), which may be contrasted to knowledge (that stays put).
12   Agamben follows the Roman scholar Varro's delineation in *De Lingua Latina* between *facere*/making, *agere*/acting and *gerere*/gesture (in Agamben's interpretation).

impotentiality of language; that is, the capacity *not to* speak that is inherent in the human capacity for language, and that distinguishes the human from animals who 'do not enter into language [as] they are already inside it' (2007, 59). (Recall how Chapter 4 showed how the idea of impotentiality comes into sight in a slightly different way in *The Childhood of Jesus,* in which the child who can read but prefers not to suggests an ethics of reading based on the impotentiality of 'study', the valuable – but not productive – state of being not-yet-committed in a certain direction.) Put differently, infancy is the uniquely human experience of being '*in a relationship to* ... language' rather than to any specific utterance; in other words, infancy refers to the experience of language taking place (Willemse 2018, 11; emphasis added).

Intriguingly, the notion of *making visible* the taking place of language as such also provides us with a way to understand the strange deictic references 'he, Simón' – *showing* rather than saying anything in particular – that are such a singular linguistic feature of *The Schooldays of Jesus*. Agamben, taking his point of departure in Emile Benveniste's work on deixis, notes that it is through such 'shifters' that 'language refers to its own taking place' (2005b, 66).[13] Conventionally, and as William Watkin points out, linguistic devices showing '*how* language indicates' are 'almost invisible within discourse: he, she, it, that, this, now, then, thus, as and so on' (2014, 96–7; emphasis added). In *The Schooldays of Jesus*, however, the 'he, Simón' is not invisible, but *made visible*, just as in the final scene the unfolding of the dance is made visible in Simón's mind – and just as, in *The Childhood of Jesus*, Coetzee's overt foregrounding of the play with Spanish, English and German, too, draws attention to the taking place of language as such.

Being like a child: '*The revocation of every vocation*'

I have proposed that the final moment of *The Schooldays of Jesus* can be understood as redemptive insofar as it manifests the condition of infancy. In

---

13 As part of her discussion in *Countervoices* on the correlation between linguistics and ethics in Coetzee, Clarkson (2009) highlights several moments in *Doubling the Point* in which Coetzee reflects on deictics: in the discussion of Émile Benveniste in his Achterberg essay as well as in his essays on Beckett (53, 138).

order to fully make this point, a further exploration of Agamben's thought on language and infancy is required. Agamben writes, following Walter Benjamin and his ideas on the philosophy of language (laid out in important essays including 'Theses on the Philosophy of History', 'On Language as Such and the Language of Men', and 'The Task of the Translator'), that the 'original sin for which humans are driven out of Paradise is … the fall of language from being a language of insignificant and perfectly transparent names to signifying speech as the means of an external communication' (Agamben 1999b, 52). In Agamben's understanding, redemptive potential can be found in the 'expressionless word', the 'pure language in which all communication and all meaning are extinguished' (53). Accordingly, he writes that the '*messianic vocation is the revocation of every vocation*'; in other words, the task for the human in search of redemption is to regress to an infantile state beyond saying this or that (2005b, 23; emphasis in original). This state, as we recall, is the state of the 'neotenic infant':

> His voice still free from any genetic prescription, and having absolutely nothing to say or express … he could, like Adam, *name* things in his language. In naming, man is tied to infancy, he is for ever linked to an openness that transcends every specific destiny and every genetic calling. (Agamben 1995, 96–7)

Other than David/Davíd, whose obsession with 'naming' I will return to shortly, a figure in Coetzee's work who comes to mind as '[transcending] every destiny' is, of course, the never-committing Michael K; he is, in the medical officer's eyes, a 'soul blessedly untouched by doctrine' (*MK* 151).[14]

Colby Dickinson, who traces Agamben's sustained engagement with Judeo-Christian theology, observes that for Agamben it is out of the removal from our 'genetic calling' that language, politics, and religion arise (2011, 145). It is 'paradoxical', writes Dickinson, that our separation from our 'genetic calling'

> *simultaneously gives rise to a reflective capacity,* and *yet leaves us with an acute sense of alienation* from our common animal species, so acute that we attempt to atone for it through our 'second nature' – that is, our

---

14 For a reading of Michael K 'as a figure in which the caesuras that Agamben argues cross the human being … are brought to visibility', see Mills (2006).

linguistic being. We *invent vocational callings, hence, as a way to try and atone for this initial separation*, as a fleeting chance to perhaps reacquire something of what we had once lost. If we follow this logic to its end, religion would therefore appear as the supreme attempt on the part of humanity to (symbolically, linguistically) atone for this separation from our calling. (2011, 145; emphasis added)

In other words, it is the specifically human predicament of being in a relationship to language – the condition of infancy, that is – that engenders *curiosity and reflection*, on the one hand, and the *invention of vocations* such as religion – or trying to write one's way towards truth – on the other. Again we are reminded that the idea of infancy offers us a way to understand the interplay in Coetzee's poetics between, on the one hand, 'freedom … irresponsibility' and, on the other hand, the 'responsibility toward something that has not yet emerged' that is implied in the idea of 'vocational callings' (*DP* 246).

I suggested earlier that in *The Schooldays of Jesus*, Simón is burdened by the polarization between irreconcilable positions; in the confrontation between rational and passionate approaches to being – represented, for example, by the debate between Moreno and Arroyo – he seems to find neither account fully satisfactory, always retaining an uneasy remainder of doubt and curiosity. My intuition is that the final dance scene gestures towards, in Agamben's terms, the '*revocation of every vocation*' as the remedy for this predicament – which, I believe, is how we might think of the nonposition of the child, the fool, the outsider as exemplified by Michael K, or, indeed, the writer (2005b, 23). In this innocent condition, there are no divisions between reason and passion, or, for that matter, between religion and the secular (or between the postreligious and the postsecular, as it were).

But how to reach such a childlike state? After all, as Simón tells Davíd, 'no one in this world grows small' (238). It seems difficult to imagine a realistic trajectory towards an infantile condition 'beyond all forms of language, religion and law' (Dickinson 2011, 107). Interestingly, though, Dickinson finds in Agamben's gesture towards 'an infancy we can hardly fathom' an 'uncanny echo' of the enigmatic passage in the Gospel in which Jesus says that if we are to enter the Kingdom of God, we must become like little children (Mt. 18.1-4). Both Jesus and Agamben, writes Dickinson, are intimating 'a similar movement beyond the representations of this world in which we are otherwise continuously mired. They are both pointing in fact to an 'impossible' realm of existence that we are yet called to' (108).

Agamben's redemption does not require us to '*do*' anything in particular, explains Dickinson, but rather to 'stop creating the representations of ourselves and our bodies that continue to plague us and to weigh us down' (2011, 139). Leland de la Durantaye describes this redemptive condition as a matter of accepting the limits of language and no longer 'pining for an unsayable or sacred speech beyond the one we know' (2009, 136). Revelation in Agamben's thought, he explains, is never the discovery of this or that, but '*an opening of the field of possibility rather than its narrowing*', revealing simply 'that there is *no final secret thing* that we discover in this world' (143; emphasis added). Put differently, the redemptive potential in Agamben's infancy lies in no longer feeling the need to capture meaning or truth. Indeed, Agamben's own words on revelation, just like his words on infancy, point simply towards the 'very fact that language … exists':

> If the theological tradition has … always understood revelation as something that human reason cannot know on its own, this can only mean the following: *the content of revelation is not a truth that can be expressed* in the form of linguistic propositions about a being (even about a supreme being) *but is, instead, a truth that concerns language itself, the very fact that language … exists*. (1999b, 40; emphasis added)

Arthur Willemse glosses this for us: In highlighting the '*experimentum linguae*, the experience of the existence of language such', he writes, Agamben 'turns thought toward its own potential, its remaining infancy and innocence, thus circumvents discourse and its fallenness, and aspires to a state of redemption' (2018, 19). The revelatory potential, then, lies in experiencing the *existence* of language.

Infancy and ethics

In his exploration of the diverging approaches to the messianic in Derrida and Agamben, Willemse writes that

> Agamben rejects the human being as the rational animal to whom language is given, as it implies the theological presupposition of language: in the beginning was the word. Implied in Agamben's response is the theological notion of the Fall: the human being is fallen from absolute language, and has to reclaim it, learn it, as knowledge; however, the human being always retains its paradisiacal capacity for not-speaking – and in this way, Agamben commences his messianic trajectory.
>
> In stark contrast to Derrida, then, for Agamben philosophy refers back to itself, prior to this or that *vocabulary* or *vocation*. (2018, 12; emphasis in original)[15]

Willemse contrasts Agamben as 'the philosopher in touch with the *infancy* of language, with the creature capable of language' with Derrida as 'the philosopher attuned to the *particularity* of language [that] is always already being spent and circulated through distinct vocabularies' (12; emphasis added). Importantly, whereas Derrida writes *in response to* 'a call, an event, a name, a date', Agamben's *experimentum linguae*, his attempt to think the experience of language itself, is 'not in response to a prior *logos*', and thus does not imply an ethics of responsibility (Willemse 2018, 8).[16] Fundamentally, then, Agamben's notion of infancy is characterized by an 'irresponsible' openness, in contrast to a Derridean responsibility towards the trace of an always presupposed other.

It bears repeating that while infancy, here, does not intend the developmental phase of childhood, it 'repeats the infant experience of discovering a world that is yet to be named' (13). Infancy, in other words, provides us with a way of understanding how for the child David/Davíd, the *act of naming* is important – 'I can name them all', he claims apropos the numbers in *The Childhood of Jesus* (150) – whereas Simón cannot grasp why Davíd 'finds names so significant'; to Simón, in contrast, names are arbitrary and can never

---

15 Willemse argues that Agamben's main critique of Derrida is that 'the latter's thought leaves the structure of presupposition intact – in Derrida's work there is always a prior word, an older trace, to which philosophy is occasioned to respond' (2018, 94). 'Agamben's work', writes Willemse, 'is at its profound level a confrontation with the theological underpinnings of philosophy, exposing our philosophical theology … Agamben conducts the *experimentum linguae* in order to expose the particularly theological heritage of philosophy that onto-theology, hermeneutics, and deconstruction never fully conceived: the existence of language' (15).

16 Equally, as Willemse points out, Derrida's sense of responsibility to the presupposed *logos* of the other 'rules out the possibility of infancy' (8).

grasp the thing itself: 'Our so-called true names, the names we had before *Davíd* and *Simón*, are only substitutes … for the names we had before them, and so on backwards' (*SJ* 198).

As I have argued, I believe that the *Jesus* novels ultimately privilege infancy – as in the open possibility of thought – over responsibility to the other, although both dynamics are at play, as in Simón's and Davíd's respective approaches to naming. The idea of infancy, then, implies an ethics based not on hospitality to difference, but on *indifference*; not, importantly, in the sense of apathy or lack of concern but in the sense of *before differentiation*. What could this mean in Coetzee? In *The Coming Community*, Agamben writes that the point of departure for any ethics is that

> there is no essence, no historical or spiritual vocation, no biological destiny that humans must enact or realize. This is the only reason why something like an ethics can exist, because it is clear that if humans were or had to be this or that substance, this or that destiny, no ethical experience would be possible – there would be only tasks to be done. (1993, 43)

What Agamben is outlining for us here is that infancy – the absence of a particular vocation – is the starting point of an openness within which ethical choices can be made.[17] It seems to me that this way of understanding infancy approaches, in Coetzee, the 'position which is not a position' that his texts so often incline towards – the ironic remainder, and confusion, that has ethical force (*GO* 99).

Writing and redemption

What, then, are the implications for writing, if the redemptive potential in infancy is, as I have argued, to be found in moments of holding thought open, rather than in the 'writing your way towards something'? In his essay on Patrick White's *The Solid Mandala*, Coetzee highlights 'one of the great scenes of the book' in which the character Arthur 'dances the golden mandala … for

---

17 Patrick Hayes similarly argues that Coetzee's approach to politics is 'anti-foundational', suggesting also that 'Coetzee's fiction is most amenable to what Jean-Luc Nancy speaks of as a democracy without foundations' (2010, 28–9).

as he has learned ... the mysteries can more easily be explored through the physical, intuitive, non-rational medium of dance than through the rational medium of language':

> The dance scene, which shows White at the peak of his powers as an artist in prose, establishes Arthur as the true spiritual hero of the book but also *exposes a tragic paradox for White himself, namely that the art he practices will not take him to the heart of the mystery of life*. It is not the writer but the dancer, the holy fool whose dance can only be danced, cannot be done in words except from the outside, who leads us and shows us the way. (*LE* 241; emphasis added)

In his reading of this scene, which clearly resonates with the final page of *The Schooldays of Jesus*, Coetzee finds a 'tragic paradox' for White in the latter's elevation of dance, as opposed to writing, as the key 'to the heart of the mystery of life'. The question arises: Are we similarly to read Simón's dance scene as Coetzee's tragic admission to the failure of writing?

As I have argued in this chapter, I believe that the opposite is true. In his introduction to *Strong Opinions* (2013), Chris Danta cites Agamben's remark that 'redemption is nothing other than a potentiality to create that remains pending, that turns on itself and "saves" itself'.[18] Danta suggests that in Coetzee's later fiction, 'we see him paying greater attention to this idea of a potentiality to create that remains pending', and locates in Coetzee's 'postmodern reflexivity ... a desire for redemption, a desire to secrete in the book a moment of ineliminable or unrealizable – and therefore redemptive – potential' (2013, xix). As I have shown, it is precisely such a redemptive 'potential to create that remains pending' that is highlighted in Simón's dance scene. Indeed, the foregrounding of the *taking place* of language throughout *The Schooldays of Jesus* demonstrates how writing can manifest the redemptive nonposition of the child – a state of infantile curiosity, reflection and openness in which the *vocation* of writing has been abandoned, at least for a moment.

---

18   Danta quotes Agamben's essay 'Creation and Salvation' in *Nudities* (2011).

Coda

This study began with *Boyhood's* child figure John creating fictions in his attempt to reach a truer understanding of himself and the world; it ends with the *Jesus* novels' adult figure Simón abandoning the idea of writing as a path towards truth, trying instead to be like a child. With these two characters we are brought full circle, beginning and ending with the idea of the child and its relation to writing. Importantly, while these two characters evince the persistent *centrality* of the idea of the child in Coetzee's writing, they also make visible a certain *shift in emphasis* with regard to the child in his poetics; a shift from an impossible responsibility towards the self, the other, and the world, to the affirmation of the ethical and aesthetic possibilities in irresponsibility. This shifting emphasis in Coetzee's work is reflected in Simón's trajectory from trying to be a responsible adult, in relation first to the child and the world that have both befallen him and later to his own soul – to his eventual embrace of what I have called the childlike nonposition of infancy.

This gradual privileging of irresponsibility over responsibility is a change in balance rather than a radical discontinuity. Intimations of a poetics of irresponsibility are present in different moments throughout Coetzee's oeuvre. For example, I have mentioned Michael K as an early incarnation of a childish figure of impotentiality; the idea of the nonposition is evoked in the 'Erasmus: Madness and Rivalry' essay; and Elizabeth Costello's approval of the idea of 'negative capability' as a figure for her writerly calling, too, points quite explicitly in the direction of irresponsibility. I have also argued that responsibility and irresponsibility can be understood as two sides of the same coin; indeed, the child makes visible how they coexist as figures of imaginative potential in Coetzee. The often-described resistance to closure in Coetzee can be understood both in terms of the failure to reach the child and in terms of the endless opening to thought that is also always present through the child.

These continuities notwithstanding, certain important differences within the oeuvre deserve to be highlighted. In the novels discussed in my first three chapters, the child figure is evoked in explicitly *worldly* (albeit not always historically recognizable) contexts: the quest towards an authentic self in the child's approach to the world (*Boyhood*); encounters with the historically specific (post)colonial other child (*Dusklands, In the Heart of the Country, Disgrace, Age of Iron*); and the ensuring of continued transmissibility between generations and the emergence of the new (*Waiting for the Barbarians, Age of Iron, Disgrace, The Master of Petersburg, Slow Man*). In each of these cases, child figures surface as part of a world. The child reminds us that authentically approaching the self takes place in dialogue with others; that alongside a responsibility to radical alterity, there is also the responsibility towards the not-so-other within history; and that the anticipation of the future always takes place in relation to a world that is already there. Moreover, in each of these cases, the child evokes the reader's desire to actualize potential meaning, although that actualization is deterred by the playful indeterminacies – also evoked by the child – inherent in the relation to the self, the other, and history. In the *Jesus* novels, the presence of a world is less prominent, and the child points rather towards a deliberate withdrawal from the actualization of meaning, directing us instead towards moments of openness. Signalling the redemptive possibilities inherent in such moments, the child in these later novels presents an invitation towards a fundamentally experimental mode of reading, writing and being in the world. Importantly, the freedom of such a nonposition (deemed irresponsible by one strand in early Coetzee criticism) is responsible precisely in how it holds open thought's possibilities.

*

In this study, Agamben's idea of infancy has emerged as a singularly productive way of approaching the writing and reading of Coetzee's work. With its distinctive quality of holding thought in suspense, infancy forms a nexus in which the ethically productive uncertainty of irony, the creative tension in the interregnum, and the resistance implicit in impotentiality – all so fundamental in Coetzee – converge. But Agamben's infancy has implications also beyond the linguistic, and, in Coetzee, beyond his poetics.

In *The Disappearance of Literature: Blanchot, Agamben, and the Writers of the No*, Aaron Hillyer traces a constellation of writers – Anne Carson, Enrique Vila-Matas, and César Aira – who 'imagine a new human innocence or infancy in which … "the creature from limbo lifts up its fragile arm against the historical tragedy of a language in a hopeless gesture, in a silent confrontation whose outcome cannot be easily understood"' (2013, 97).[1] What these writers share, Hillyer suggests, is a new form of writing that 'continually points beyond itself, not to an ineffable transcendence, but toward a new form of being outside of being, a new way of life that breaks through the constraints of identity that are upheld by linguistic signification' (98). To Hillyer, this tendency should be understood not merely in terms of 'the disappearance of literature' and 'the erasure of the subject', but chiefly as the potential for opening 'new avenues of interrogation ... for community, philosophy, art, and language' (98). To my mind, countless such 'new avenues of interrogation' appear in the intersection between Agamben and Coetzee. I referred in Chapter 5 to how Agamben, in *The Coming Community*, sketches the embryo of a politics arising out of infancy, an ethics that does not find its origin or destiny in difference, but that finds its basis, instead, in the very absence of any 'essence ... historical or spiritual vocation' (1993, 43). In the light of such an – admittedly vague – idea of community, it seems worthwhile to explore, again, Coetzee's remark, 'I am not a herald of community, or anything else' (*DP* 341). Moreover, as an extension of this thought, Agamben's infancy, reincarnated in *The Open* (2002) as a zone of indistinction between humans and non-human animals, invites further thinking about the responsibility of indifference also beyond the human world that has been my focus here.[2]

*

Above all, the child in Coetzee makes visible the tensions at work in the writing and reading of fiction – between responsibility and irresponsibility, between impossibility and possibility. This poses the question of the affordances of literature as a privileged realm for the working through of complex thinking. Crucially, Coetzee evokes the child to remind us that the only possible notion of innocence – the never-fully-but-always-partly-knowing – applies also to the adult: 'I try not to lose sight of the reality that we are children, unreconstructed' (*DP* 249). It is this mode of epistemological uncertainty that prompts the creation of new stories of selves and of the world; this is where the ethical force of irony is at play; where the interregnum between the old and the new gives intimations of freedom; and where impotentiality – the

---

1 Hillyer is quoting Agamben's *The End of the Poem* (1999a, 132).
2 See Frances Restuccia (2017) on how Coetzee's *Lives of Animals* 'lends poetic embodiment to Agamben's conception of the messianic' (414).

capacity not to commit – is not dismissed but embraced. Possibly, it is also in this state of incomplete innocence that something approaching grace might appear, a possibility Coetzee gestures towards when he says that, as 'children, unreconstructed', we should 'be treated with the charity that children have due to them'; charity, he suggests, being 'the way in which grace allegorizes itself in the world' (*DP* 246). In other words, while the child highlights the predicament of never-quite-knowing, it also helps us see that openness and experimentation are conditions to be embraced.

*

This book has taken its cue from the question asked of Elizabeth Costello at the gate to the afterlife: 'What about children?' I have shown that children are everywhere in Coetzee. Indeed, the question that has presented itself to me with increasing insistence during the course of this study is not how does one *find* the child, but, rather, how does one *leave* it?

Writing this book, I have felt the impossible urge – and responsibility – to pin down, once and for all, the meaning of Coetzee's children. Even more so, however, I have experienced a sense of 'joyful' freedom in the constant emergence of new possible ways of thinking about the child in Coetzee. Paying attention to Coetzee's children has made clear to me that the sense of childish experimentation that seems to fuel Coetzee's writing also defines the ever-engaging experience of responding to his work. In fact, reading and writing about the child in Coetzee has involved, at different stages of this study, instances of each aspect of Coetzee's poetics of the child: navigating between fictions of childhood, probing my own responses to ironic representations of not-so-other children, experiencing the failure to imagine the new and landing, finally, in childlike openness and childish irresponsibility as the only possible responsible stance. The writer Ceridwen Dovey articulates precisely this attitude in a recent piece on her experience of reading Coetzee, when she suggests that 'by returning us to this childlike, childish state, maybe Coetzee is asking us to learn, as we did as infants, how to manage uncertainty, how to live with complexity: the project of a lifetime' (2018, 10).

Finally, and given the difficulties in leaving the child that points perpetually towards experimentation, it seems appropriate to end this study with a gesture towards the experience of study itself, in the words that, to my mind, best capture Coetzee's poetics of the child: 'Not only can study have no rightful end, [it] does not even desire one' (Agamben 1995, 64).

References

Agamben, Giorgio. 1993. *The Coming Community*. Translated by Michael Hardt. Minneapolis: University of Minnesota Press.

Agamben, Giorgio. [1985] 1995. *Idea of Prose*. Translated by Michael Sullivan and Sam Whitsitt. Albany: State University of New York Press.

Agamben, Giorgio. [1996] 1999a. *The End of the Poem*. Translated by Daniel Heller-Roazen. Stanford, CA: Stanford University Press.

Agamben, Giorgio. 1999b. *Potentialities: Collected Essays in Philosophy*. Edited and translated by Daniel Heller-Roazen. Stanford, CA: Stanford University Press.

Agamben, Giorgio. [2002] 2004. *The Open: Man and Animal*. Translated by Kevin Attell. Stanford, CA: Stanford University Press.

Agamben, Giorgio. [2003] 2005a. *State of Exception*. Translated by Kevin Attell. Chicago, IL: University of Chicago Press.

Agamben, Giorgio. [2000] 2005b. *The Time That Remains: A Commentary on the Letter to the Romans*. Translated by Patricia Dailey. Stanford, CA: Stanford University Press.

Agamben, Giorgio. [1978] 2007. *Infancy and History: On the Destruction of Experience*. Translated by Liz Heron. London: Verso. Radical Thinkers.

Agamben, Giorgio. [2009] 2011. *Nudities*. Translated by David Kishik and Stefan Pedatella. Stanford, CA: Stanford University Press.

Alryyes, Ala A. 2001. *Original Subjects: The Child, the Novel, and the Nation*. Harvard: Harvard University Press.

Arendt, Hannah. [1958] 1998. *The Human Condition. Second Edition*. Chicago, IL: University of Chicago Press.

Arendt, Hannah. [1961] 2006. *Between Past and Future: Eight Exercises in Political Thought*. New York: Penguin.

Arendt, Hannah. [1951] 2017. *The Origins of Totalitarianism*. St Ives: Penguin.

Ariès, Philippe. [1960, in French] 1962. *Centuries of Childhood: A Social History of Family Life*. Translated by Robert Baldick. New York: Vintage.

Attell, Kevin. 2015. *Giorgio Agamben: Beyond the Threshold of Deconstruction*. New York: Fordham University Press.

Attridge, Derek. 2004a. *J.M. Coetzee and the Ethics of Reading: Literature in the Event*. Chicago, IL: University of Chicago Press.

Attridge, Derek. 2004b. *The Singularity of Literature*. London: Routledge.

Attridge, Derek. 2015. *The Work of Literature*. Oxford: Oxford University Press.
Attwell, David. 1993. *J.M. Coetzee: South Africa and the Politics of Writing*. Berkeley: University of California Press.
Attwell, David. 2009. 'J.M. Coetzee and the Idea of Africa'. *Journal of Literary Studies/Tydskrif vir literatuurwetenskap* 25 (4): 25–41.
Attwell, David. 2014. 'Writing Revolution: The Manuscript Revisions of J.M. Coetzee's *Waiting for the Barbarians*'. *Life Writing* 11 (2): 201–16.
Attwell, David. 2015. *J.M. Coetzee and the Life of Writing: Face to Face with Time*. Johannesberg: Jacana.
Attwell, David. 2019. '"A New Footing": Re-reading the Barbarian Girl in Coetzee's *Waiting for the Barbarians*'. In *Reading Coetzee's Women*. Edited by Sue Kossew and Melinda Harvey, 55–65. London: Palgrave Macmillan.
Augustine. [1991] 2008. *Confessions*. Translated by Henry Chadwick. Oxford: Oxford University Press.
Babuk, Aleksandr. 2015. 'The Myth of Childhood as an Embodiment of the Golden Age in Dostoevsky's Oeuvre'. *Russian Studies in Literature* 51 (2): 33–53.
Bachelard, Gaston. [1971] 1992. *The Poetics of Reverie. Childhood, Language, and the Cosmos*. Translated by Daniel Russell. Boston, MA: Beacon Press.
Barnard, Rita. 2014. 'Prologue: Why Not to Teach Coetzee'. In *Approaches to Teaching Coetzee's Disgrace and Other Works*. Edited by Laura Wright, Jane Poyner and Elleke Boehmer, 31–42. New York: Modern Language Association of America.
Barney, Richard A. 2016. 'On (Not) Giving Up: Animals, Biopolitics, and the Impersonal in J.M. Coetzee's *Disgrace*'. *Textual Practice* 30 (3): 509–30.
Barstow, Jane Missner. 1978. 'Charles Dickens, Marcel Proust and Günter Grass on Childhood'. *Children's Literature* 7: 147–68.
Bartnik, Ryszard. 2014. 'On South African Violence through Giorgio Agamben's Biopolitical Framework: A Comparative Study of J.M. Coetzee's *Disgrace* and Z. Mda's *Ways of Dying*'. *Studia Anglica Posnaniensia* 49 (4): 21–36.
Bataille, Georges. [1973] 2012. *Literature and Evil*. Translated by Alastair Hamilton. London: Penguin.
Baudrillard, Jean. 2002. 'The Dark Continent of Childhood'. In *Screened Out*. Translated by Chris Turner, 102–6. London: Verso.
Beard, Margot. 2007. 'Lessons from the Dead Masters: Wordsworth and Byron in J. M. Coetzee's *Disgrace*'. *English in Africa* 34 (1): 59–77.
Bell, Michael. 2007. *Open Secrets: Literature, Education, and Authority from J.J. Rousseau to J.M. Coetzee*. Oxford: Oxford University Press.

Benjamin, Walter. [1968] 1999. *Illuminations*. Edited by Hanna Arendt and translated by Harry Zorn. London: Pimlico.

Bertolini, Paolo. 2011. 'Infancy'. In *The Agamben Dictionary*. Edited by Alex Murray and Jessica Whyte, 105. Edinburgh: Edinburgh University Press.

Bhabha, Homi. 1994. 'Sly Civility'. *The Location of Culture*, 132–44. London: Routledge.

Blake, William. [1794] 2011. *Songs of Innocence and Experience*. Oxford: Oxford University Press.

Boas, George. 1966. *The Cult of Childhood*. London: Warburg Institute. Studies of the Warburg Institute, vol. 29.

Bowen-Moore, Patricia. 1989. *Hannah Arendt's Philosophy of Natality*. Basingstoke: Macmillan Press.

Broch, Hermann. [1945] 1995. *The Death of Virgil*. Translated by Jean Starr Untermeyer. New York: Vintage International.

Broggi, Alicia. 2018. ' "A Language I Have Not Unlearned": Cultivating an Historical Awareness of J.M. Coetzee's Engagement with Christianity'. *Literature and Theology* 32 (4): 452–74.

Bunge, Marcia, editor. 2001. *The Child in Christian Thought*. Grand Rapids, MI: Eerdmans.

Caselli, Daniella. 2005. 'The Child in Beckett's Work: Introduction'. *Historicising Beckett/Issues of Performance: Beckett dans l'histoire/En jouant Beckett* (*Samuel Beckett Today/Aujourd'hui*) 15: 259–60.

Castañeda, Claudia. 2002. *Figurations: Child, Bodies, Worlds*. Durham, NC: Duke University Press.

Caton, Steven C. 2006. 'Coetzee, Agamben, and the Passion of Abu Ghraib'. *American Anthropologist* 108 (1): 114–23.

Chapman, Michael. [1996] 2003. *Southern African Literatures*. Pietermaritzburg: University of Natal Press.

Chesney, Duncan McColl. 2007. 'Towards an Ethics of Silence: *Michael K*'. *Criticism* 49 (3): 307–25.

Clarkson, Carrol. 2009. 'J.M. Coetzee and the Limits of Language'. *Journal of Literary Studies* 25 (4): 106–24.

Clarkson, Carrol. [2009] 2013. *J.M. Coetzee: Countervoices*. Basingstoke: Palgrave Macmillan.

Coetzee, J. M. [1986] 1987. *Foe*. London: Penguin.

Coetzee, J. M. 1988. *White Writing: On the Culture of Letters in South Africa*. London: Yale University Press.

Coetzee, J. M. 1992. *Doubling the Point: Essays and Interviews*. Edited by David Attwell. London: Harvard University Press.
Coetzee, J. M. 1996. *Giving Offense: Essays on Censorship*. London: University of Chicago Press.
Coetzee, J. M. [1990] 1998. *Age of Iron*. London: Penguin.
Coetzee, J. M. [1997] 1998. *Boyhood: Scenes from Provincial Life*. London: Vintage.
Coetzee, J. M. [1983] 1998. *Life and Times of Michael K*. London: Vintage.
Coetzee, J. M. [1999] 2000. *Disgrace*. London: Vintage.
Coetzee, J. M. [2001] 2002. *Stranger Shores: Essays 1986–1999*. London: Vintage.
Coetzee, J. M. [2002] 2003. *Youth*. London: Vintage.
Coetzee, J. M. [1974] 2004. *Dusklands*. London: Vintage.
Coetzee, J. M. [2003] 2004. *Elizabeth Costello*. London: Vintage.
Coetzee, J. M. [1977] 2004. *In the Heart of the Country*. London: Vintage.
Coetzee, J. M. [1994] 2004. *The Master of Petersburg*. London: Vintage.
Coetzee, J. M. [1980] 2004. *Waiting for the Barbarians*. London: Vintage.
Coetzee, J. M. [2005] 2006. *Slow Man*. London: Vintage.
Coetzee, J. M. [2007] 2008. *Diary of a Bad Year*. London: Vintage.
Coetzee, J. M. [2007] 2008. *Inner Workings: Literary Essays 2000–2005*. London: Vintage.
Coetzee, J. M. [2009] 2010. *Summertime: Scenes from Provincial Life*. London: Vintage.
Coetzee, J. M. 2012. Graduation ceremony, University of the Witwatersrand, 10 December. Honorary doctorate acceptance speech.
Coetzee, J. M. 2013. *The Childhood of Jesus*. London: Harvill Secker.
Coetzee, J. M. 2014. 'In the Heart of the Country', *Two Screenplays*, edited by Herman Wittenberg. Cape Town: UCT Press.
Coetzee, J. M. 2014. Foreword in *Academic Freedom in a Democratic South Africa: Essays and Interviews on Higher Education and the Humanities*, by John Higgins, xi–xv. London: Bucknell University Press.
Coetzee, J. M. 2016. 'On Literary Thinking'. *30@30: The Future of Literary Thinking*, special issue of *Textual Practice* 7: 1151–2.
Coetzee, J. M. 2016. *The Schooldays of Jesus*. London: Harvill Secker.
Coetzee, J. M. 2017. *Late Essays: 2006–2017*. London: Harvill Secker.
Coetzee, J. M. 2019. *The Death of Jesus*. Melbourne: Text Publishing.
Coetzee, J. M., and Attwell, David. 2003. 'An Exclusive Interview with J.M. Coetzee'. *Dagens Nyheter*. 8 December. https://www.dn.se/kultur-noje/an-exclusive-interview-with-j-m-coetzee/. Accessed 4 October 2018.

Coetzee, J. M., and Attwell, David. 2006. 'All Autobiography Is *Autre*-biography'. *Selves in Question: Interviews on South African Auto/biography*. Edited by Coullie, Meyer, Ngwenya and Olver, 213–18. Honolulu: University of Hawaii Press.

Coetzee, J. M., and Auster, Paul. 2013. *Here and Now: Letters 2008–2011*. London: Faber and Faber.

Coetzee, J. M., and Brink, André, editors. 1986. *A Land Apart: A South African Reader*. London: Faber and Faber.

Coetzee, J. M., and Kurtz, Arabella. 2015. *The Good Story: Exchanges on Truth, Fiction and Psychotherapy*. London: Harvill Secker.

Coetzee, J. M., and Rhedin, Folke. [1982] 1984. 'Interview'. *Kunapipi* 6 (1): 6–11.

Coetzee, J. M., and Scott, Joanna. 1997. 'Voice and Trajectory: An Interview with J.M. Coetzee'. *Salmagundi*, no. 114/115: 82–102.

Coetzee, J. M., and Wittenberg, Hermann. 2017. 'Remembering Photography'. *Photographs from Boyhood (Exhibition Catalogue)*.

Colebrook, Claire. 2004. *Irony*. London: Routledge.

Coveney, Peter. 1967. *The Image of Childhood: Individual and Society: A Study of the Theme in English Literature*. Harmondsworth: Penguin.

Cunningham, Hugh. 2005. *Children and Childhood in Western Society Since 1500*. Harlow: Pearson.

Danta, Chris. [2011] 2013. 'Introduction. J.M. Coetzee: The Janus Face of Authority'. In *Strong Opinions: J.M. Coetzee and the Authority of Contemporary Fiction*. Edited by Chris Danta, Sue Kossew and Julian Murphet, xi–xx. London: Bloomsbury.

Deleuze, Gilles, and Guattari, Félix. [1980] 1987. *A Thousand Plateaus: Capitalism and Schizophrenia*. Translated by Brian Massumi. Minneapolis: University of Minnesota Press.

Derrida, Jacques. [1997] 2000. *Of Hospitality: Anne Dufourmantelle Invites Jacques Derrida to Respond*. Translated by Rachel Bowlby. Stanford, CA: Stanford University Press.

Derrida, Jacques. [1993] 2006. *Specters of Marx: The State of the Debt, the Work of Mourning and the New*. Translated by Peggy Kamuf. New York: Routledge Classics.

De la Durantaye, Leland. 2009. *Giorgio Agamben: A Critical Introduction*. Stanford, CA: Stanford University Press.

DeVries, Dawn. 2001. '"Be Converted and Become as Little Children": Friedrich Schleiermacher on the Religious Significance of Childhood'. In *The Child in Christian Thought*. Edited by M. Bunge, 329–49. Grand Rapids, MI: Eerdmans.

Dickinson, Colby. 2011. *Agamben and Theology*. London: T&T Clark.
Dimitriu, Ileana Șora. 2015. '"Attachment with Detachment": A Postsecular Reading of J.M. Coetzee's Recent Fiction'. *British and American Studies* 21:133–41.
Diprose, Rosalyn, and Ziarek, Ewa. 2013. 'Time for Beginners: Natality, Biopolitics, and Political Theology'. *philoSOPHIA* 3 (2):107–20.
Diprose, Rosalyn, and Ziarek, Ewa. 2017. *Arendt, Natality and Biopolitics: Toward Democratic Plurality and Reproductive Justice*. Edinburgh: Edinburgh University Press.
Dooley, Gillian. 2010. 'Parents and Children'. In *J.M. Coetzee and the Power of Narrative*, 151–70. New York: Cambria Press.
Dovey, Ceridwen. 2018. *On J.M. Coetzee: Writers on Writers*. Carlton: Black.
Dubow, Saul. 2014. *Apartheid, 1948-1994*. Oxford: Oxford University Press.
Dudley, Jack. 2017. '"Along a Road That May Lead Nowhere". J.M. Coetzee's *Disgrace* and the Postsecular Novel'. *Studies in the Novel* 49 (1):109–30.
Durrant, Sam. 2003. *Postcolonial Narrative and the Work of Mourning: J.M. Coetzee, Wilson Harris, and Toni Morrison*, 23–51. Albany: State University of New York Press.
Durrant, Sam. 2006. 'J.M. Coetzee, Elizabeth Costello, and the Limits of the Sympathetic Imagination'. In *J.M. Coetzee and the Idea of the Public Intellectual*. Edited by Jane Poyner, 118–34. Athens: Ohio University Press.
Edelman, Lee. 2004. *No Future: Queer Theory and the Death Drive*. Durham, NC: Duke University Press.
Faulkner, Joanne. 2010. 'Innocence, Evil and Human Frailty: Potentiality and the Child in the Writings of Giorgio Agamben'. *Angelaki: Journal of the Theoretical Humanities* 15 (2): 203–14.
Faulkner, Joanne. 2016. *Young and Free. [Post]colonial Ontologies of Childhood, Memory and History in Australia*. London: Rowman & Littlefield.
Geertsema, Johan. 1997. '"We Embrace to Be Embraced": Irony in an Age of Iron'. *English in Africa* 24 (1): 89–102.
Geertsema, Johan. 2011. 'Coetzee's *Diary of a Bad Year*: Politics, and the Problem of Position'. *Twentieth-Century Literature* 57 (1): 70–85.
Giddings, Robert. 1991. *Literature and Imperialism*. Basingstoke: Macmillan.
Gottlieb, Susannah Young-ah. 2003. *Regions of Sorrow: Anxiety and Messianism in Hannah Arendt and W.H. Auden*. Stanford, CA: Stanford University Press.
Hanawalt, Barbara A. 2003. 'The Child in the Middle Ages and the Renaissance'. In *Beyond the Century of the Child: Cultural History and Developmental Psychology*. Edited by Willem Koops and Michael Zuckerman, 21–42. Philadelphia: University of Pennsylvania Press.

Hayes, Patrick. 2010. *J.M. Coetzee and the Novel: Writing and Politics after Beckett*. Oxford: Oxford University Press.

Hayes, Patrick, and Wilm, Jan, editors. 2017. *Beyond the Ancient Quarrel: Literature, Philosophy, and J.M. Coetzee*. Oxford: Oxford University Press.

Head, Dominic. 2010. *J.M. Coetzee*. Cambridge: Cambridge University Press.

Helgesson, Stefan. 2004. *Writing in Crisis: Ethics and History in Gordimer, Ndebele and Coetzee*. Pietermaritzburg: University of KwaZulu-Natal Press.

Hesiod. 2008. *Theogony and Works and Days*. Translated by M. L. West. Oxford: Oxford University Press.

Heyns, Michiel. 2000. 'The Whole Country's Truth: Confession and Narrative in Recent White South African Writing'. *Modern Fiction Studies* 46 (1): 42–66.

Hillyer, Aaron. 2013. *The Disappearance of Literature*: Blanchot, Agamben, and the Writers of the No. London: Bloomsbury.

Hinsdale, Mary Ann. 2001. ' "Infinite Openness to the Infinite": Karl Rahner's Contribution to Modern Catholic Thought on the Child'. In *The Child in Christian Thought*. Edited by M. Bunge, 406–45. Grand Rapids, MI: Eerdmans.

Honeyman, Susan. 2005. *Elusive Childhood: Impossible Representations in Modern Fiction*. Columbus: Ohio State University Press.

Hugo, Victor. [1877] 2012. *How to Be a Grandfather (L'Art d'être Grand-Père)*. Translated by Timothy Adès. London: Hearing Eye.

Hutcheon, Linda. 1988. *A Poetics of Postmodernism: History, Theory, Fiction*. London: Routledge.

James, Allison, and Prout, Alan. 1990. *Constructing and Reconstructing Childhood*. London: Falmer.

Jasinski, Igor. 2018. *Giorgio Agamben: Education without Ends*. Cham: Springer.

Jay, Martin. 2011. 'Historical Explanation and the Event: Reflections on the Limits of Contextualization'. *New Literary History* 42 (4): 557–71.

Jenks, Chris. 2005. *Childhood*. Second edition. Abingdon: Routledge.

Kaplan, Brett Ashley. 2011. *Landscapes of Holocaust Postmemory*. New York: Routledge.

Kennedy, David. 1995. 'Notes on the Philosophy of Childhood and the Politics of Subjectivity'. *Proceedings of the Twentieth World Congress of Philosophy*. Boston, 10–15 August.

Kennedy, David. 2002. 'The Child and Postmodern Subjectivity'. *Educational Theory* 52 (2): 155–67.

Kennedy, David. 2006. *The Well of Being: Childhood, Subjectivity, and Education*. Albany: State University of New York Press.

Kincaid, James. 1998. *Erotic Innocence: The Culture of Child Molesting*. Durham, NC: Duke University Press.

Kohan, Walter Omar. 2011. 'Childhood, Education and Philosophy: Notes on Deterritorialisation'. *Journal of Philosophy and Education* 45 (2): 339–57.

Kossew, Sue. 2017. 'J.M. Coetzee and the Parental Punctum'. In *J.M. Coetzee's The Childhood of Jesus: The Ethics of Ideas and Things*. Edited by Jennifer Rutherford and Anthony Uhlmann, 149–64. London: Bloomsbury.

Kunene, Mazisi. [1980] 1986. 'The Rise of the Angry Generation'. Translated by Mazisi Kunene. In *A Land Apart: A South African Reader*. Edited by André Brink and J. M. Coetzee, 68. London: Faber and Faber.

Laszlo, Katharina. 2018. 'Childhood, Pedagogy and Education'. In *Franz Kafka in Context*. Edited by Caroline Duttlinger, 241–8. Cambridge: Cambridge University Press.

Lenta, Margaret. 2003. '*Autre*biography: J.M. Coetzee's *Boyhood* and *Youth*'. *English in Africa* 30 (1): 157–69.

Lesnik-Oberstein, Karín. 1994. *Children's Literature: Criticism and the Fictional Child*. Oxford: Oxford University Press.

Levitt, Deborah. 2011. 'Gesture'. In *The Agamben Dictionary*. Edited by Alex Murray and Jessica Whyte, 79–82. Edinburgh: Edinburgh University Press.

Lewis, Tyson E. 2013. *On Study: Giorgio Agamben and Educational Potentiality*. Abingdon: Routledge.

Locke, John. [1693] 1996. *Some Thoughts Concerning Education*. Indianapolis, IN Hackett.

Locke, Richard. 2011. *Critical Children: The Use of Childhood in Ten Great Novels*. New York: Columbia University Press.

López, María J., and Wiegandt, Kai. 2016. 'Introduction: J.M. Coetzee, Intertextuality and the Non-English Literary Traditions'. *European Journal of English Studies* 20 (2): 113–26.

Lyotard, Jean-François. [1988] 1991. *The Inhuman: Reflections on Time*. Translated by Geoffrey Bennington and Rachel Bowlby. Stanford: Stanford University Press.

Lyotard, Jean-François. [1988] 1992. *The Postmodern Explained: Correspondence 1982–1985*. Edited by Julian Pefanis and Morgan Thomas. Translations by Don Barry, Bernadette Maher, Julian Pefanis, Virginia Spate and Morgan Thomas. Minneapolis: University of Minnesota Press.

Marais, Mike. 2009. *Secretary of the Invisible: The Idea of Hospitality in the Fiction of J.M. Coetzee*. Amsterdam: Rodopi.

Maxwell, Jason. 2011. 'Ethics'. In *The Agamben Dictionary*. Edited by Alex Murray and Jessica Whyte, 63–5. Edinburgh: Edinburgh University Press.

McGavran, James Holt. 1999. *Literature and the Child: Romantic Continuations, Postmodern Contestations*. Iowa City: University of Iowa Press.

Mehigan, Tim, and Moser, Christian, editors. 2018. *The Intellectual Landscape in the Works of J.M. Coetzee*. Rochester, NY: Camden House.

Mills, Catherine. 2006. 'Life beyond Law: Biopolitics, Law and Futurity in Coetzee's *Life and Times of Michael K*'. *Griffith Law Review* 15 (1): 177–95.

Monticelli, Daniele. 2016. 'From Dissensus to Inoperativity: The Strange Case of J.M. Coetzee's *Michael K*'. *English Studies* 97 (6): 218–37.

Nandy, Ashis. 1987. *Traditions, Tyranny, and Utopias: Essays in the Politics of Awareness*. Oxford: Oxford University Press.

Natov, Roni. 2003. *The Poetics of Childhood*. New York: Routledge.

Niemi, Minna. 2017. 'Totalitarian Politics and Individual Responsibility: Revising Hannah Arendt's Inner Dialogue through the Notion of Confession in J. M. Coetzee's *Waiting for the Barbarians*'. *South African Journal of Philosophy* 36 (2): 223–38.

Ou, Li. 2009. *Keats and Negative Capability*. London: Bloomsbury.

Pattison, Robert. 2008. *The Child Figure in English Literature*. Athens: University of Georgia Press.

Pawlicki, Marek. 2013. *Between Illusionism and Anti-Illusionism: Self-Reflexivity in the Chosen Novels of J.M. Coetzee*. Newcastle upon Tyne: Cambridge Scholars.

Pecora, Vincent P. 2015. *Secularization without End: Beckett, Mann, Coetzee*. Notre Dame, IN: University of Notre Dame Press.

Pifer, Ellen. 2000. *Demon or Doll: Images of the Child in Contemporary Writing and Culture*. Charlottesville: University of Virginia Press.

Pippin, Robert B. 2017. 'What Does J.M. Coetzee's Novel, *The Childhood of Jesus* Have to Do with the Childhood of Jesus?'. In *J.M. Coetzee's The Childhood of Jesus: The Ethics of Ideas and Things*. Edited by Jennifer Rutherford and Anthony Uhlmann, 9–31. London: Bloomsbury.

Pitkin, Barbara. 2001. '"The Heritage of the Lord": Children in the Theology of John Calvin'. In *The Child in Christian Thought*. Edited by M. Bunge, 160–93. Grand Rapids, MI: Eerdmans.

Plato. 1997. *Complete Works*. Edited by John Cooper. Indianapolis, IN: Hackett.

Plotz, Judith. 2001. *Romanticism and the Vocation of Childhood*. New York: Palgrave.

Poetzsch, Markus. 2014. 'Between the "Abyss of Idealism" and the Hard Wall of "Reality": Lessons of the Wordsworthian Child'. *New Review of Children's Literature and Librarianship* 20: 15–25.

Poplak, Richard. 2013. 'Disgrace: JM Coetzee Humiliates Himself in Johannesburg. Or Does He?'. *Daily Maverick*. 3 January.

Postman, Neil. [1982] 1994. *The Disappearance of Childhood*. New York: Vintage.
Restuccia, Frances. 2017. 'Agamben's Open: Coetzee's Dis-grace'. *Comparative Literature* 69 (4): 413–29.
Romano, Claude. [1998] 2009. *Event and the World*. Translated by Shane Mackinlay. New York: Fordham University Press.
Rose, Jacqueline. [1984] 1993. *The Case of Peter Pan or The Impossibility of Children's Fiction*. Philadelphia: University of Pennsylvania Press.
Rousseau, Jean-Jacques. [1762, in French; 1896] 2003. *Émile, or, Treatise on Education*. Translated by William H. Payne. New York: Prometheus Books.
Rowland, Ann Wierda. 2012. *Romanticism and Childhood: The Infantilization of British Literary Culture*. Cambridge: Cambridge University Press.
Rutherford, Jennifer. 2017. 'Thinking through Shit in *The Childhood of Jesus*'. In *J.M. Coetzee's The Childhood of Jesus: The Ethics of Ideas and Things*. Edited by Jennifer Rutherford and Anthony Uhlmann, 59–81. London: Bloomsbury.
Rutherford, Jennifer, and Uhlmann, Anthony, editors. 2017. *J.M. Coetzee's The Childhood of Jesus: The Ethics of Ideas and Things*. London: Bloomsbury.
Ryan, Pam. 2005. 'A Woman Thinking in Dark Times?: The Absent Presence of Hannah Arendt in J. M. Coetzee's "Elizabeth Costello and the Problem of Evil"'. *Journal of Literary Studies* 21 (3–4): 277–95.
Schiller, Friedrich. [1966] 1984. *Naïve and Sentimental Poetry*. Translated by Julius A. Elias. New York: Frederick Ungar.
Schiller, Friedrich. [1954] 2004. *On the Aesthetic Education of Man*. Translated by Reginald Snell. Mineola, NY: Dover.
Shattuck, Sandra D. 2009. 'Dis(g)race, or White Man Writing'. In *Encountering Disgrace: Reading and Teaching Coetzee's Novel*. Edited by Bill McDonald, 138–47. Rochester, NY: Camden House.
Smuts, Eckard. 2014. 'Displaced Romanticism: Searching for the Self in J.M. Coetzee's Autobiographical Fiction', PhD dissertation, University of Cape Town.
Snoek, Anke. 2012. *Agamben's Joyful Kafka: Finding Freedom beyond Subordination*. London: Bloomsbury.
Splendore, Paola. 2003. '"No more Mothers and Fathers": The Family Sub-Text in J.M. Coetzee's Novels'. *Journal of Commonwealth Literature* 38 (3): 148–68.
Steedman, Carolyn. 1995. *Strange Dislocations: Childhood and the Idea of Human Interiority 1780-1930*. London: Virago.
Steiner, Rudolf. [1956] 1977. *Eurythmy as Visible Music Eight Lectures Given at Dornach, 19 to 27 February 1924*. Translated by J. Compton-Burnett. Sussex: Rudolf Steiner Press.

Stockton, Kathryn. 2009. *The Queer Child, or Growing Sideways in the Twentieth Century*. Durham, NC: Duke University Press.

Su, John J. 2011. *Imagination and the Contemporary Novel*. Cambridge: Cambridge University Press.

Tarc, Aparna Mishra. 2020. *Pedagogy in the Novels of J.M. Coetzee: The Affect of Literature*. New York: Routledge.

Van der Vlies, Andrew. 2017. *Present Imperfect: Contemporary South African Writing*. Oxford: Oxford University Press.

Vermeulen, Pieter. 2007. 'Wordsworth's Disgrace: The Insistence of South Africa in J.M. Coetzee's *Boyhood* and *Youth*'. *Journal of Literary Studies* 23 (2): 179–99.

Vloeberghs, Katrien. 2004. 'Constructions of Childhood and Giorgio Agamben's *Infantia*'. In *New Voices in Children's Literature Criticism*. Edited by Sebastien Chapleau, 71–8. Lichfield: Pied Piper.

Vloeberghs, Katrien. 2007. 'Babbling Redemption: Agamben's Messianic Infancy'. In *On the Outlook: Figures of the Messianic*. Edited by Thomas Crombez and Katrien Vloeberghs, 115–20. Newcastle: Cambridge Scholars.

Wall, John. 2010. *Ethics in Light of Childhood*. Washington, DC: Georgetown University Press.

Wallace, Jo-Ann. 1994. 'De-Scribing the Water-Babies: "The Child" in Post-colonial Theory'. In *De-Scribing Empire: Post-Colonialism and Textuality*. Edited by Chris Tiffin and Alan Lawson, 171–84. London: Routledge.

Watkin, William. 2010. *The Literary Agamben: Adventures in Logopoeisis*. London: Continuum.

Watkin, William. 2014. *Agamben and Indifference: A Critical Overview*. London: Rowman & Littlefield.

Weber, Barbara. 2011. 'Childhood, Philosophy and Play: Friedrich Schiller and the Interface between Reason, Passion and Sensation'. *Journal of Philosophy of Education* 45 (2): 235–50.

Wiegandt, Kai. 2018. 'The Creature-Feeling as Secular Grace: On the Religious in J.M. Coetzee's Fiction'. *Literature & Theology* 32 (1): 69–86.

Willemse, Arthur. 2018. *The Motif of the Messianic: Law, Life, and Writing in Agamben's Reading of Derrida*. London: Lexington.

Williams, James S. [2014] 2015. 'Silence, Gesture, Revelation: The Ethics and Aesthetics of Montage in Godard and Agamben'. In *Cinema and Agamben: Ethics, Biopolitics, and the Moving Image*. Edited by Henrik Gustafsson and Asbjørn Grønstad, 27–54. London: Bloomsbury.

Wilm, Jan. 2016. *The Slow Philosophy of J.M. Coetzee*. London: Bloomsbury.

Woessner, Martin. 2017. 'Beyond Realism: Coetzee's Post-Secular Imagination'. In *Beyond the Ancient Quarrel: Literature, Philosophy, and J.M.Coetzee*. Edited by Patrick Hayes and Jan Wilm, 143–59. Oxford: Oxford University Press.

Wordsworth, William. [1984] 2008. 'Ode'. In *The Major Works*. Edited by Stephen Gill. Oxford: Oxford University Press.

Zakin, Emily. 2017. 'Between Two Betweens: Hannah Arendt and the Politics of Education'. *Journal of Speculative Philosophy* 31 (1): 119–34.

Zimbler, Jarad. 2011. 'Caring, Teaching, Knowing: Spivak, Coetzee and the Practice of Postcolonial Pedagogies'. *Parallax* 17 (3): 19–31.

Zimbler, Jarad. 2014. *J.M. Coetzee and the Politics of Style*. Cambridge: Cambridge University Press.

Index

Agamben, Giorgio
  and Derrida 15–16, 16 n.11, 18, 28, 126–7, 134, 162–3, 163 nn.15, 16
  impotentiality 7, 15–16, 34, 39, 88 n.16, 123, 125, 132, 138–47, 152, 157, 159, 167–9
  infancy 14–18, 15 n.10, 29, 35–6, 39, 93, 116 n.15, 123, 125–6, 131–3, 136–8, 137 n.6, 138 n.7, 140, 142–5, 147, 152–3, 157–64, 163 n.16, 167–9
  see also infancy
  kairos 36 n.39
  messianic, conception of the 14, 36 n.39, 132–5, 138, 138 n.7, 143, 160, 162–3, 169 n.2
  potentiality 15, 17–18, 34, 36, 131–2, 138–9, 165
  study 123, 125–8, 131–6, 138, 140, 143–7, 159, 170
Age of Iron 2, 4, 12, 22 n.20, 24, 34, 46, 49, 49 n.4, 70, 81–93, 98, 109–10, 110 n.11, 113–14, 119 n.16, 126, 155–6, 168
Aira, César 168
A Land Apart 30 n.28, 90, 90 n.21
Alryyes, Ala 104
amor mundi 18, 38, 110–12, 114, 117, 122
  see also Arendt
anthroposophy 154 n.5 *see also* Steiner and Waldorf
apartheid 12, 45 n.2, 49, 55, 65, 67, 70, 74, 81, 83, 90, 107 n.10, 113
Aquinas, Thomas 33
Arendt, Hannah 18–19, 19 n.14, 27, 38–9, 98–102, 101 nn.3, 4, 102 n.7, 104, 106, 111–12, 116–18, 120, 130
  amor mundi 18, 38, 110–12, 114, 117, 122
  and Derrida 18, 101–2, 101 n.4
  and education 18–19, 38, 98, 111–12, 117–18

  and event 18, 101–2
  natality 7, 18–19, 27, 38. 98–103, 101 n.4, 102 n.7, 103 n.8, 106, 112–13, 116–17, 120, 123
  plurality 100, 103, 112
Ariès, Philippe 30, 30 n.29
Aristotle 33–4, 138, 158
Attell, Kevin 16 n.11
Attwell, David 68, 71 nn.3, 4, 74, 77 n.10, 79 n.12, 89 n.19, 95 n.1
  Life of Writing 4–5, 5 n.2, 11, 41, 42, 46–8, 62 n.13, 63, 82–3, 107, 107 n.10
Attridge, Derek
  ethics of reading 5–6, 8–9, 67, 68, 115, 126, 127, 137, 145, 150 n.1 *see also* hospitality
  event 18, 101–2, 102 nn.5, 6
Augustine 18, 25, 32, 32 n.33, 99, 99 n.2
Auster, Paul 116–17

Bachelard, Gaston 23 n.21
Ballantyne, J. M. 73 n.8
Barnard, Rita 13 n.9, 88 n.16
Barney, Richard 16 n.13
Barstow, Jane M. 28 n.26
Bartleby (Melville's character) 11, 125, 132, 141, 141 n.9
Bartnik, Ryszard 16 n.13
Bataille, Georges 4 n.1
Baudrillard, Jean 31 n.30
Beckett, Samuel 4, 4 n.1, 151, 159,
Bell, Michael 13 n.9
Benjamin, Walter 36 n.39, 134–5, 160
Benveniste, Émile 15 n.10, 159, 159 n.13
Bhabha, Homi 73, 73 n.9
Bible 4, 32, 32 n.33, 101, 136, 137 n.6, 161
birth 10, 26, 98–9 *see also* natality
Blake, William 14, 27–8, 47
Blanchot, Maurice 5
Boas, George 72 n.5
Bowen-Moore, Patricia 103 n.8, 112, 120

Boyhood 2, 3, 4, 23, 24, 26, 28, 38, 42–6, 48, 51–63, 62 nn.12, 13, 75, 118, 121, 167–8
Brink, André 30 n.28, 90
Broggi, Alicia 150 n.2
Buber, Martin 15 n.10

Calvin, Jean 32, 34, 45, 46, 54 n.8, 73, 121, 150 n.2, 151 n.3
Carson, Anne 168
Castañeda, Claudia 36, 36 n.40, 72
Caton, Steven 16 n.13
Chapman, Michael 110, n.12
Chaucer, Geoffrey 47
Chesney, Duncan 141 n.9
child
   and adult/hood 4, 20, 21, 23–37, 23 n.21, 24 n.22, 30, 30 nn.29, 30, 33 n.35, 34 n.36 and n.37, 51–2, 54–60, 55 n.9, 69–70, 74–8, 85, 92, 103, 103 n.8, 136–7, 142, 147, 149, 151, 157, 161, 163, 167, 169
   and ambiguity 20, 23 n.22, 24, 34, 49, 66, 69, 84, 92, 113 *see also* child and irony
   angelic 47, 49–50, 84, 151
   and authenticity 23, 42–4, 50, 53, 55 n.9, 56–7, 59–60, 62–3, 67, 168
   and autobiography 24, 25, 41, 53
   basic conceptions of 29–35
   and confession 25, 32, 42, 55, 153
   as construct 2, 19, 30, 23–4, 23–4 n.22, 30–1, 30 n.30, 35, 38, 42, 54, 57–8, 66, 68, 70–1, 74, 78, 81, 83, 92, 113
   and continuity 13, 22 n.19, 23 n.21, 35, 80, 90–1, 93, 96, 98, 103–13, 110 nn.11, 12, 115, 117–18, 130
   and desire 10–11, 13, 16, 21–5, 29, 35, 42, 52, 57–8, 104, 115, 168 *see also* child and writing
   and determinism 29, 35, 99, 111
   and Enlightenment 27, 34–6, 72, 154
   and foundational fictions 35, 54, 56–7, 71–2, 83, 104
   and history 5, 7, 12–13, 29, 36, 47–8, 68–70, 72, 78 n.11, 86, 88, 95–100, 105, 110–18, 126, 134–5, 164, 168
   and hope *see* hope
   and ignorance 26, 54, 58, 61, 88 n.16, 89, 118–19, 123
   and imagination 21, 25, 27, 43–4, 53, 58, 60, 72
   and imperialism 19, 70, 72–3, 78, 111 *see also* child, (post)colonial
   innocent 13, 21, 23, 27–9, 32, 34 n.36, 35, 46–59, 55 n.9, 66, 73, 78–9, 83–8, 92, 113, 169 *see also* innocence, Coetzee on innocence
   and irony 2, 49–50, 66–7, 69–70, 70 n.2, 74, 76, 78, 81, 84–5, 88–9, 92, 106, 113, 152, 164, 168 *see also* child and ambiguity
   and language 22 n.19, 23, 26, 28–9, 34 n.37, 35, 37, 47–8, 56, 156–63 *see also* infancy
   and learning 4, 13, 37, 49–50, 111, 118, 121, 125–6, 130, 132, 138–41 *see also* Agamben and study, education
   and lies 41, 44, 53, 58–9 *see also* child and imagination, child and storytelling
   lost (child/hood) 5, 5 n.2, 7, 10, 12–13, 21, 24–5, 28, 55, 65–6, 82, 85, 107, 115, 126, 144
   and meaning 21–2
   modern idea of 20, 27, 33, 35, 56 n.10
   and nature 27–8, 28 n.27, 33, 46, 48, 48 n.3, 73, 75, 151
   and original sin 25, 31–2, 32 n.33, 160
   and otherness/alterity 5–6, 9–10, 12–13, 23–4, 23 n.22, 63–80, 87, 92–3, 119, 126, 147, 164
   and play *see* play
   and politics 19–20, 67–8, 86, 93, 107, 113–17 *see also* infancy and politics
   post(colonial) 13, 19, 24, 49, 65–92
   postmodern 20, 36–7, 36 n.40
   and primitivism 21, 47, 72, 72 n.5, 73
   and psychoanalysis *see* Freud
   queer 19 n.15
   and rationality/reason 23, 27, 31–4, 47, 56, 121, 154, 157, 161, 165
   and redemption 25, 27–9, 35–6, 123 n.17, 136 *see also* redemption, infancy
   and religion 31–34, 45–6, 54 n.8, 58–9, 73, 121, 151, 161
   and representation *see* child and writing
   and resistance 37, 46–8, 83, 88, 88 n.16, 90, 104, 118–19, 126, 130, 138, 142

Romantic 4, 23, 23 n.22, 27–9, 27 n.4,
33, 35, 35 n.38, 43, 45, 47–52, 55–6,
60, 62, 63, 70 n.2, 72, 84–5, 151
and self 13, 22–6, 34, 37–8, 41–4, 50,
56–8, 61–4, 65–6, 71–81, 85–6, 92–3,
113, 167–8, *see also* child and adult/
hood
and storytelling 53, 60, 63, 169 *see also*
child and writing
and teleology 29, 31, 35
and theology 25, 31–5, 151 *see also*
infancy and theology
and transcendence 3, 15, 28, 46–7, 52,
61, 101, 151–3
and truth 23–5, 28, 42–4, 52–8, 60–3,
157, 162, 167
unborn 7, 10, 12, 47, 49, 79–81, 84, 92,
103, 109
and universalizing 69, 74, 78, 84,
86, 92–3
and violence 2, 12, 47, 49, 71–92, 78 n.11
and world 12–13, 18–19, 26, 26 n.23,
37, 43–4, 52, 55–8, 60–1, 63, 97–102,
102 n.7, 104–6, 111–14, 117–18, 122,
130, 161–2, 167 *see also amor mundi*,
Arendt
and writing 3, 6–11, 13, 16, 19–29, 29,
38, 42–3, 47, 56, 60, 62–3, 66, 113–17,
119, 126, 146–7, 160, 163–5, 167–9
childhood *see* child
childish vs childlike 11–12, 145
childlessness 5 n.2, 86, 104 *see also*
parenthood
Clarkson, Carrol 15 n.10, 43, 43 n.1, 68, 79,
159 n.13
Coetzee, J. M.
on authenticity 23, 42–4, 55 n.9 *see also*
child and authenticity
and auto-/*autre*biography 24, 41–2, 53
childhood of 45–6, 54 n.8, 60
on childhood openness to experience 51,
54–5, 61–2, 62 n.13
on childhood photography 62–3
'Confession and Double Thoughts'
(essay) 22, 41–2, 82, 153
on education 13, 13 n.9, 20 n.16, 34, 47,
117–22, 130, 132 *see also* education
'Erasmus: Madness and Rivalry' (essay)
10, 119, n.16, 167

and Eurocentrism 29 n.28
'Four Notes on Rugby' (essay) 73 n.7,
120–1
on freedom 8
on Freud 22–3, 22 n.20
on games 73, n.7, 120, 127
on grace 150–1, 150 n.1, 151 n.3, 170
on innocence 33 n.35, 34–5, 54–7, 82–3,
169 *see also* child, innocent
Jerusalem Prize Acceptance
speech 74, 81
on Oedipal compromise 121
'On Literary Thinking' (essay) 27 n.25, 156
and 'nonposition' 10, 39, 93, 152, 155–7,
161, 165, 167–8
'Patrick White: *The Solid Mandala*'
(essay) 164–5
on play 73 n.7, 119–21 *see also* play
on redemption 150, 170 *see also* child
and redemption
and South Africa 29 n.28, 54 n.8, 74,
81–2, 84, 114
'Taking Offense' (essay) 54–6, 83
on teaching 51, 118–19, 121
on truth 23, 41–4, 52, 56–7, 60, 62–3, 82,
150, 150 n.3, 152–3
Witwatersrand (speech) 4, 34, 50–1,
142, 152
on writing and (ir)responsibility 7–9, 14,
119, 125–6, 161
Colebrook, Claire 66–7
continuity (historical/across generations)
35, 90–1, 93, 96, 98, 103–11, 113, 115,
117–18, 130
Coveney, Peter 27
Cunningham, Hugh 30 n.29

dance 137, 149, 153–4
 as gesture 157–9
 and writing 164–5
Danta, Chris 17, 165, 165 n.18
death 19, 91, 99–100, 103, 103 n.8, 106–7,
111, 114–15, 117, 157 n.10 *see also*
mortality
deixis 159, 159 n.13
Deleuze, Gilles, and Guattari, Félix 36
Derrida, Jacques 6, 9, 14–16, 16 n.11, 18,
24, 26 n.23, 28, 39, 68, 101–2, 101
n.4, 119 n.16, 126–8, 134, 146, 152

n.4, 162–3, 163 n.15; n.16 see also
  hospitality
 and Agamben 15–16, 16 n.11, 18, 28,
  126–7, 134, 162–3, 163 n.15
 and Arendt 18, 101–2, 101 n.4
developmentalism 72, 72 n.5
Diary of a Bad Year 2, 3, 50, 85, 155
Dickens, Charles 28 n.26
Dickinson, Colby 18, 160–2
Dimitriu, Iliana Şora 156 n.9
Diprose, Rosalyn, and Ziarek, Ewa 99, 101
  n.4, 113
Disgrace 2, 13, 14 n.9, 22 n.20, 24, 48, 70,
  78–81, 79 n.12, 92, 98, 107, 114, 126,
  150 n.1, 151, 168
Dooley, Gillian 5 n.2, 107 n.9
Dostoevsky, Fyodor 4, 4 n.1, 41, 153
Dovey, Ceridwen 170
Dubow, Saul 83
Dudley, Jack 150–1, 150 n.1
Durantaye, Leland de la 36 n.39, 134, 162
Durrant, Sam 22 n.20, 86 n.15, 123 n.17
Dusklands 2, 7, 13, 24, 35, 41, 46, 70–8, 70
  n.4, 73 n.9, 81, 88, 107 n.9, 168

Edelman, Lee 19 n.15
education 13, 18–19, 72–3, 98, 102,
  111–12, 117–22, 125, 130, 132–3, 135,
  138–44, 149 see also Agamben on
  study, Arendt on education, Coetzee
  on education, teaching
 in Coetzee criticism 13 n.9
 philosophical/theological approaches to
  31–5, 37
 and play 117–22, 130
Elizabeth Costello 1, 7, 13, 19 n.14, 52, 100,
  117, 137, 146–7, 156, 167, 170
Erasmus 33, 34, 155–6
Erlkönig (Goethe's ballad) 52, 61, 129
ethics see also *amor mundi*, hospitality
 of indifference 69, 92–3, 116 n.5,
  163–4, 169
 and irony 67, 83, 88, 92
 and natality 18, 19 n.14, 101–2, 106,
  112–13, 118–19, 168
eurythmy 154 n.5 see also Steiner

Faulkner, Joanne 18, 25
Foe 12, 47–8, 126, 150 n.1

Foucault, Michel 36
Freud, Sigmund 4, 22–3, 22 nn.19, 20, 45

Gadamer, Hans 26 n.23
Geertsema, Johan 82 n.13, 155
Giddings, Robert 73 n.8
Goethe, Johann Wolfgang von 4, 52, 129,
  129 n.1
Gordimer, Nadine 114
Gospel, the (New Testament) 32, 101,
  136, 161
Gramsci, Antonio 114, 114 n.13
Grass, Günter 28 n.26

Haeckel, Ernst 73 n.7
Hanawalt, Barbara 30 n.29
Hayes, Patrick 9–10, 9 n.6, 93, 93 n.23, 119
  n.16, 145, 155, 155 n.6, 164 n.17
Head, Dominic 49 n.4
Helgesson, Stefan 6 n.4
Heraclitus 37 n.41
Herder, Johann Gottfried von 33
Hesiod 89, 89 n.17
Heyns, Michiel 55
Higgins, John 20 n.16, 27 n.25
Honeyman, Susan 23, 23 n.22, 25–6, 35
  n.38, 56 n.10
hope 13, 17, 52, 86, 97, 99, 101, 103,
  112–13, 134
hospitality (Derrida/Levinas) 5–6, 9, 16,
  18, 24, 39, 68, 101 n.4, 115, 125–8,
  134, 144, 146–7, 152 n.4, 164
Hugo, Victor 48, 80, 109
Hutcheon, Linda 71 n.4

ignorance 24 n.22, 26, 54, 58, 61, 88 n.16,
  89, 118–19, 123
imagination see child and imagination
impotentiality 7, 15–16, 34, 39, 88 n.16,
  123, 125, 132, 138–47, 152, 157,
  159, 167–9
infancy 14–18, 15 n.10, 29, 35–6, 39, 93,
  116 n.15, 123, 125–6, 131–3, 136–8,
  137 n.6, 138 n.7, 140, 142–5, 147,
  152–3, 157–64, 163 n.16, 167–9 see
  also Agamben
 and ethics 163–4, 169
 and play 138
 and history 123

and (im)potentiality 138
vs innocence 29
and language 15, 137, 140, 156–65
and naming 163–4
and natality 122–3
and politics 17, 93, 155–7, 164, 169
and redemption 36, 140, 157,
  161–2, 164–5
and study 123, 126, 131–3, 138, 143–4
and theology 160–3, 163 n.15
and truth 157, 162
and vocation 136, 159–64
and writing 161, 163–5
innocence *see also* child, innocent
  adult 33 n.35
  etymology of 54
  as foundational fiction 54
  and ignorance 24 n.22, 54, 58
  and writing *see* child and writing
interregnum 27, 38, 39, 113–17, 114 n.13, 168
In the Heart of the Country 2, 47, 65–6, 74,
  111, 168
irony *see* child and irony
ir/responsibility, interplay between 3, 6–16,
  18, 27, 29, 39, 43, 115, 119, 125–6,
  145–7, 161, 167

James, Henry 23 n.22
Jay, Martin 114, 114 n.14
Jenks, Chris 20
Jesus (in the *Bible*) 32, 161

Kafka, Franz 4, 4 n.1, 17
Kant, Immanuel 8
Kaplan, Brett 22 n.20
Kearney, Richard 26 n.23
Keats, John 146
Kennedy, David 37
Kincaid, James 21 n.18
Kohan, Walter Omar 37, 37 n.41
Kossew, Sue 5 n.2
Kristeva, Julia 37
Krog, Antjie 3
Kunene, Mazisi 89–91
Kurtz, Arabella 5, 23, 41, 121

language 9–12, 14–17, 22 n.19, 28–9, 34
  n.37, 35, 37, 47–8, 56, 67–8, 98, 104,
  129, 135, 135 n.4, 137, 140, 153,
  155–63, 165 *see also* child and
  language, infancy
Lamb, Charles 28 n.26
Lesnik-Oberstein, Karin 21 n.18, 69
Lessing, Doris 62
Levinas, Emmanuel 5, 6, 6 n. 4, 9, 14–16,
  18, 24, 101 n.4, 126, 146, 152 n.4 *see
  also* hospitality
Lewis, Tyson 18, 132, 132 n.3, 135, 143–4
Life and Times of Michael K 10–12, 12 n.8,
  16, 17, 47, 88 n.16, 119 n.16, 126, 141,
  141 n.9, 160, 160 n.14, 161, 167
Lives of Animals 101 n.3, 155, 169 n.2
Locke, John 34, 34 n.36
Lopez, María J. 29 n.28
Luther, Martin 32
Lyotard, Jean-François 34 n.37, 36

Marais, Eugène 70 n.2
Marais, Mike 5–8, 10–12, 24, 78 n.11, 126
Melville, Herman 125, 141, 141 n.9, 144
messianic time *see* Agamben, messianic
Mills, Catherine 17, 141 n.9, 160 n.14
Montessori (pedagogy) 45, 121
Monticelli, Daniele 17, 141 n.9
mortality 19, 102 *see also* death
Moser, Christian 119 n.16

Nabokov, Vladimir 4, 55
Nancy, Jean-Luc 164 n.17
Nandy, Ashis 20, 72
natality 7, 18–19, 27, 38. 98–103, 101 n.4,
  102 n.7, 103 n.8, 106, 112–13, 116–17,
  120, 123 *see also* Arendt
  and ethics 18, 19 n.14, 101–2, 106,
    112–13, 118–19, 168
  and event 18, 101–2
  and infancy 122–3
  as miracle 100–2
  and mortality 19, 102
  and play 96–7, 99–100, 120, 122
Natov, Roni 20, 28
negative capability 146, 146 n.11, 167
Nietzsche, Friedrich 36
non-human animals 16, 16 n.13, 101 n.3,
  102 n.7, 137, 155, 159, 169

original sin 25, 31–2, 31 n.33, 160
Ovid 89

parenthood/parental responsibility 5 n.2, 7, 10, 78 n.11, 88, 90, 107, 107 n.9, 110, 115 see also childlessness
Pattison, Robert 25, 28
Paul (New Testament) 32
Pawlicki, Marek 71, 71 n.3
Pecora, Vincent 140 n.8, 150 n.2, 151 n.3, 152
pedagogy see education
Pifer, Ellen 21 n.18
Pippin, Robert B. 135, 135 n.4, 137 n.6,
Plato 4, 31–2, 32 n.32, 130, 158 n.11
play 8–9, 26, 26 n.23, 37 n.41, 63, 67–8, 73 n.7, 74, 76, 96–7, 99–100, 113, 117–22, 119 n.16, 130, 135 n.4, 138–40, 151, 159
  and infancy 138
  and irony 67–8
  and natality 96–7, 99–100, 120, 122
  and pedagogy 117–22, 130
  and study (Agamben) 140
  and writing 8–9, 63, 67–8, 119, 159
Plotz, Judith 28 n.26
plurality 100, 103, 112 see also Arendt
Postman, Neil 30 n.30
potentiality 31, 33–4, 34 n.36, 138–9 see also Agamben and im/potentiality
Proust, Marcel 28 n.26

Rahner, Karl 32
recapitulation theory 72
redemption 147, 149–65
  and infancy 140, 161, 164–5
  and innocence 161
  and potentiality 132
  and writing 164–5
responsibility 98, 102 see also Arendt, ethics, hospitality, ir/responsibility, natality
  and vocation 161
Restuccia, Frances 16 n.13, 169 n.2
Rhedin, Folke 97
Robinson Crusoe 33 n.34, 46
Romano, Claude 114 n.14
Rose, Jacqueline 21–3, 21 n.17, 22 n.19
Rousseau, Jean-Jacques 25, 33, 33 nn.34, 35, 34 n.36, 41, 45, 73, 89
Rowland, Ann 27–9, 72
Rutherford, Jennifer 125, 131

Schiller, Friedrich 26–7
Schleiermacher, Friedrich 32
Schulz, Bruno 61
Scott, Joanna 42, 120
self see child and self
Shakespeare, William 118
Slow Man 2, 7, 49–50, 49 n.5, 98, 102–6, 107 n.10, 151, 155 n.6, 168
Smuts, Eckard 27 n.24, 48 n.3, 110 n.11
Snoek, Anke 17
South African contexts 55, 63, 65, 67–8, 71–93, 98, 107, 107 n.10, 110, 113–14
  Coetzee's childhood in 45
  as material for Coetzee 29 n.28
Steedman, Carolyn 24, 43
Steiner, Rudolf 45, 47, 49 n.5, 121, 154 n.5
Stockton, Kathryn 19 n.15
study see Agamben and study, infancy and study

Tarc, Aparna 14 n.9, 156 n.8
teaching 13, 13 n.9, 50–1, 111–12, 118–19, 121, 135, 139, 142 see also education
teleology 29, 31, 35
The Childhood of Jesus 2, 4, 5, 11, 34–5, 39, 51–2, 61–2, 88 n.16, 98, 109–10, 121–3, 125–36, 135 n.4, 137 n.6, 138–145, 149, 152, 156, 156 n.9, 159, 163
The Good Story 5, 23, 41, 51, 55 n.9, 57, 60, 119, 121
The Master of Petersburg 2, 12, 98, 109, 114–16, 126, 168
The Schooldays of Jesus 4, 39, 51–2, 58, 61, 93, 110, 136, 147, 149–65
Tolstoy, Leo 41
transcendence 3, 6–7, 28, 42, 46–7, 52, 61, 101, 151–3, 169

Uhlmann, Anthony 125

Van der Flies, Andrew 113
Vila-Matas, Enrique 168
Virgil 89, 157 n.10
Vloeberghs, Katrien 18, 35–6, 138 n.7
vocation see infancy and vocation, responsibility and vocation

Waiting for the Barbarians 2, 16, 19 n.14, 22, 22 n.20, 48, 78 n.11, 95–100, 102–3, 107 n.10, 111–12, 122–3, 126, 168
Waldorf (pedagogy) 47, 49 n.5 *see also* anthroposophy and Steiner
Wall, John 26 n.23
Wallace, Jo-Ann 19, 19 n.15, 72, 72 n.6
Watkin, William 16 n.11, 18, 159
White, Patrick 62, 164–5
Wiegandt, Kai 29 n.28, 150 n.1, 151
Willemse, Arthur 15–16, 18, 159, 162–3, 163 nn.15, 16
Wilm, Jan 10, 103, 141 n.9, 144–5, 155

Winnicott, D. W. 26
Wittenberg, Herman 63
Woessner, Martin 150, 150 n.1
Wordsworth, William 4, 25, 27–8, 28 n.27, 47–8, 55–6, 60, 62, 85
world *see* Arendt, *amor mundi*, child and world

Young-ah Gottlieb, Susannah 101

Zakin, Emily 104, 112
Zimbler, Jarad 14 n.9, 29 n.28, 68, 150, 150 n.1

www.ingramcontent.com/pod-product-compliance
Lightning Source LLC
Chambersburg PA
CBHW070639300426
44111CB00013B/2169